BARRY KERNFELD

What to Listen For in Jazz

Yale University Press   New Haven and London

Published with assistance from the foundation established
in memory of Philip Hamilton McMillan of the class of 1894,
Yale College.

Designed by Sonia L. Scanlon.

Set in Bodoni type by The Composing Room of Michigan, Inc.

Printed in the United States of America by Vail-Ballou
Press, Binghamton, New York.

Library of Congress Cataloging-in-Publication Data

Kernfeld, Barry Dean, 1950–

    What to listen for in jazz / Barry Kernfeld.

      p.   cm.

    Includes discography (p.   ) and index.

    ISBN 0-300-05902-7 (alk. paper)

      0-300-06162-5 (CD)

    1. Jazz—Analysis, appreciation. I. Title.

ML3506.K47   1995

781.65'17—dc20   94-18324

           CIP

           MN

A catalogue record for this book is available from
the British Library.

The paper in this book meets the guidelines for
permanence and durability of the Committee on
Production Guidelines for Book Longevity of the
Council on Library Resources.

10 9 8 7 6 5 4 3

Contents

Music Examples

CD Tracks

Track 1. Louis Armstrong and his Hot Five. *Hotter than That*. 1927. Composer credit: Lillian Hardin Armstrong.

Track 2. Count Basie and his orchestra. *Jumpin' at the Woodside*. 1938. Composer credit: Count Basie.

Track 3. Ornette Coleman and Prime Time. *Honeymooners*. 1987. Composer credit: Ornette Coleman.

Track 4. John Coltrane orchestra. Excerpt from *Ascension* (edition II). 1965. Composer credit: John Coltrane.

Track 5. Miles Davis quintet. *'Round Midnight*. 1956. Composer credit: Bernie Hanighen, Cootie Williams, and Thelonious Monk.

Track 6. Duke Ellington and his orchestra. *Ko-Ko* (take 2). 1940. Composer credit: Duke Ellington.

Track 7. Duke Ellington and his orchestra. *Trumpet No End* (originally issued as *Blue Skies*). 1946. Composer credit: Irving Berlin.

Track 8. Dizzy Gillespie and his orchestra. *Manteca*. 1947. Composer credit: Dizzy Gillespie, Gil Fuller, and Chano Pozo (Luciano Pozo y Gonzales).

Track 9. Herbie Hancock quintet. Excerpt from *Maiden Voyage*. 1965. Composer credit: Herbie Hancock.

Track 10. Coleman Hawkins quartet. *The Man I Love*. 1943. Composer credit: George Gershwin and Ira Gershwin.

Track 11. Earl Hines. *Sweet Sue*. 1965. Composer credit: Victor Young and Will J. Harris.

Track 12. Billie Holiday. *Georgia on My Mind* (take 1). 1941. Composer credit: Hoagy Carmichael and Stuart Gorrell.

Track 13. Charles Mingus and his Jazz Workshop. Excerpt from *Fables of Faubus*. 1959. Composer credit: Charles Mingus.

Track 14. Thelonious Monk quartet. *Misterioso* (take 1). 1948. Composer credit: Thelonious Monk.

Track 15. Jelly Roll Morton's Red Hot Peppers. *Black Bottom Stomp*. 1926. Composer credit: Jelly Roll Morton.

Track 16. New Orleans Rhythm Kings. *Tin Roof Blues* (take B). 1923. Composer credit: Leon Roppolo, Paul Mares, Benny Pollack, George Brunies, Mel Stitzel, and Walter Melrose.

Track 17. Charlie Parker quintet. *Koko* (take 2). 1945. Composer credit: Charlie Parker.

Track 18. Sonny Rollins quartet. Excerpt from *St. Thomas.* 1956. Composer credit: Sonny Rollins.

Track 19. Sun Ra and his Solar Arkestra. Excerpt from *Outer Nothingness.* 1965. Composer credit: Sun Ra.

Track 20. Kid Thomas Valentine and his Creole Jazz Band. *Panama.* 1959. Composer credit: William H. Tyers.

Track 21. Weather Report. *Birdland.* 1976. Composer credit: Josef Zawinul.

Acknowledgments

In 1989 Ed Tripp of Yale University Press asked if I would be willing to write a book called *What to Listen For in Jazz*. Several months later I submitted a plan for which Frank Tirro supplied enthusiastic and helpful criticisms. From that point the book was in the hands of Fred Kameny, with whom I had worked earlier on a large jazz dictionary. I was delighted to work with him again. He supplied penetrating comments on the manuscript, coordinated the making of the compact disc that accompanies this book, and secured two readers, whose criticisms greatly improved the manuscript. I hope these anonymous readers will discover my appreciation here. My thanks to Karen Gangel, the manuscript editor, for the many ways she improved the clarity of the text.

On the strength of his distinguished career as a record producer, George Avakian gave invaluable advice on the business aspects of creating a historical anthology of recordings. Subsequently, when Sony Music Special Products took over the project, Lynne Frost, John Muller, and Tom Laskey handled areas in which Fred and I were complete novices: licensing the recording rights and manufacturing the compact disc. Johnny Simmen, Arild Wilderöe, and Don Waterhouse helped to resolve an especially difficult problem concerning permissions. Sony Music Special Products, the arts library of the Pennsylvania State University, and Blue Train (a compact disc store in State College, Pennsylvania), provided the music tracks that went into the making of that disc. Sam Aldrich, of Audio Etc. (a high-fidelity equipment store in New Haven), graciously volunteered to make digital audio tapes of two tracks that, at the time of writing, had appeared only on LP. The master tape was engineered by Gene Kimball of the Fred Plaut Recording Studios in New Haven.

For help in identifying copyright holders and obtaining copies of original sheet music, I am grateful to Calvin Elliker, head of the Music Library at the University of Michigan; William L. Schurk, archivist for sound recordings at the Popular Culture Library of Bowling Green State University; Victor T. Cardell and Henry Rivero, respectively head and assistant to the head of the Archive of Popular American Music at the University of California, Los Angeles; David Sanjek of the BMI Archives; and Dave Berger, who generously supplied free copies of his scores of Count Basie's *Jumpin' at the Woodside* and Duke Ellington's *Ko-Ko* and who offered, unsolicited, an insight into the creation of Ben Webster's tenor saxophone part on *Ko-Ko*. Dan Morgenstern, director of the Institute of Jazz Studies, patiently answered assorted discographical questions. Burt Fenner, professor of music at the Pennsylvania State University, kindly took time to introduce me to the Finale music-notation software program and, late in the project, helped iron out a notational problem.

In this, my third book, the acknowledgments end in the now-usual manner, with a special note of thanks to my loving wife and "patron," Sally McMurry, whose flourishing career as associate professor of history at the Pennsylvania State University allows me to pursue free-lance jazz writing.

Sources and Permissions
for Music Examples

Included in the book are a few excerpts from published songs, listed below. I have used an excerpt from an unsigned arrangement of *Blue Skies* (attributed to Mary Lou Williams), held in the archives of the Smithsonian Museum of American History, and several excerpts from Dave Berger's published score of Duke Ellington's *Ko-Ko,* which Berger created with the aid of individual instrumental parts held in that same museum. All of the remaining examples come directly from recordings. Included are passages notated by Berger, Charles Blancq, Franz Kerschbaumer, Thomas Owens, and the late John Mehegan; their contributions are indicated in captions to the examples. Except where these names are indicated, all transcriptions from recordings into music notation are my own.

For the purposes of comparative description, all examples in the book are in concert pitch, and all versions of a title are in the same key. Consequently the pitches of certain pieces are transpositions, not replicas, of materials detailed below.

I am grateful to the publishers and researchers listed below for permission to reproduce copyrighted material. Every effort has been made to trace copyright holders, and I apologize to anyone whose name may have been omitted.

Seven fragments from Josef Zawinul's *Birdland* appear by permission of Mr. Zawinul and Mulatto Music. Fuller details of copyright appear beneath example 12 in chapter 2 and example 30 in chapter 3.

Two fragments from the melody of Irving Berlin's *Blue Skies* appear by permission of the Irving Berlin Music Company. Fuller details of copyright appear beneath example 33.

The melody and piano accompaniment of Ray Noble's *Cherokee* appear by permission of Shapiro, Bernstein, and Co., Inc. These have been taken from the original sheet music, a copy of which was supplied by the UCLA Archive of Popular American Music. Fuller details of copyright appear beneath example 24 in chapter 3.

A transcription of portions of the theme of Charles Mingus's *Fables of Faubus*, as recorded in 1959, appears by permission of Susan Graham Ungaro Mingus and the Charles Mingus Institute.

The melody and lyrics of *Georgia on My Mind*, by songwriter Hoagy Carmichael and lyricist Stuart Gorrell, appear by permission of CPP/Belwin, Inc. Fuller details of copyright appear beneath example 52 in chapter 6.

A number of fragments from Count Basie's *Jumpin' at the Woodside*, as recorded in 1938 and as transcribed by Dave Berger, also appear by permission of Warner/Chappell Music, Inc. Fuller details of copyright appear beneath example 40 in chapter 4. Berger's score has been published by King Brand Products, Inc., New York.

A number of fragments from Duke Ellington's *Ko-Ko*, as recorded in 1940 and as preserved in a score prepared by Dave Berger, appear by permission of CPP/Belwin, Inc. Fuller details of copyright appear beneath examples 37 and 38 in chapter 4; examples 42 and 43 in chapter 5; and example 55 in chapter 6. Berger's score has been published in two contexts: separately, by King Brand Products, Inc., New York; and as one of many diverse items in *The Norton Scores: An Anthology for Listening*, volume 2, edited by Roger Kamien (New York: Norton, 1990), pp. 1084–1102.

The transcription of the first 48 bars of the piano and string bass accompaniment to Charlie Parker's solo choruses on take 2 of *Koko* (1945) was prepared by Thomas Owens. It first appeared in his "Charlie Parker: Techniques of Improvisation" (Ph.D. dissertation, University of California, Los Angeles, 1974). It reappears here by permission of Dr. Owens.

A theme from William H. Tyers's *Panama*, as published by Leo Feist in New York in 1911, has been taken from the original sheet music, a copy of which was supplied by the UCLA Archive of Popular American Music.

The melody of *'Round Midnight* appears by permission of Warner/Chappell Music, Inc. Fuller details of copyright appear beneath example 11 in chapter 2. Transcriptions of Miles Davis's solos on two versions of *'Round Midnight* (both from 1956) were first published in Franz Kerschbaumer, *Miles Davis: Stilkritische Untersuchungen zur musikalischen Entwicklung seines Personalstils* (Graz, Austria: Institut für Jazzforschung, 1978). They reappear here by permission of the Institute and its head, Dr. Kerschbaumer.

Charles Blancq's transcription of Sonny Rollins's solo on *St. Thomas* appeared in his "Melodic Improvisation in American Jazz: The Style of Theodore 'Sonny' Rollins, 1951–1962" (Ph.D. dissertation, Tulane University, 1977). An excerpt appears here by permission of Dr. Blancq.

Two fragments of the melody of Victor Young's *Sweet Sue—Just You* appear by permission of Shapiro, Bernstein and Co., Inc., New York. Fuller details of copyright appear beneath example 21 in chapter 3.

Transcriptions from the New Orleans Rhythm Kings' recordings of three takes of *Tin Roof Blues* appear by permission of Edwin H. Morris and Co., a division of MPL Communications, Inc., New York. Fuller details of copyright appear beneath example 20 in chapter 3 and examples 44 and 45 in chapter 6.

What to Listen For in Jazz

1 INTRODUCTION

Jazz can be blatantly exhilarating and exciting. A performance such as Duke Ellington's *Trumpet No End* has exactly this sort of immediate attraction. It moves along from the first note with relentless drive and ends with Cat Anderson cleanly popping out an unbelievable high note on the trumpet in a moment of true virtuosity. This sort of listening requires no explanation. Let the music wash over you. Play it again, louder. Tap your foot. Listen in awe.

Jazz may also be subtle and profound, its understanding requiring years of experience and careful listening. Perhaps an explanation of the process of making jazz—in the form of this book—will help too. Even a performance such as *Trumpet No End*, with all its showy and accessible qualities, rewards close study: how does clarinetist Jimmy Hamilton's brief solo fit into the formal scheme; how does that little solo encapsulate the melodic expression of swing rhythm; how has arranger Mary Lou Williams woven an existing melody into the accompaniment during the trumpet solo that follows Hamilton? And if *Trumpet No End* supplies, through its raw vitality, a good starting point for listening to jazz, it also supplies a focus for a searching ending—the question of how to distinguish the personal sounds of the five trumpet soloists. Don't just let the music wash over you. Tap your foot, listen in awe, and think about what you hear.

What to Listen For in Jazz is organized around seven topics: rhythm, forms, arrangement, composition, improvisation, sound, and style. To lend substance to these topics, examples have been drawn from twenty-one recorded selections. For convenience of reading and listening, these tracks have been collected on a compact disc, with timings keying the text and the notated music examples to the minutes and seconds of the recorded music. The discography of this CD (given in appendix 2) lists personnel, instrumentation, and place and date of recording for each of these twenty-one selections, and it identifies the CD or LP issue from which each track has been dubbed. The discography also identifies issues of several additional recordings that amplify a particular point in the text.

The intent is not to work exhaustively through all twenty-one selections for all topics but to choose moments that best illustrate a concept or procedure or style—so that the reader may in effect use these musical excerpts as firm stepping stones along the path into the vastness of jazz. The focus is on fundamental examples, some requiring no special knowledge, others requiring the ability to read music and a rudimentary acquaintance with music theory. Yet this book does not shy away from complexity. For each topic, there are challenging examples and, when necessary, references to sophisticated analytical concepts. In particular, an excerpt from Earl Hines's recording of *Sweet Sue* (chap. 2, ex. 17) should prove challenging even to the most accomplished musicians. I count in weeks the amount of time it took to transcribe these fourteen seconds of jazz into music notation.

The following chapters speak for themselves and should need no further introduction. What might be mentioned before embarking on this tour of musical concepts, procedures, and styles is a topic that is not of concern here: listening for a program. In the popular imagination, jazz musicians are valued for their ability to "tell a story." As in many types of music, playing jazz is a highly emotional business. In some sense it expresses life. But jazz does not depend heavily on lyrics, and thus opportunities are tightly circumscribed for reaching any general agreement on just how an ensemble or an individual expresses that life.

To be sure, there are specific accounts of how programs have provided the inspiration for performance, none more so than in the music of Duke Ellington, who was as programmatic as a composer can be. One such story was told in a series of interviews on BBC Radio 3, broadcast in advance of drummer Max Roach's concert at Queen Elizabeth Hall in London on October 3, 1989. In conversation with jazz writer Charles Fox, Roach described an example of Ellington's programmatic method in a trio session with bass player Charles Mingus. Ellington conjured up an image of piles and piles of money, which the three men then translated into an emotional and musical response that became *Money Jungle*.[1]

Although this approach to creation may be crucially important to the musicians involved in that creation, it seems far less important—and often of no help at all—to the subject of this book. While listening to a track, should one be able to identify a meaningful musical relationship between the program and the resulting sound? In comparing *Money Jungle* to other performances on a monetary or jungle theme, should one expect to find a unifying musical character and emotion? Performers may well share programmatic ideas, which help shape the creation of a piece, but for listeners, jazz programs are entirely subjective and individual. Those who feel the need for a direct connection between sound and story would do better to invent a personal interpretation rather than to look for stories in a book such as this.

There are times, though, when the title of a piece seems to be expressed directly in sound. Among the twenty-one selections in this book, two titles are particularly instructive—one because it cautions us not to give too much weight to programmatic titles, the other because the title seems to help listeners understand the music making, which is not usually the case.

The first of these two pieces, Mingus's *Fables of Faubus*, conveys a mocking, satirical emotion, even in the version that Mingus recorded for Columbia in 1959, a version that omits the lyrics. It might therefore seem crucial to know that Faubus was Orval Faubus, the governor of Arkansas who in 1957 sent the National Guard into Little Rock to prevent the integration of the school system. *Fables* could therefore be considered a musical commentary on this and other landmarks of the emerging civil rights movement. But too much can be made of the political reference, for the program goes only a short way toward explaining why *Fables of Faubus* is such a remarkable piece of jazz. A more substantial answer lies in its form and composition. In addition, an uncomfortable circumstance surrounds the political interpretation. According to Mingus's drummer, Dannie Richmond, Mingus had already created the music when, during a performance, the two men began to improvise lyrics. From there the title and program followed.[2]

The contrasting example is Sun Ra's *Outer Nothingness*. Interpreted within the context of this musician's eccentric personality and musical methods, the title may be understood as a programmatic instruction to his band. The description of what that instruction might mean musically is reserved for discussions of collective improvisation and group timbres (see, respectively, chaps. 6 and 7). For the moment, it is enough to say that the imagined program seems to provide the single best analytical clue to how this enigmatic piece of jazz operates. The recording presents, as it were, a musical story of outer nothingness.

The book now turns to its true concern, sound. The aim is to present musical concepts and procedures that explain how jazz works and then to provide an introduction to the understanding of style.

2 RHYTHM

A bass should play nice four-beat rhythm that can be heard, but no slapping. I can't stand bass players when they slap the strings.

I want the drummer to be straight with the section. He's messing with the rhythm when he drops those bombs. In small groups, I like the drummer to play a little tinkety-boom on that one cymbal, four-beats on the pedal. Just little simple things.
—Lester Young

For all the changes that jazz has undergone in its headlong rush through the twentieth century, the music first played in the streets, dance halls, and saloons of New Orleans continues to make itself felt, not only by being recreated, revised, and adapted, but more broadly by underpinning certain basic assumptions about jazz performance. The most important assumption has to do with rhythm: except in some types of free jazz, the vast majority of musicians agree on the need to keep feet tapping, walking, marching, and dancing. Even when the New Orleans style has been transformed into a drastically different art music and concert music, jazz rhythm still provides a simple, reliable framework for performance.

This chapter begins with a list of rhythmic concepts that occur unsystematically: four-beat, two-beat, backbeat, double-time, break, and stop-time. From there it proceeds to two grand approaches emanating from the bedrock principle that the music have a beat. One approach utilizes patterns of accentuation and triplet subdivision that developed within jazz. In the early 1930s this rhythm came to be known as "swing," after having been around for at least a decade. The other uses patterns of accentuation and duple subdivision borrowed from various musical forms over the years: the ragtime and parade rhythms that inspired jazz; the Charleston and Black Bottom of the 1920s; the Caribbean and Brazilian dances that influenced jazz throughout its history, but particularly from the mid-1940s on; and the rock, funk, soul, disco, and rap rhythms of the past three decades.

The expression of these patterns varies considerably, with performers pounding out the beat or manipulating rhythm in wondrously subtle ways. The chapter ends with a close look at some of the subtler possibilities: nuances of rhythmic placement, unpredictable syncopation, superimposed meter, and rhythm freed from the beat.

The Four-Beat

Countless performances have not merely a steady beat but an explicit steady beat known as a four-beat, because jazz is overwhelmingly dominated by pieces in $\frac{4}{4}$ time. It may take the form of a "nice four-beat rhythm" and "four-beats on the pedal," as Lester Young requested in his instructions to bass players and drummers. (By the way, Young was referring to the bass-drum pedal, not to the pedal of the hi-hat cymbal.) Or the beat may fall on the shoulders of other members of the "rhythm section," a wide-ranging label that applies to diverse combinations of chordal, bass, and percussion instruments.

The rhythm section of Count Basie's big band (Young's fellow bandsmen) emphasizes a four-beat on *Jumpin' at the Woodside* (track 2). To begin, pianist Basie pounds out an on-the-beat pattern. He was renowned for his ability to set up the perfect tempo for a given piece by means of fingers on the keyboard rather than by conducting or by counting 1-2-3-4. Once having established that tempo, he would take up a less rigid rhythm, with timekeeping duties handed over to his sidemen. In this instance, the sidemen are Freddie Green, who strokes four-beat guitar chords, and Walter Page, who plucks a four-beat bass line. Drummer Jo Jones plays something more than a four-beat, although his swing pattern (of the type discussed below) also involves striking on each beat. Although Decca's murky recording makes it difficult to hear exact details (no music example appears here), the lack of detail has no effect on the four-beat swing. These musicians made up the finest rhythm section of their era, and *Jumpin' at the Woodside* is an irresistible example of them at their best.

The Two-Beat

Accents on beats 1 and 3 constitute a two-beat. From its name, the two-beat would seem to be a sort of parallel or alternative to the four-beat, but the two are different. Whereas the four-beat can occur anywhere in the rhythm section, the two-beat is anchored mainly by bass playing. This rhythm might involve the string bass, electric bass guitar, tuba, bass saxophone, bass register of the piano, organ bass pedal, synthesized bass, or even a bass drum, which one hears thumping out a two-beat that begins at bar 13 of Ornette Coleman's *Honeymooners* (track 3, 0:21). The exact instrument does not matter, so long as there is a firm splat, thump, or honk on the appropriate beats.

The two-beat is often associated with early styles of jazz in which bass instruments expressed the "oom" in the oom-pah oom-pah rhythms heard in the marches and rags that inspired much of the music. But any evolutionary account that proposes a general transition from two-beat jazz to four-beat jazz should be viewed skeptically. For one thing, the two-beat carried over into later styles, becoming a standard device for ballads; this is evident in the recording of *'Round Midnight*, discussed below in the section on double-time. For another, the two-beat and four-beat often go hand in hand. Bass notes might sound on one and three, while a chord sounds on each beat; or the bass line might dance between a two-beat and a four-beat.

John Lindsay gives a good demonstration of this last variation in slapping out the string bass line on Jelly Roll Morton's *Black Bottom Stomp*. The clearest examples are during the first, second, and fifth statements of the piece's second theme, which is 20 bars long. (See ex. 26 in chap. 3 for a succinct diagram of the structure of *Black Bottom Stomp*.) During the second statement, which features Omer Simeon on clarinet, Lindsay sticks to a two-beat, except when he and the other accompanists stop playing during the solos at bars 7–8 and 19–20 (track 15, 1:14). During the first statement, for the full ensemble, and the fifth, featuring a banjo solo, Lindsay plays an identical pattern: a two-beat in bars 1–2, 5, and 9 and a four-beat elsewhere—again, except for the solos at bars 7–8 (track 15, 0:55 and 2:09).

While *Black Bottom Stomp* is cued up, listen to how Johnny St. Cyr's banjo playing operates at a rhythmic pace different from Lindsay's. When St. Cyr is not playing an irregular, arranged pattern (as in the pairing of clarinet and banjo during the third statement of the 16-bar opening theme), he variously plays a four-beat and eighth notes (the latter constituting what might be called an eight-beat). Taken together, the rhythms of Lindsay and St. Cyr confirm a time-honored principle: speed and excitement are not necessarily related. The fast-moving banjo part, for example, is not especially interesting. When, after the interlude between the two main themes, Lindsay enters with a two-beat that is somehow driving and relaxed at the same time, *Black Bottom Stomp* positively bursts with excitement (track 15, 0:51). These simultaneous yet differing levels of rhythmic activity, a commonplace event in the music, also serve as a further warning against any rigid discussion of four-beat jazz and two-beat jazz.

Backbeat

Strong accents on beats 2 and 4 constitute a backbeat—an effect sometimes used to add intensity. In the climactic section that ends *Black Bottom Stomp*, a backbeat rhythm on the tom-tom drum provides an extra push (track 15, 2:47). During the last minute or so of Weather Report's *Birdland*, backbeat hand clapping serves a similar purpose, although here, as the recording is about to fade out, the clapping quadruples in speed from a backbeat to continuous eighth notes, to crank the rhythmic intensity up yet another notch (track 21, 4:24).

Alternatively the backbeat may be used as a fundamental rhythmic pattern. A snappy backbeat anchors the last minute of Coleman's *Honeymooners* (track 3, 3:21). Also, about a minute and a half into this piece, there is a rhythmically disorienting moment when the bass drum, having earlier played a two-beat rhythm, now thumps out a backbeat rhythm (track 3, 1:36). The conventional association between two-beat and bass drum is so strong that it almost seems here as if the meter had turned around, beats 1 and 3 becoming beats 2 and 4, though in fact the meter remains constant.

Double-Time

Double-time involves a doubling of tempo in the rhythm section, a doubling of the general speed of the melody line, or both. This musical device is usually obvious—particularly when a melody suddenly picks up speed—but not always. Recognizing double-time requires one to pin down the tempo. Identifying the beat can sometimes be difficult, even in the most toe-tapping styles, not because of any irregularity in the music or incompetence in its performance but because musicians present two tempos. By using the simultaneously differing levels of rhythmic activity noted in *Black Bottom Stomp*,, though in a subtler way, performers can leave open the issue of distinguishing between time and double-time.

Charles Mingus's *Fables of Faubus* offers straightforward examples of double-time, along with other basic rhythmic devices: a two-beat and a walking four-beat on the bass, played by Mingus, and swing rhythms on the cymbals, played by Dannie Richmond. About two minutes into the theme, the tempo shifts, as the alto saxophone improvisation, walking bass line, and swinging cymbal patterns all double in speed to create the impression of eight rather than four measures at bars 56–59. (See ex. 41 in chap. 5 for a diagram of the theme and a full transcription of the double-time passage.)

Double-time in Coleman Hawkins's version of *The Man I Love* is just as straightforward, but with a twist: the entire piece is in double-time, the harmonies having been stretched out to make a swinging romp through a cyclic 64-bar theme out of what was originally a 32-bar ballad (track 10, 0:09–1:20, 1:20–2:35, 2:35–3:50, 3:50–end). One needs to know standard versions of *The Man I Love*, taken at its usual slow pace, to recognize that Hawkins's group has doubled that pace throughout.

The interpretation of *'Round Midnight* by the Miles Davis quintet (recorded for Columbia in 1956) uses double-time as more than a rudimentary means of generating activity. In this recording, it becomes a sophisticated device that subtly undermines the opening tempo and is in turn subtly undermined. At the start, the ballad is quietly interrupted by a couple of closely related double-time patterns, the first sounded by pianist Red Garland and drummer Philly Joe Jones in the second half of bars 2 and 4, the second, with bassist Paul Chambers added, filling bars 7–8 (ex. 1). In the course of Davis's muted trumpet solo, Jones, playing with brushes, sneaks in a double-time feeling at the midpoint of the 32-bar solo (bars 15–20; track 5, 1:32) and again during the last phrase (bars 25–30; track 5, 2:10). Meanwhile Chambers pulls in the other direction by playing mainly a two-beat bass line, although he does not stick to it rigorously. As Davis's solo ends, Jones rolls a soft whir on the drums to smooth the transition away from the original tempo, and Garland then "counts off" the new pulse by tinkling the keys from octave to octave. Jones lays down his brushes in favor of drumsticks, and the band launches into double-time with a fanfare (ex. 2). The double-time feeling continues through John Coltrane's tenor saxophone solo, but Chambers is not so willing to let the ballad go. He plays the same patterns heard during Davis's solo: notes placed on the new beats 1 and 3, the occasional additional note on beat 4, and intermittent dancing figures. How should this be heard, as a two-beat in double-time or as a four-beat at the original pace? Why not hear it both ways?

Example 1. A double-time pattern in the introduction to Miles Davis's *'Round Midnight,* as recorded for Columbia in 1956. Track 5, 0:23.

Rhythm
10

Example 2. The fanfare at the midpoint of Davis's *'Round Midnight,* as recorded for Columbia in 1956. Track 5, 2:39.

42

The Break

A break is a momentary interruption of the accompaniment, during which a soloist steps to the fore. A break has two components: one formal, delineating the midpoint or end of a theme (see chap. 3); the other rhythmic. Although texturally a performance must change at a break, rhythmically the beat keeps moving. The tempo may become implicit, because the timekeeping instruments have been interrupted, but the force of jazz rhythm is such that often a melodic player feels compelled to take up the slack and approach melody as if beating a drum. An example of this occurs in Louis Armstrong's trumpet break, following Kid Ory's trombone solo on *Hotter than That* (ex. 3). Armstrong's rising melody fills the silence with a drumlike succession of continuous eighth notes. He keeps the line from becoming monotonous by grouping the eighth notes into a pattern of accentuation that twice doubles in speed: two groups of four notes, two groups of two notes, two single notes.

Example 3. Louis Armstrong's trumpet break on *Hotter than That*. Track 1, 2:33.

Stop-Time

A close cousin of the break is stop-time, a technique in which a normal accompaniment is interrupted in favor of a repeated pattern of stark accents. Like the break, stop-time supplies textural contrast and presumes the continuation of an implicit, steady beat. "Time" (the beat) does not actually stop.

Black Bottom Stomp, a virtual compendium of rhythmic jazz devices, includes a stop-time passage between Morton's piano solo and St. Cyr's banjo solo. While cornetist George Mitchell plays a solo, the rest of the band repeats a 2-bar-long syncopated pattern (ex. 4), interrupted by Mitchell's break in bars 7–8 of the chorus. (Syncopation is discussed later in the chapter.)

Example 4. The rhythm of the stop-time chorus in Jelly Roll Morton's Black Bottom Stomp. Track 15, 1:50.

Although Black Bottom Stomp is an extraordinary performance, the stop-time section falters in that the band's syncopated rhythm is not as tightly coordinated as Morton meant it to be. Such flaws bring to mind one of the basic concepts of jazz: some jazz musicians may put a great premium on perfect unity of execution (Benny Goodman was a renowned perfectionist), whereas others may find the musical interest elsewhere. Jazz is therefore not the sort of music in which a performance is necessarily ruined because of a mistake in detail. In ambitious performances, inspired interpretation may preclude perfection.

The little catalog of rhythmic devices—four-beat, two- beat, backbeat, double-time, break, and stop-time—will continue to make its presence felt in rhythmic topics that follow, as well as in later chapters addressing structure and procedures (forms, arrangement, composition, and improvisation). But the focus now turns to the two grand rhythmic systems in jazz: swing rhythm and duple rhythm. The discussion centers on how they work separately, coalesce, and sometimes disappear altogether, giving way to music freed from the beat.

Swing Rhythm

Swing in its broadest sense involves the simultaneous interaction of rhythmic components of articulation, duration, note placement, contour, dynamics, and vibrato. That is to say, layers of rhythmic pulsation are piled on top of one another. The musician articulates one note crisply, another gently, another imperceptibly, in an infinitely varied succession of pulsations. The relative length of adjacent notes or silences creates a second layer of pulsation. Placement of notes in relationship to the under-lying beat—on the beat, between the beat, ahead of it (by a lot, by a little), behind it (by a lot, by a little)—creates a third layer of pulsation. Against these three layers, pitches move—high note, low note, in between, back up, higher still—and the resulting contours of melody, countermelody, or bass line create another infinitely varied pulsation, defined by the pace at which pitches (or general areas of pitch) recur. These same pitches (or areas of pitch) vary in loudness, perhaps in a clichéd manner—high and loud, low and soft—but often in a marvelously ingenious and unpredict-able manner, thereby creating yet another infinitely varied pulsation. Fi-nally, a steady or a changing vibrato, if present, pulsates in relationship to the ground beat, perhaps moving in phase with that ground beat but more often defining, as it were, a different and variable beat. When these layers are presented in the right way—whatever that may be—the result swings. It is as if the patterns of human speech that yield sense had been translated by analogy into an equivalent, subtle, complex musical rhythm, yielding swing.

Swing is a subject of eternal disagreement. Insofar as the disagreement stems from perceptions of subtle, complex rhythm, it seems genuine: the fine details of swing can be hard to hear, and invariably these details defy precise analysis and rational notation. But among jazz fans a snobbish tradition sometimes makes the subject exclusive: if you don't already know what swing is, we're certainly not going to tell you. Accessible, musically rational qualities are sometimes ignored or belittled: take the simplest swing rhythm, with none of the intricacies of sophisticated jazz-samba or jazz-funk rhythmic patterns (those based on duple rhythms rather than on swing), and someone will call that swing rhythm unfathomable. And the concept "swing" is sometimes use in a stylistically vague and almost per-verse manner, so that "it swings" seems to mean little more than "the rhythm sounds good to me."

In terms of a speechlike, multifaceted layering of rhythm, *Black Bottom Stomp* swings madly, as does *Jumpin' at the Woodside*, but the present chapter distinguishes between these pieces, by focusing on just a few of these rhythmic components, ones that are not particularly hard to hear or to describe and that are the source of two grand rhythmic streams. From this more restrictive perspective, Basie's performance swings, but Mor-ton's emphatically does not. To fail to make the distinction is to fail to perceive the two most widespread and fundamental rhythmic traditions in jazz.

The essential properties of a simple swing rhythm can be summarized by Lester Young's concise definition, the rhythmic phrase "tinkety boom." Simple swing should meet three criteria:

1. Some beats are explicitly subdivided into three parts (tin ke ty).
2. The first and third parts receive emphasis (TIN ke TY).
3. The third part sounds as if it were connected more to the following beat than to its own (TIN ke TY-BOOM) and thus pushes the rhythm forward.

It might also be useful to spell out what these criteria are not. On the one hand, triple subdivision of the beat is not, in and of itself, sufficient for swing. Accentuation matters as well, just as it does in distinguishing, say, a duple subdivision in calypso from a duple subdivision in disco. A common African drum rhythm in $\frac{6}{8}$, for example, uses the age-old device called hemiola, in which every other note (in triple meter) receives emphasis (TIN-ke-TY tin-KE-ty). This compelling and hypnotic pattern of triplet subdivision creates a back-and-forth motion that melds poorly with the continuous propulsion of swing.

On the other hand, it is not necessary to split every beat to evoke the swing feeling. A continuous triplet subdivision called "shuffle rhythm" (tinkety tinkety tinkety tinkety) developed in jazz during the late 1930s, but it became more characteristic of the rhythmically stricter rhythm-and-blues style than of jazz, because it lacked suppleness. Indeed, a swing rhythm need not be consistent or symmetrical. A drummer might mix up the presentation of *tinkety*s and *boom*s, with the result that emphasized beats change from measure to measure. Or a drummer might play a long series of accents strictly on the beat and then a single "tinkety," which alone evokes the long-standing and potent rhythmic tradition standing behind that little rhythmic pattern.

Coleman Hawkins's *The Man I Love* offers a clear example of percussive swing rhythm. During the piano and tenor sax solos that frame the piece, Shelly Manne uses wire brushes on the snare drum to provide an insistent but subdued accompaniment. His rhythm might be described as shinkety swish, to paraphrase Young. In the middle of the piece, during Oscar Pettiford's string bass solo, Manne switches over to the hi-hat cymbal, which he keeps closed (the pedal pressed down), the result being something along the lines of tippety tap.

Jazz musicians do not usually notate swing rhythm the way that it sounds, because indications of a triplet subdivision of the beat clutter the page. Instead, the long-short triplet pair (TINke TY) is written as a pair of even ("straight") eighth notes or—alternatively and far less often—as a dotted eighth and sixteenth pair. A brief instruction may appear at the top of the page ("swing," "swing feel," "swing eighths," "jazz eighths," or the like); or there may be no instruction whatsoever, the performer being expected to know that the rhythm is not to be played literally. The upper staff of example 5 presents Manne's swing rhythm in its cumbersome triplet notation; the lower staff presents that same rhythm in even eighths, together with the instruction "swing eighths." (Examples used in this book follow the latter approach.) Readers might also take a second look at examples 1 and 2, double-time passages from *'Round Midnight* in which the swing feeling operates at the sixteenth-note level rather than at the eighth-note level—hence "swing sixteenths."

Example 5. A literal transcription of the swing rhythm that Shelly Manne plays on Coleman Hawkins's *The Man I Love* (upper staff); this same rhythm as it would normally be notated (lower staff). Track 10, 0:08.

The single-mindedness that Manne exhibits is appreciated in many types of drum, bass, guitar, and piano playing but finds less favor when one steps out of the rhythm section. When acting as a fellow contributor to timekeeping, a melodic player may be tempted to play an outpouring of continuous notes, as Armstrong does on *Hotter than That* and as Jimmy Hamilton does in the clarinet break that finishes the introduction to Duke Ellington's *Trumpet No End* (ex. 6).

Example 6. Jimmy Hamilton's clarinet break on Duke Ellington's *Trumpet No End*. Track 7, 0:06.

But in this sort of example, when the melodic player takes up the burden of maintaining an explicit beat, another consideration—the need for variety in the contour and articulation of a melody—requires that swing melody be more complex than Manne's drumming. Hamilton's contrasts of higher and lower pitches, and of attacked and slurred notes, operate along with the swing eighths to create several levels of rhythmic action, thereby sustaining the listener's interest. In a solo break that moves away from the beat, and in any lengthy melody, there is additionally the need for variety in the duration of notes and silences. Vibrato may also be at work as a rhythmic device, supplying a continuous undulation (not necessarily in phase with the beat) or changing in speed and intensity with individual notes. As mentioned earlier, all these devices used together create a multilayered, speechlike rhythmic pattern far more complex and intangible than the simplest swing drumming. Yet this complexity does not mean that it is always difficult to assess the melodies that swing and the ones that don't.

The distinction seems clear-cut in the first half of *Hotter than That*, in which Armstrong's playing and singing surround Johnny Dodds's clarinet solo. The piece does not move at a particularly fast tempo, but in 1927 swing had not yet achieved wide currency, and Armstrong had the then-rare ability to maintain the swing feeling while creating a relaxed and tuneful line at medium speed. As great a player as Dodds was, he could not come close to matching his leader in this area.

Example 7 presents the trumpet and clarinet solos, as well as the beginning of Armstrong's "scat singing" (vocalizing with nonsense syllables rather than with lyrics). The concern here is rhythmic placement, and less attention has been given to exact duration, especially when a note on the beat is followed by a silence off the beat. In Armstrong's portions the instruction "swing eighths" is in operation. There are rhythmic patterns that run through dance-oriented music, and on this recording Armstrong is, as musicians would say, "locked into the groove" of the swing pattern. He is so comfortable with it, in fact, that he is able to drift away momentarily (at bar 14 of the piece) in a manner that heightens the rhythmic tension without disrupting the swing.

In Dodds's hot and frenetic solo, an attempt has been made to spell out the details of straight eighths, swing eighths, and (occasionally) dotted eighths. Readers are welcome to argue with the particulars. Dodds himself seems to have been unable to make up his mind. Sometimes he falls into the straight style of ragtime; sometimes he produces swing eighths, though without the relaxation characteristic of Armstrong's playing; and sometimes his rhythmic needle skips across the solo, failing to land in either groove. (Boxed italic letters in ex. 7 refer to the structure described in chap. 3.)

Example 7a. Louis Armstrong's trumpet solo on *Hotter than That.* Track 1, 0:08.

Example 7b. Johnny Dodds's clarinet solo on *Hotter than That*. Track 1, 0:42.

Rhythm
18

Example 7c. The start of Armstrong's vocal solo on *Hotter than That*. Track 1, 1:18.

Dip deh doop da,   doe doe doe doe.   Dah dew dah   doot doot dew,

Duple Rhythms

The question of jazz that swings, and jazz that doesn't, need not involve judgments of quality, as in the claim that Armstrong's melody is better than Dodds's, in part because it swings. Rather, the distinction may involve an opposition between swing rhythm and duple rhythm, neither having an inherent advantage over the other.

Duple rhythm circumscribes a grab bag of styles that are in many other respects incompatible: early jazz styles, Caribbean and Brazilian styles, and fusions with popular music. Chronologically last and rhythmically most systematic among these are the hyphenated styles that take their rhythms and their names from popular music: jazz-funk, jazz-soul, jazz-disco, jazz-rap. Jazz-rock may be added to the list as well, although despite frequent use of the label, strict rock rhythms fused with jazz are less usual than the other inventions, jazz having tilted its rhythmic head more toward African-American dances than toward English and white American rock beats. In these styles, swinging cymbal patterns and walking four-beat bass lines sound meek and inappropriate. Instead, the drummer slices the beat apart symmetrically into two or four parts, while the bass repeats, and perhaps varies, syncopated patterns.

Weather Report's *Birdland* provides an emphatic example (track 21). At the beginning, Joe Zawinul plays a synthesized bass line that is heavily syncopated: he attacks each held note on the last eighth note of a measure and carries it through the downbeat of the next measure. After three statements of this pattern, a constant disco beat gets under way: while Manolo Badrena shakes out continuous sixteenth notes on the tambourine, accenting each beat by tapping on the beat, Alex Acuña plays continuous eighth notes on an alternately closed and open hi-hat cymbal, accenting each offbeat by striking the open cymbal. When a counterpoint between synthesized chords and an electric bass guitar line begins 16 bars later, Acuña adds a click on each beat by striking the metal edge of the snare drum. Hence quarter notes, eighth notes, sixteenth notes—a beginner's music lesson, all the more so because of the click, which brings the group as close to playing along with a metronome as they could get. But some of the most forceful dance rhythms are the simplest ones, and when in a live version (for details of this recording, see appendix 2) Weather Report "dresses up" *Birdland* by substituting a swinging shuffle rhythm for the disco beat, the whole piece drags down, as if someone had attached a lead weight to the rhythm section.

The second stylistic collection, Caribbean and Brazilian dance rhythms, spans the history of jazz. There have been many milestones along the way: Jelly Roll Morton's frequently cited use of the "Spanish tinge"; beginning in the mid-1940s, Dizzy Gillespie's work with Afro-Cuban jazz; beginning in 1956, Sonny Rollins's improvisations on West Indian calypso music; during the mid-1960s, a craze for Brazilian "cool" samba rhythms (bossa nova); and since the 1970s, the incorporation of "hot" samba rhythms into fusion. The connection between samba and fusion rhythms is natural, because both utilize duple subdivisions of the beat, which makes their integration seamless. Yet there is also a link between swing and Afro-Cuban, Afro-Brazilian, and West Indian dance patterns, because the leading practitioners of these three jazz rhythms were for many years deeply involved in jazz that swings and searching for ways to bring the two systems together.

Gillespie's *Manteca* and Rollins's *St. Thomas* clearly illustrate Caribbean dance rhythms and their confluence with swing. In tracing these threads through *Manteca*, as Gillespie recorded it for RCA in 1947, it is helpful to present a structural design, which will be further elaborated in chapter 3:

Example 8a. The form of Dizzy Gillespie's recording of *Manteca* for RCA in 1947. Track 8.

Opening (0:00)
28 bars

Chorus 1 (0:38)
40

a   a   b   b'   a
8 + 8 + 8 + 8 + 8

Interlude (1:33)
10

Chorus 2 (1:47)
40

c   c   b   b'   a
8 + 8 + 8 + 8 + 8

Ending (2:42)
16

At the opening, four ostinatos (brief and persistently repeated patterns) enter successively on the conga drum, string bass, baritone sax, and trombones (ex. 8b). Kenny Clarke's drumming roughly doubles the conga, though exact details are not easy to hear. In this segment of the piece, the focus is on rhythm, with the harmony comprising only three pitches, B♭, F, and A♭; even Chano Pozo, on the conga, has taken care to tune his drum to these pitches. The rhythm of the ostinato builds upon a steady flow of eighth notes sounded by Pozo. As in all Caribbean and Brazilian popular styles (except reggae), everyone accents this flow of eighth notes in irregular groupings rather than on every beat or on a two-beat or on a backbeat. The result forms a revolving, blinking collection of accentuations.

Example 8b. Four ostinatos at the opening of *Manteca.* Track 8.

Duple rhythm continues throughout the opening, the first chorus, and the interlude, although there are nods in the direction of swing during segments *b* and *b'*, with Al McKibbon's walking bass line accompanying the occasional use of triplet rhythms in the sax section and in Gillespie's trumpet solo (track 8, 0:18). These isolated elements foreshadow the second chorus, which leaps into swing for segments based on the chord progression of *I Got Rhythm* and stays there for the return of segments *b*

and *b'*. The cymbal patterns, the walking bass line, the rhythms of the tenor sax solo, the ensemble lines, and Gillespie's trumpet solo all exemplify swing (track 8, 1:47); only Pozo refuses to go along, steadfastly maintaining his ostinato until everyone comes back into his camp for the remainder of the performance.

Rollins's *St. Thomas* begins with drummer Max Roach playing his interpretation of a calypso rhythm. In a parallel to the work of Pozo and Clarke on *Manteca*, Roach combines tuned and untuned percussion in a repeated pattern of irregularly grouped duple subdivisions of the beat (ex. 9; untuned pitches have crossed note heads). Roach's pattern incorporates a drumming formula that was current in the hard-bop style of the 1950s: a crisp backbeat, achieved by closing the hi-hat pedal. Although other elements of a characteristic hard-bop drum pattern have given way to calypso rhythm and although the hi-hat backbeat fits just as well into that calypso rhythm, it is entirely reasonable that Roach should have had his ear cocked toward swing rhythm as it was being expressed in hard bop. At the time he was coleader with trumpeter Clifford Brown of one of the three best hard-bop groups.

Example 9. Max Roach's drum pattern at the start of Sonny Rollins's *St. Thomas*. Track 18.

Rollins shared Roach's rhythmic conception. (Not coincidentally, he was a sideman in the Brown-Roach quintet when *St. Thomas* was recorded.) In his first tenor saxophone solo, Rollins supports Roach by building ideas mainly on an implicit flow of steady eighth notes, but he cannot completely hold back a propensity for swing, and thus the occasional fast run of swing eighths comes popping out. Meanwhile Doug Watkins takes a noncommittal approach, playing neither a syncopated nor a walking line but a two-beat (plus some additional notes on beat 4), which can fit into calypso or swing patterns.

In the course of Roach's drum solo, the rhythmic feel changes to swing (see chap. 6, ex. 46). When Rollins reenters with an abundance of swing eighths in his running melody, supported by Watkins's walking bass and Roach's tinkety boom cymbal patterns, the dance between calypso and swing rhythm has resolved itself unequivocally in favor of the latter.

A different cultural synthesis occurs in Herbie Hancock's *Maiden Voyage*, recorded in 1965. Hancock explained his idea this way: "My purpose in writing *Maiden Voyage* was to write a tune that had even eighth notes but didn't have the same kind of rock & roll back beat that I had been hearing around that time."[1] He seems to have taken the rhythmic pattern of the stereotypical Brazilian bossa nova (ex. 10, upper staff), which was all the rage in the mid-1960s, and displaced it in relation to the meter (ex. 10, lower staff). The resulting accompanimental rhythm forms the backbone of the piece. Pianist Hancock, bassist Ron Carter, and drummer Tony Williams do not adhere strictly to this rhythm, but it recurs throughout the piece.

Example 10. The stereotypical bossa nova rhythm (upper staff) and Herbie Hancock's transformation of it in his composition *Maiden Voyage* (lower staff). Track 9, 1:53.

Like *Manteca* and *St. Thomas*, *Maiden Voyage* also goes back and forth between swing eighths and straight eighths, but in a freer and less systematic way, with all the players participating in this dance between rhythmic streams. There is not a sense, as with Dodds on *Hotter than That*, of an improviser struggling frenetically to lock into the rhythmic groove. Rather, a sense of relaxation and mastery pervades the piece, with one musician suggesting a polymetric idea or a change of rhythmic feeling, and another responding immediately to that suggestion. One instance of the dance between rhythmic systems is notated later, in the discussion of modal improvisation (chap. 6, ex. 51): trumpeter Freddie Hubbard swings the eighth notes during the third 8-bar phrase of his solo and then returns to a duple rhythmic feeling.

Within the two rhythmic systems, the least systematic distinctions are found in a network of performances that meanders through the realm of brass bands, ragtime-based piano, New Orleans jazz, continuations of that style in dixieland bands, and revivals of New Orleans jazz from the late 1930s onward. One or the other rhythmic system may present itself piece by piece, instrument by instrument, or phrase by phrase.

Chronology has only a shaky bearing on the question. In the spring of 1923, when few of the African-American creators of New Orleans jazz had yet recorded, the white New Orleans Rhythm Kings showed themselves fully capable of achieving a lilting swing on *Tin Roof Blues*. (For transcriptions of portions of the piece, see chap. 3, ex. 20, and chap. 6, exx. 44 and 45.) It seems that even if swing rhythm took some years to develop, it was nonetheless already making its way. Three and a half years later, in September 1926, Jelly Roll Morton recorded *Black Bottom Stomp*. Morton was, paradoxically, as conservative as he was creative, and his composition adheres almost entirely to strict duple subdivisions of the beat. The only hint of swing comes in segments of George Mitchell's cornet melody. Perhaps this deviation from Morton's preference is not surprising, given what was at the time the overwhelming impact of Louis Armstrong upon jazz cornet playing.

In the area of rhythmic nuance, jazz regularly achieves a richness, complexity, subtlety, and depth that are profound. Such nuances involve microscopic variation in placing a melody against a steady beat, unpredictable syncopation, the superimposition of a new meter upon a prevailing meter, and freedom from conventional tempo, beat, and meter.

Microscopic Note Placement

Before a case can be made for varying fine details of melodic rhythms, it is best to look at another example of rhythm in standard accompaniment, to assure that there be no confusion between wobbly rhythm and pliant rhythm. In Kid Thomas's recording of *Panama*, the drum and piano rhythm wobbles because of the playing, not because of some glitch in the recording process. Like the stop-time chorus in *Black Bottom Stomp*, however, the wobbliness is not terribly important. This imperfection is overshadowed by the players' rhythmic enthusiasm, especially the joyful parade drumming. Nonetheless, this sort of accompaniment feels uncomfortable to anyone with a good ear for a steady beat.

The same reasoning need not apply to melody. Of course melody may wobble just as much as accompaniment, and some melodies might benefit from a greater rhythmic regularity (for example, Dodds on *Hotter than That*), but this does not mean that all great soloists must strap themselves to the beat. On the contrary, at the most rarefied level of jazz performance, soloists may toy with melody as if it were connected to the beat by means of a short, sturdy piece of elastic: the melody remains in the vicinity of the beat but floats on either side, without restriction. As it strays further from the beat, or into the territory of adjacent beats, tension increases, to be relieved only when the soloist snaps the melody back into place.

Miles Davis was a master of this technique. With a rock-steady rhythm section beneath him, he manipulated attack, dynamics, and duration, all in the service of rhythmic subtlety. It is not difficult to explain the principles at work, but it is nearly impossible to capture the details. A note slides in from silence. When did it begin? Another note arrives abruptly, crisply, but slightly off the beat. Where did it land? Pitches meld in glides, steps, and leaps. Where did each fall? Notes form odd partnerships, not straight eighths, not swing eighths, not dotted eighths, but some other elusive proportion. What was it exactly?

Consequently, the task of notating Davis's trumpeting, with the incompatible goals of precision and clarity, is an exercise in frustration, particularly when one is dealing with a slow-paced piece, such as Thelonious Monk's 'Round Midnight. The upper staff of example 11 presents Monk's melody as interpreted by trumpeter Cootie Williams on the first recording of this piece, done in 1944. Williams presents it more strictly than most jazz musicians might, sprinkling a few ornaments throughout his solo, but otherwise repeating his ideas literally. The first 8-bar phrase is the same as the second and last (except for its ending). Williams begins bars 17–24 exactly as he had ended the first a section (compare bars 7–8, 17–18, 19–20). His rhythms are deliberate and reasonably easy to hear (if you can find a copy of the record!). They serve as a perfect foil for Davis's approach.

The remainder of example 11 presents Franz Kershbaumer's transcription of Davis's versions of Monk's melody, as recorded for Columbia in September 1956 (middle staff) and again for Prestige in November of that same year (lower staff). Except for several spurts of newly improvised ideas, Davis clearly keeps the original tune in mind, but he toys with all aspects of the rhythm, including the aforementioned microscopic nuances. Any careful reader and listener is certain to wince at discrepancies between the notations of rhythm on paper and the true rhythms of Davis's trumpeting. This comment should not be taken as a criticism of Kershbaumer's work; one could hardly do better. The point is, rather, that Davis is too sophisticated a rhythm maker to be pinned down by any straightforward system of notation.

Example 11. Cootie Williams's statement of the melody of *'Round Midnight* as recorded in 1944 (upper staff; transcribed by Barry Kernfeld). Versions recorded by Miles Davis for Columbia (middle staff) and Prestige (lower staff) in 1956 (transcribed by Franz Kerschbaumer). Track 5, 0:30. Boxed italic letters indicate segments of the *aaba* form described in chapter 3.

Rhythm
26

Rhythm
28

'Round Midnight

Cootie Williams, Bernie Hanighen, Thelonious Monk

Copyright © 1944 Warner Bros. Inc. (renewed) and Thelonious Monk Publishing Designee.

Unpredictable Syncopation

Finding syncopation in jazz is about as difficult as finding water in the ocean. It is the cornerstone of one of the principal sources of jazz rhythm, ragtime melody, so much so that to "rag a melody" and (a decade or so later) to "jazz up a melody" meant, in part, to syncopate it. Later defini-
tions of jazz became more expansive and more cautious, but syncopation remained a normal event, to the point of losing its force. Technically, to syncopate is to attack a note in a rhythmic position weaker than one through which it carries, for example, an attack on beat 4, carrying through the start of the next measure, or an attack off the beat, carrying through the following beat. Emotionally, syncopation ought to mean rhythmic surprise, but in a music laced with weak and offbeat accents and known for breaking down conventional notions of rhythm (remember the backbeat, with accents on beats 2 and 4), technical syncopations are often tuneful and memorable but not at all surprising. It takes no great effort to learn the opening theme of *Birdland,* with its numerous offbeat accents in the melody and the bass (ex. 12). Joe Zawinul's composition has such a strong hook that the difficulty, if any, is getting the rhythm out of your head. Its emotional appeal is to make people want to dance, not to startle.

Example 12. The opening melody and bass line of Joe Zawinul's *Birdland,* recorded by Weather Report in 1977. Track 21, 0:18.

In his improvisations, Lester Young sometimes included a gesture that reverses these technical and emotional qualities. Evidently having recognized how syncopation can lose its shock value, Young turned the conventional definition on its head, as exemplified in his solo on Count Basie's *Doggin' Around.* Although this piece is not included among the twenty-one tracks collected here, it is available on many reissues of Basie's early recordings (for a brief listing, see appendix 2.)

Young follows Basie on this track. After the pianist reiterates an offbeat treble note, Young lands right on the downbeat of the first measure of his solo. Through this elegantly simply gesture, he syncopates the syncopation: technically, he accents the most classically proper (and seemingly the most unhip) of all rhythmic positions, a structural downbeat; emotionally, in the context of weak- and offbeat accents, his downbeat surprises, even after repeated hearings. Although the gesture became a mannerism in Young's improvisations and in the work of his many imitators, and therefore lost some of its effect, it nevertheless provided a breath of fresh air within a conventionally syncopated atmosphere.

In spite of such well-established precedents, many opportunities remain for truly surprising syncopation in jazz. Thelonious Monk, for example, consistently inserted unpredictable phrases into his piano playing. His *Misterioso* provides a sample of his peculiar gift to jazz rhythm.

The excerpt transcribed as example 13 comes at the end of the first and longer of two takes of *Misterioso* recorded on July 2, 1948. While vibraphonist Milt Jackson leads a restatement of the theme, Monk outlines B♭ dominant ninth and E♭ dominant ninth chords in a stark progression of chordal tones. Note that his rhythmic material has none of the complexity of Davis's. Apart from the first triplet eighth note, every note is strictly a duple subdivision at the quarter-note level (that is, eighth notes on or off the beat) or a triplet subdivision at the next level down (that is, swing sixteenths). What is extraordinary is the pattern of appearance of these individually simple rhythms. Before studying the transcription carefully, listen, and try to guess where the next piano note will fall.

Example 13. Unpredictable syncopations in Thelonious Monk's piano accompaniment at the end of take 1 of *Misterioso*, recorded in 1948. Track 14, 2:39.

59

Superimposing One Meter on Another

Within the large and predominant body of jazz pieces with a steady beat, a small portion of the repertory moves in waltz time. Apart from Fats Waller's *Jitterbug Waltz* (recorded in 1942), these jazz waltzes began to work well only in the 1950s, when some brilliant drummer discarded the traditional "boom chuck chuck" pattern (graceful in a true waltz but horrid and lumpy in jazz) and instead invented an asymmetrical version of a swing beat: in effect, Lester Young's "tinkety boom" became "boom tinkety swish." A smaller portion, inspired mainly by African-American gospel rhythms, moves in $\frac{6}{8}$ time and exhibits a pattern that closely resembles a swinging waltz, but with the fourth beat receiving less emphasis than the first: to continue paraphrasing Young, "boom tinkety swish, tack tinkety swish." And there are the occasional pieces that move in odd meters, ranging from simple $\frac{5}{4}$ to zany fractional meters borrowed from Bulgarian folk music.

Most jazz with a steady beat—that is to say, most jazz—uses common time, or $\frac{4}{4}$. (As a small but representative sample, eighteen of the twenty-one selections chosen for this book are in $\frac{4}{4}$ time.) Evidently varied meter is not terribly important in jazz. But increasingly over the years, musicians have achieved momentary polyrhythmic effects by superimposing another meter on common time.

This rhythmic innovation had roots in turn-of-the-century ragtime. Beginning around 1905 (with isolated examples before that), ragtime composers began creating melodies that moved in successions of three-note groups at the eighth-note level, giving the impression of $\frac{3}{8}$ time laid across common time. By 1926, when Johnny St. Cyr used the pattern in his banjo solo on Morton's *Black Bottom Stomp* (track 15, 2:10), this rhythmic device had become commonplace in ragtime, popular songs, novelty piano pieces, and jazz. It eventually became known as secondary rag (ex. 14).[2]

Example 14. Secondary rag rhythm.

While secondary rag was commonplace, a parallel process developed in jazz, involving the superimposition of $\frac{3}{4}$ time on $\frac{4}{4}$ time. An early, and justifiably famous, example occurs in Armstrong's scat-singing solo on *Hotter than That* (ex. 15). This passage, a highlight of Armstrong's career, still seems fresh. It was not long, though, before maintaining a pattern of "three against four" had become just another thing to be expected of any decent jazz musician. Because of the fairly inflexible nature of this device, it soon threatened to become a musical gimmick. Thus, when Rollins inserts passages of $\frac{3}{4}$ time into *St. Thomas* (ex. 16), he seems to be spinning his wheels before the end of what is otherwise one of his greatest improvisations.

Example 15. The superimposition of $\frac{3}{4}$ time on $\frac{4}{4}$ during Armstrong's scat-singing solo on *Hotter than That*. The example begins at the midpoint of the theme labeled *A3* in the structural diagram in chapter 3. Track 1, 1:38.

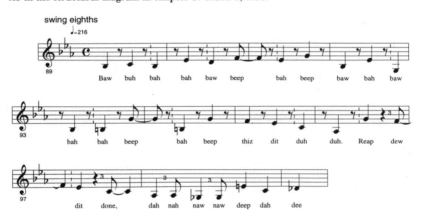

Example 16. The superimposition of $\frac{3}{4}$ time on $\frac{4}{4}$ in Rollins's improvisation on *St. Thomas*. Track 18, 4:42.

Like syncopation, however, the superimposing of meters need not become prosaic through overuse or misuse. As a delicate example, listen to the start of Herbie Hancock's piano solo (following the trumpet solo) on *Maiden Voyage* (track 9, 2:14). In the fourth bar Hancock and drummer Tony Williams simultaneously begin to sound every eighth note, with Hancock giving out an ascending staircase-shaped solo line and Williams tapping a cymbal accompaniment. From the downbeat of the next bar, bassist Ron Carter begins playing a series of dotted quarter notes, which has the effect of momentarily transforming Hancock's altered bossa nova pattern in $\frac{4}{4}$ time into a waltz in $\frac{3}{8}$ time. The rhythm section of Hancock, Carter, and Williams is renowned as one of the most sensitive and interactive in jazz. This little passage of waltz time is but one of the many moments in *Maiden Voyage* when the three men subtly alter subdivisions of the meter and the beat.

A technically and conceptually spectacular example of polymetric playing occurs roughly at the midpoint of Earl Hines's recording of *Sweet Sue*. Proceeding at lightning tempo, Hines's improvisation is so magnificently difficult that some readers may not be able to follow its notation, though looking at the transcription (ex. 17) while listening to the recording should at least produce a smile. For those as foolhardy as the transcriber, a brief description of Hines's performance follows.

This *Sweet Sue* consists of seven 32-bar choruses. (A jazz chorus, introduced in chapter 3, is one complete statement of a repeating harmonic and metric progression.) To facilitate getting started, the transcription begins at bar 5 of the fourth chorus, where Hines plays a firmly planted two-handed chromatic scale. At bar 9 Hines takes off. He accelerates the tempo slightly, and while arpeggiating skittering chords in the right hand, he tenaciously bangs out a series of dotted quarter notes in the left. On paper these resemble Armstrong's polymetric scat-singing rhythms, but Hines phrases the dotted quarter notes as if he were playing quarter notes at a slower tempo, thus generating four new beats where six had been before (that is, "four against six" rather than Armstrong's and Rollins's "three against four"). In another musical genre, outside of jazz, this would be called metric modulation.

The difficulty is magnified at bar 13, where a little rhythmic hiccup occurs: after pausing roughly half a beat, Hines resumes the series of skittering arpeggios and dotted quarter notes, one growing rhythmically more independent of the other. At bars 18–19 the proceedings whirl to an end in a descending scale that has somehow swallowed a whole beat. With a couple of emphatic chords, Hines then moves back into tempo and back into swing. All this in fourteen seconds. Don't blink or cough.

Example 17. A polymetric passage in Earl Hines's *Sweet Sue*. Track 11, 1:25. Boxed italic letters indicate segments of the *aaba* form described in chapter 3.

118

Free Rhythm

Until the late 1950s the only normal avenue for separating jazz from its beat was in an introduction. Ad-lib rhythm served as a foil to the emotional and structural moment when, at last, the beat would begin. Referring to one of the leading practitioners, pianist Art Tatum, Ralph Berton called this the "it-feels-so-good-when-he-stops device."[3]

In the late 1950s, musicians in the emerging free-jazz style began to reject traditional jazz forms in favor of new compositions and improvisations created in an ad hoc manner. They ignored the harmonies that went along with traditional forms in favor of atonality and drones. They discarded conventional notions of playing in tune in favor of blues-based and non-Western tuning systems. They liberated melodic rhythm from the beat. Nonetheless a considerable amount of rhythmic caution prevailed, because all these stylistically revolutionary elements were undergirded by the then-conventional accompaniments typical of hard-bop bassists and drummers: walking bass lines, swinging rhythmic patterns played on the ride cymbal, and a metronomic backbeat sounded on the hi-hat cymbal.

Jazz was reaching the end of a long period of rapid change, and by the early 1960s some instrumentalists had taken that most dangerous final step from a music based on a steady body rhythm, pulse, to a music based on a variable body rhythm, energy. The accompaniment no longer had a beat.[4]

Sun Ra's *Outer Nothingness* and John Coltrane's *Ascension*, both recorded in 1965, demonstrate ways of presenting free rhythm. The gentler of the two, *Outer Nothingness,* is rhythmically the more radical, with its scrupulous avoidance of a pulse. There is a carefully varied yet spontaneous ebb and flow of events, with held notes giving way to busy passages and then returning. This irregular ebb and flow does not necessarily mean that some astonishing transcendence of conventional rhythm is at work. Instead, what seems likely is that Sun Ra and his musicians have jiggled the building blocks of jazz, tilting the emphasis away from rhythm.

In Coltrane's *Ascension* conventional patterns are assimilated into a broad, free conception that summarizes, and goes beyond, the rhythmic systems and devices presented in this chapter. *Ascension* was recorded in two versions, each roughly forty minutes long. The excerpt described below comprises Coltrane's tenor saxophone solo with rhythm section accompaniment, plus fragments of the surrounding ensemble passages, from the version that came to be known as Edition II (track 4).[5]

Because there is no useful way to reproduce the passage in musical notation, the description is keyed to minutes and seconds of the performance. In the excerpt issued with this book, the 0:00 mark falls two minutes and ten seconds from the start of Edition II. At this point a sudden shift of tonal center occurs (insofar as there is a tonal center), with an F♯ from one of the string bass players and a resounding descending figure, starting four octaves higher, from one of the trumpeters.

0:00—The excerpt begins with a momentary interruption of what had been a dense thicket of accentuations produced by seven wind instruments (two trumpets, two alto saxophones, three tenor saxes) and four rhythm instruments (piano, two basses, drums). The thicket of overlapping wind lines resumes. Cymbals and drums crash and roll. The piano drones on with a repeated chord.

0:26—When the nebulous tonal center shifts again, drummer Elvin Jones fleetingly goes into a swinging cymbal pattern, with a backbeat rhythm on a closed hi-hat cymbal (as Roach does on *St. Thomas*) at a tempo of 240 beats per minute. Immediately Jones returns to crashes and rolls, but this moment of bop drumming foreshadows what is to come, particularly in that it sets a recurring tempo (240).

0:34—Over the next half minute, the beat is in Jones's hands (and feet), while everyone else challenges it in the continuing thicket of notes. Initially the beat pokes its head out in the guise of a brief pattern in $\frac{3}{4}$, with cymbal crashes on each downbeat (ex. 18).

Example 18. A fragment of $\frac{3}{4}$ rhythm in Coltrane's *Ascension*. Track 4, 0:34.

0:44—Jones transforms the pattern into a steady, ponderous oom-pah in $\frac{2}{4}$.

1:00—As the ensemble drops away and Coltrane begins his solo, the tenor saxophonist locks into the drum rhythm and begins to play a 2-bar-long figure that he repeats with small variations. Jones in turn supports the leader: the oom-pah mutates into a syncopated Latin pattern, including a thundering accent dropped into the gaps between statements of Coltrane's repeated figure (ex. 19).

Example 19. A repeated rhythm at the beginning of Coltrane's solo on *Ascension.* Track 4, 1:00.

1:15—Over the next twenty seconds or so, the swing beat, hinted at earlier, reemerges more persistently. It is keyed mainly by the cymbals, but tempo and meter also influence the bountiful irregular accents coming from the rest of Jones's drum kit. He is joined by McCoy Tyner, who intermittently supplies metered piano chords (at first moving strictly in half notes), and by one of the bassists, Jimmy Garrison, who supplies snippets of walking motion. The soloist Coltrane feels no obligation to improvise in step with the rhythm section.

1:23 and 1:35—Tyner twice plays a succession of chords in dotted quarter notes, creating the same sort of "three against four" pattern heard on *Hotter than That* and *St. Thomas.*

1:39—With an emphatic chordal downbeat, the rhythm section moves back into free playing.

2:01—As if to pick up the baton of rhythmic stability, Tyner sounds a chord every three beats, marking out 25 bars of quasi $\frac{3}{4}$ time, if the underlying tempo of 240 beats per minute still obtains. Alternatively, Tyner's chords may be taken as individual pulses at a new, slower tempo of 80 beats per minute, in what amounts to an oblique passage of metric modulation.

2:21—Tyner breaks out of the pattern.

2:29—A brief tonal unison and rhythmic respite takes hold in the piano and bass, with Jones supplying even briefer support before resuming his flurry of activity. Tyner then resumes the succession of chords on the downbeat of a fast $\frac{3}{4}$ meter, and these continue with few interruptions for the remainder of Coltrane's solo. Bass and drums roam freely.

3:00—Jones goes back to what is, in the context, a somewhat conventional swing cymbal pattern.

3:15—His ears continually directed toward the leader, Jones begins rumbling on lower-pitched drums as Coltrane's solo reaches a climax.

3:38—The ensemble returns, but the $\frac{3}{4}$ swing of the rhythm section pushes its way into the thicket. Those familiar with the work of Coltrane's quartet during the 1960s will recognize in this last minute and a half the rhythmic essence of the group's best-known and most frequently played piece, *My Favorite Things*, with all its thematic sugar stripped away and with its patterns of $\frac{3}{4}$ time integrated into, and challenged by, aperiodic events.

If this account elucidates some of the rhythmic organization of *Ascension*, it does so by picking out conventional elements buried within layers of freedom. Admittedly such analytical mining leaves a mountain of unexplained musical motion. This problem—made all the more difficult by the lack of a handy vocabulary for describing free rhythm—is accompanied by a nagging doubt. Is there such a thing as free rhythm? If it is not in some sense regular, is it rhythmic?

Whatever the answer to these questions, it is tempting to argue that despite the overwhelming energy put forth by the massed winds and rhythm section, rhythm is no more important in *Ascension* than in *Outer Nothingness*. As representatives of profound investigations of improvisation and timbre, such pieces serve well. For profound rhythmic work, listen to tunes with a beat. The scat singing and trumpet solo of Louis Armstrong, the relaxed swing of the Count Basie orchestra, the churning time and double time of the Miles Davis quintet, the mad gallop of Earl Hines—these seem nearer the apotheosis of jazz rhythm.

3 FORMS

In the summer Kirk's band worked only from nine to twelve at night, and afterwards we would drive by the Sunset—John Williams and me and the five or six that rode with us. Pete might be playing something like *Sweet Georgia Brown* or *Indiana* when we got there. I'd go home to bathe and change, and when I got back, ten to one Pete would still be jamming the same tune, and maybe some of the guys wailing along with him.
—Mary Lou Williams

The repertory of jazz consists of at least several thousand pieces (perhaps more than ten thousand), and—except for those players who have forthrightly rejected tradition to play in a style in which a conventional repertory is insignificant or irrelevant—any respected jazz musician is expected to be able to deal with hundreds of these at a moment's notice. In fact, established musicians often put newcomers to this test, and the resulting anecdotes are endless: at a jam session in Kansas City, the young Charlie Parker had a cymbal tossed at him for his inept attempt to make his way through a tune he did not know; at Jimbo's Bop City, in San Francisco, Frank Foster, with his soldier suit and battered silver saxophone, looked every bit the hick musician as he asked to sit in with Dexter Gordon's group and then proceeded to tear the place up with a lightning-fast romp through *Cherokee*; at the Cafe Bohemia, in New York, a visiting saxophonist from Florida, Cannonball Adderley, sat in on *I'll Remember April* with Oscar Pettiford's quintet, astonishing the bop community.

The quickest way of approaching this intimidatingly large collection is to break it into formal categories. Like the second of the two rhythmic systems (duple rhythm), standard jazz forms have been brought into the music from without: from the metric and harmonic progressions of African-American blues and gospel songs; from popular song forms used by George Gershwin, Cole Porter, Jerome Kern, and their colleagues; from the multithematic forms of ragtime piano compositions and brass-band marches; from the repetitive patterns of some Latin American dances; and, later, from the repetitive patterns of some rock and soul music.

Form can be an extremely sophisticated and complex building block of music. The concept of form embraces any aspect of music (harmony, melody, counterpoint, timbre, rhythm, theme, motive, variation, development, and so forth) that contributes to the organization of a specific piece. The concept also embraces abstract and sometimes intricate structural models generated by the analysis of interrelationships among pieces. But in jazz, specific forms of the vast majority of pieces in the standard repertory, and generalized forms abstracted from this repertory, are simple. Such simplicity allows each form to serve as a framework for improvisation. It could not be otherwise. How can a soloist be loose and creative, how can accompanists make impromptu variations, if everyone is worrying where the form is going?

Because of this simplicity, the standard forms are easy to learn. Gaining a grasp of the entire repertory is a laudable goal, but once one learns the basic forms and a few dozen tunes, a large portion of jazz becomes easier to hear. The key to identification lies above all in the domains of harmony and rhythm: a sequence of chords tied to a metric scheme. In jazz, metric schemes are easy to understand, but harmony gets rather involved. Hence this subject merits a brief digression, to identify the harmonic vocabulary used in analyses of forms. That vocabulary is drawn from two systems of notation.

Fake-book notation offers jazz and popular music a useful shorthand for identifying individual harmonies. A fake-book symbol defines the general makeup of a chord (for example, Bb^7 is shorthand for the pitches Bb, D, F, Ab).

Roman numeral notation has been adapted to jazz from an analytical system developed for classical music. Like a fake-book symbol, a roman numeral symbol defines the general makeup of a chord, but it further designates how chords relate to one another within a key. (Readers unfamiliar with either or both of these notational systems should consult appendix 1 of this volume.)

Chorus Forms

In those pieces with only a single continuously recurring form, one complete statement of the harmonic and metric progression is called, in jazz parlance, a chorus. For example, after the 2-bar introduction to *Georgia on My Mind*, Billie Holiday sings the first 32-bar chorus, Eddie Heywood plays a piano solo through the first half of the second 32-bar chorus, and Holiday returns to sing the second half; hence this is a performance comprising an introduction and two choruses. The New Orleans Rhythm Kings' *Tin Roof Blues* has a 4-bar introduction and then a series of 12-bar choruses, featuring the ensemble (12 + 12 + 12 bars), a trombone solo (12 bars), a clarinet solo (12 bars), and the ensemble again (12 bars, which are extended an additional 2 bars to bring the piece to an end).

Repeating a Chorus Form

Every chorus, whether the ordinary 32-bar popular song and the 12-bar blues (as in these examples) or something less ordinary, has a common element: the design allows it to repeat. This is achieved through a lack of coincidence between two points of arrival—the cadence on a tonic chord, which falls 2 (sometimes 4) bars before the end of a chorus, and the strongest metric downbeat, which falls on the first bar of the next chorus. The result is a formal instability that perpetually energizes a piece, pushing it toward a simultaneous resolution of harmony and rhythm but never allowing it to reach that resolution. Infrequent exceptions are found in those jazz compositions built upon static sounds or weakly related successions of chords. Unlike blues and American popular song, each of which characteristically uses a functional (that is, strongly related) chord progression offering a clear sense of tonal center (from which the harmony departs and to which it cadences), a jazz composition such as Herbie Hancock's *Maiden Voyage* avoids harmonic resolution altogether, thereby enhancing the restlessness of chorus form still further. Such restlessness, in which the tail keeps chasing after the head, is perfectly suited to performances of flexible, indefinite length.

In many jazz performances the number of repetitions of a chorus is determined by practical considerations of time and tempo that have nothing to do with fancy notions of form. If the tempo is fast, play the strain again. If the tempo is slow, there may be no time to repeat. If people want to keep dancing, repeat a chorus over and over again. If you want people to stop dancing, cut off the piece. An extreme example of this option was the so-called taxi dance (or dime-a-dance) of the swing era, in which repetitions of the chorus were determined by financial considerations. It worked this way: male customers were required to pay a dime (the taxi fare) for the privilege of dancing one tune with a woman employed by the dance hall. To keep the dimes rolling in, the tune was kept short, lasting perhaps only half a minute. The band played as many choruses, or as much of a single chorus, as could be squeezed into that time. (Changing tunes every thirty seconds was, by the way, an excellent way for a jazz musician to learn the huge repertory).

From 1917, when the Original Dixieland Jazz Band cut its first recordings into a wax 78 RPM disc, to 1950, when the technology for making tapes and LPs became firmly established in the industry, the length of the record placed even greater restrictions on repetitions of a chorus. The standard medium for jazz recording, the 10-inch 78 RPM disc, allowed roughly three minutes of music. A jazz band had the choice of either fitting a given number of choruses to the record or, more casually, watching for a studio light that signaled the end of the recording.

During the same period other technologies allowed a longer playing time. A type of recording called a broadcast transcription was developed for the purpose of broadcast over the radio rather than for home use; each broadcast transcription was done on a 16-inch 33 1/3 RPM disc that held about fifteen minutes of music. A movie soundtrack (not a record, but a recording nonetheless, and a rich source indeed for documenting jazz) could be as long as the filmmaker wanted it to be; during and beyond the era of the 78 RPM disc (until the advent of home video), movies were not intended for home use. In 1931–32 the Victor company experimented with long-playing 33 1/3 discs meant for home use, but the reception was disappointing. Later in the decade, some jazz began to be recorded on 12-inch 78 RPM discs, which held about five minutes of music.

In spite of these technological possibilities, the influence of the 10-inch 78 RPM disc was so pervasive that its three-minute limit came to dictate the length of performances, even when there was no technological reason for such a restriction. Jazz broadcasts, accordingly, consisted of sets of short pieces rather than of one long piece, and filmmakers of the era evidently felt there would be no audience for an extended jazz performance. In short, technological factors gave way to artistic or popular arguments: the merit or interest of a tune diminished if it went on too long.

In the early 1950s the 78 RPM record was replaced by the long-playing disc (LP), made possible by new microgroove technology. A 10-inch 33 1/3 RPM LP could hold about ten or twelve minutes on each side; a 12-inch LP, which soon became standard, about 15 minutes on each side. As technology continued to improve over the years, that maximum length doubled. This development was a boon to classical music. No longer was it necessary to interrupt a movement by dividing it among an album of 78 RPM discs. The LP was of little consequence for Top 40 genres, however, which simply replaced 78s with a modern equivalent, the 7-inch 45 RPM disc, known as the single. Only with the advent of rock in the mid-1960s did popular albums begin to overshadow Top 40 singles.

As has been the case from many perspectives, jazz took a middle ground between classical music and popular music. Early in the history of the LP, some jazz musicians began to stretch out chorus forms. Some LPs replicated the length (and spirit) of live performances, including series released under the banners of Jazz at the Philharmonic (this series having gotten under way in the 1940s on albums of 78s) and Buck Clayton's Jam Sessions. But broadly speaking, LPs of the 1950s seldom filled an entire side with a single chorus form. Performers did not begin to take full advantage of the duration of an LP until the next decade, with the flowering of free jazz and the emergence of fusion, and when they did, they seldom used chorus forms. The most notable example is John Coltrane's *Ascension*, which comprises two sides of an LP and delivers its full impact only when heard in its entirety; indeed, this stylistically revolutionary performance was also ahead of its time technologically, because only in the 1980s, when *Ascension* was first reissued on compact disc, was it possible to hear the whole piece without having to flip over the LP.

The invention of cassettes and compact discs, either of which can hold a continuous hour of music, had no great effect on extending recordings of chorus forms. The reason seems clear. Most jazz fans would give a life's fortune to have been at the jam sessions described by Mary Lou Williams. Two or three hours of *Sweet Georgia Brown* must have flown by for those sitting in a club listening to the best of the Kansas City jazz musicians improvising one chorus after another. But on a recording, without the social amenities, without the live sound, without the interaction between musicians and audience, two or three hours of that repetitive background might overwhelm all but the most devoted listener.

Ending a Chorus Form

The forward push of chorus forms explains the heavy reliance of jazz on abrupt, tentative, awkward, corny, nebulous, and dissonant endings: by its very nature, the chorus does not allow itself to end neatly.

To be sure, there have been genuinely great and satisfying solutions to this problem, as, for example, the ecstatic final moments of Duke Ellington's *Ko-Ko* and *Trumpet No End* (the latter arranged by Mary Lou Williams) and the elegantly controlled decrescendo in Count Basie's *Jumpin' at the Woodside*. But these are not the norm. After studying many endings, listeners may recognize the value of electronic fade-outs, which neatly avoid the issue by not really ending at all.

Herbie Hancock's *Maiden Voyage*, as he recorded it in 1965, is one such piece. As the rhythm section repeats the rhythmic signature (discussed in chap. 2) and as trumpeter Freddie Hubbard plays a rapid trill, the piece gently fades away.[1] Weather Report's *Birdland* is another. Although the piece is neither standard nor simple in form (see the discussion of ad hoc forms, below), it incorporates as its final segment a chorus form—a harmonic and metric progression that is repeated over and over again (track 21, 4:48). Composer Joe Zawinul has constructed the repetitions of this chorus so that just as the volume diminishes, his synthesizer solo intensifies; meanwhile, as noted in chapter 2, the hand clapping quadruples in speed, from a backbeat rhythm (on beats 2 and 4) to continuous eighth notes. The piece then disappears from actual sound, with its denouement left to our imagination.

Within the realm of jazz performances using chorus forms, the principal models are based on African-American blues progressions and American popular songs of decades past. Other models include hymns, spirituals, and gospel music.[2]

Blues Progressions

The blues progression is a marvelously pliable device that allows itself to be stretched or squeezed, decorated or left unadorned, while retaining its unique character. Searching for the Ur-blues progression is something like reconstructing the Indo-European language: there is no concrete evidence that it ever existed, but by laying eighty or one hundred standard variants on top of one another, one can surmise what it might have been. The most common progressions join a 12-bar metric pattern (built from three 4-bar phrases) to the functional progression I - IV - I - V - I. The original might have looked like this: I - I - I - I^{b7} - IV - IV - I - I - V - V - I - I.

Moving from the abstract to the real, one finds that individual genres (blues, rhythm and blues, rock and roll, rock, jazz) and even individual styles (early down-home blues, classic blues, urban blues) have particular tendencies of form. The most imaginative rhythmic variants occur in country blues, in which the lyrics take precedence over the beat, with the result that a steady 12 bars might be thrown out the window in favor of unpredictable, asymmetrical phrasing. The most imaginative harmonic variants occur in jazz, which almost always dresses up the basic progression. At the extreme, a jazz blues may layer two or three tiers of subsidiary progressions within the basic one. Far less often, it might also stretch out the 12 measures (usually to 16).

When a vocalist sings the blues, one may identify a blues progression without actually being able to hear it, because the music will usually be tied to a rhymed couplet, the 12 bars dividing into three 4-bar phrases in the pattern *aab*. But if, as in so much of jazz, the performance is strictly instrumental, there are no tricks to learning to hear the underlying pattern.

Tin Roof Blues, recorded by the New Orleans Rhythm Kings in 1923, provides a good introduction to the form, especially in the famous and widely quoted theme heard in the second and third choruses and notated in example 20. This theme involves, above the piano accompaniment, the classic "front line" of a dixieland band: clarinet, played by Leon Roppolo; cornet, played by Paul Mares; and trombone, played by George Brunies. The emphasis on coordinated chordal playing (rather than on improvisation) helps to spell out some typical features of blues progressions in jazz.

From the downbeat of bar 1, the basic sonority is not a triad but a tonic seventh chord, I^7, which could also be spelled and heard as a secondary dominant, V^7 of IV. In B♭, the key of *Tin Roof Blues*, I^7 would be spelled B♭-D-F-A♭. The chord V^7 of IV, built on the dominant (B♭) of the subdominant (E♭), would also be spelled B♭-D-F-A♭. Although some readers may be put off by this sort of chordal calculating, the analysis is worthwhile, because it reveals a vital feature of the blues progression. The notations "I^7" and "V^7 of IV" spell the same chord (B♭-D-F-A♭), but with two different functions, and in this piece, as in numerous other blues pieces, these two functions are at work simultaneously. *Tin Roof Blues* is obviously in B♭, but from the start that sound wants to push on to E♭; thus, another unstable element, along with chorus structure, energizes the blues form.

In this elementary example of harmonic elaboration in jazz, the progression is colored by coordinated chromatic passing tones, as cornet, clarinet, and trombone slip downward between voicings of the structural chords. In his brief improvisations between each of these descents, Rop-

Example 20. The second 12-bar blues chorus of take B of *Tin Roof Blues*, recorded by the New Orleans Rhythm Kings in 1923. Track 16, 0:36.

polo sticks to basics, arpeggiating triads and seventh chords, with a lean toward a secondary dominant in the ninth bar of this chorus of the blues progression (in ex. 20, bar 25 of the piece; the dominant seventh of B♭ is the chord F-A-C-E♭, and its dominant seventh—that is to say, the secondary dominant—is the chord C-E-G-B♭, evoked here by Roppolo having played the pitch E rather than E♭). But the blues progression is also colored by a moment of striking dissonance in the final bars: as the front line makes its way from one B♭ triad to another, a quick succession of grating parallel minor ninths arises between clarinet and cornet. This pungent dissonance should not be heard as a mistake. A slight touch of planned chaos, it recurs on other choruses and takes of *Tin Roof Blues*.

The front line further alters the elementary blues harmonies by introducing blue notes: pitches that do not correspond to a conventional Western tuning system and that slide through a microscopic continuum rather than being fixed on a point (see the discussion of tuning systems in chap. 7). Example 20 calls attention to obvious blue notes in the clarinet (bar 22, beat 3) and cornet (bars 25–26), but to avoid cluttering up the notation, no attempt has been made to detail all of Roppolo's pitch bending. His playing is drenched in blue notes, especially when he slithers around in the vicinity of the major and minor third.

Another straightforward 12-bar blues is Thelonious Monk's *Misterioso*, which, conveniently, also happens to be in the key of B♭. Its principal divergence from the pattern underlying *Tin Roof Blues* is the substitution of a subdominant chord (E♭-G-B♭-D♭) for the tonic chord (B♭-D-F-A♭) in measure 2; this is a normal variant of the imagined Ur-blues.

There is a peculiar glitch in *Misterioso*. Monk, as mentioned earlier, had a special rhythmic vision that dazzled and sometimes baffled listeners and fellow musicians alike. In his solo on *Misterioso*, he seems to have inadvertently performed that same effect upon himself. Immersed in inventing a strange new melody, he loses track of the blues form during his two 12-bar choruses and adds a full measure at the turnaround from one to the next, thus soloing for 25, not 24, bars. His sidemen cover up the mistake as well as they can, but not before there is a lag between their arrival at a subdominant chord at bar 2 of his second chorus, and his arrival, one bar late.

Either of these pieces represents the ambiguity of the blues progression. Each is in a major key, but the prominence of seventh chords and blue notes undermines that sense. In what is admittedly a tautology, it might be best to refer to this ambiguous tonality of the blues as "blues tonality," for want of a more precise term.

Duke Ellington's *Ko-Ko*, recorded in 1940, offers a contrasting approach, the 12-bar blues in a minor key. Before the mid-1950s minor-key blues progressions rarely filled an entire piece. (*Ko-Ko* is exceptionally creative in this respect, as in so many others.) Instead, such progressions were used for coloristic harmonic effect, in alternation with and hence in contrast to blues tonality. Since the mid-1950s, when the sound of minor chords was perceived to be a soulful element in hard-bop and related styles, independent minor-key blues progressions have appeared routinely, dominating rather than merely coloring the harmony of a piece and thus providing a recurring alternative to blues tonality.

Popular Song Form

In jazz, the term *song form* refers to formal models borrowed from American popular songs of the 1920s to 1940s. Structurally, this body of music differs from ragtime, blues, country, bluegrass, western, rhythm and blues, rock and roll, rock, soul, Motown, funk, disco, rap, and the like, in its almost singular use of 32-bar chord progressions. Such a formula offered, alongside the blues progression, a perfect vehicle for building jazz choruses.

Of the various models, the most common one subdivides into four 8-bar phrases, in the pattern *aaba*. As an indication of the prominence of this form, over the years the *b* section has acquired four nicknames: the bridge, the channel, the release, the middle eight (never mind that the eight are not quite in the middle). Another sign of its pervasiveness is evident in the twenty-one selections presented in this book: although form was not the first consideration in deciding which tracks to choose, coincidentally ten of the twenty-one recordings have *aaba* themes. Owing to rapid tempos, two of the ten—Hawkins's *The Man I Love* and Parker's *Koko*—spread out their themes to 64 rather than 32 bars, but that sort of variation is inconsequential. Among the others, Dizzy Gillespie and Gil Fuller's composition *Manteca* ties together song form and a Latin jazz ostinato, while Charles Mingus's *Fables of Faubus* uses song form as an arch over a sophisticated structure of his own invention.

As in most jazz based on blues, popular song form may sometimes be recognized by a lyric, independent of whether one actually learns to hear the metric and harmonic underpinning. For example, in Billie Holiday's rendition of *Georgia on My Mind*, the lyrics provide clear guidelines: the first two lines begin with "Georgia," the third (the bridge) with "Other arms," and the fourth with "Georgia" (hence *aaba*; track 12).

A jazz version of a pop song may also have melodic or textural elements that supply clues to its metric and harmonic underpinning. As an example of form delineated by melody, listen to Earl Hines play a full chorus of the melody of Victor Young's hit song of 1928, *Sweet Sue—Just You*. (Hines's version uses the shortened title *Sweet Sue*.) Example 21 compares the opening phrase and the bridge of the original song and the piano recording.

Example 21a. Bars 1–8 of *Sweet Sue—Just You* (upper staff) and these same measures in Earl Hines's *Sweet Sue*, recorded in 1965 (piano staffs). Track 11, beginning.

Example 21b. Bars 17–24 of *Sweet Sue—Just You* (upper staff) and these same measures as played by Hines (piano staffs). Track 11, 0:14.

Sweet Sue—Just You
Victor Young
Copyright © 1928 Shapiro, Bernstein and Co., Inc., New York.
Copyright renewed.
Used by permission.

Hines takes liberties. From the downbeat he tells us "this is jazz harmony" as he turns a ii^7 chord (in the key of G, A minor seventh: A-C-E-G) on its head, with the root in the melody (as in Young's song) and the seventh sitting all by itself below. Then Hines drops the repeated note in Young's opening phrase into the bass and lowers the fifth of the chord, which becomes ii$^7_{b5}$ (A-C-E♭-G). He thickens up the sound, adding chromatic passing tones in either hand, letting left-hand chords ring in intervals that pulsate in sevenths and ninths against those in the right hand, and dressing up the end of the bridge with a dense contrapuntal passage. He displaces Young's melodic rhythms throughout, adding syncopation and swing. Yet in spite of the stylistic transformation, the popular song remains clear. It might prove helpful to memorize this catchy melody and keep it cycling in one's mind, while attempting to follow the ensuing six choruses of wildly complex improvisation.

Melodic cues in other examples are less complete, because—as is typical in jazz—the arranger or the improviser feels no obligation to stick to the borrowed material. Following an 8-measure-long introduction, Miles Davis plays the melody of Thelonious Monk's jazz standard *'Round Midnight* in measures 1–8, 13–16, 21–24, and 29–32 of his 32-bar solo chorus. In the gaps Davis improvises his own new melody (see chap. 2, ex. 11); by contrast, his saxophonist, John Coltrane, gives only a brief, heavily ornamented nod to the original melody before hurtling off into his own personal melodic world. As another example of melodic variation, a syncopated version of the opening melody of Irving Berlin's *Blue Skies*, as well as the melody from the bridge, leap out of the arranged accompaniment during the first chorus of Ellington's *Trumpet No End*, but not until the fourth and final chorus is there a forthright version of the familiar title phrase of the melody, now in Cat Anderson's moderately high register (see chap. 4, ex. 33d). On a recording such as Hawkins's version of *The Man I Love*, where there are nothing more than snippets of the melody (first in Eddie Heywood's piano solo and later in Oscar Pettiford's bass solo), to look for melody as a guide to the underlying form is useless.

Count Basie's *Jumpin' at the Woodside* provides an example of form delineated by texture. The recording has an 8-bar introduction built on a walking piano bass line; four 32-bar choruses; and then six consecutive statements of the *a* section, the bridge having dropped away. Whenever the bridge arrives, something new happens. The first time, alto saxophonist Earle Warren solos. The second, brass and reeds drop out. The third, saxophones begin to hold out chords beneath Buck Clayton's muted trumpet solo. And the last, the brass stop playing accompanimental figures during Lester Young's tenor sax solo.

In the end, however, none of these textual, melodic, or textural cues provides a satisfactory substitute for actually learning to hear the underpinning. Toward that goal, *Jumpin' at the Woodside* does for song form what *Tin Roof Blues* does for the blues progression, providing a simple place to start listening. Its basic progression appears in example 22, in both roman numeral and fake-book notation.

Example 22a. The basic harmonies of the *a* section of Count Basie's *Jumpin' at the Woodside*. Track 2, 0:07.

$$\text{B}\flat\text{: I}_6^9 \quad | \qquad | \qquad | \qquad | \text{ V}^9 \text{ } | \qquad | \text{ I}_6^9 \text{ } | \qquad |$$
$$\text{or B}\flat_6^9 \quad | \qquad | \qquad | \qquad | \text{ F}^9 \text{ } | \qquad | \text{ B}\flat_6^9 \text{ } | \qquad |$$

Example 22b. The basic harmonies of the bridge of *Jumpin' at the Woodside*. Track 2, 0:23.

$$\text{B}\flat\text{: V}^9/\text{IV} \text{ } | \qquad | \text{ IV}^6 \text{ } | \qquad | \text{ V}^7/\text{V} \text{ } | \qquad | \text{ V}^7 \text{ } | \qquad |$$
$$\text{or } \text{B}\flat^9 \text{ } | \qquad | \text{ E}\flat^6 \text{ } | \qquad | \text{ C}^7 \text{ } | \qquad | \text{ F}^7 \text{ } | \qquad |$$

Once again, the model is an abstraction, somewhat removed from the actual sound of any of the four choruses. Even in a performance such as this, which on the surface offers every appearance of carefully coordinated teamwork, there lurks a gentle but pointed undercurrent of personal expression in the accompaniment. (Of course the improvised solos are filled with personal expression.) Close listening will reveal the musicians having little clashes with one another's interpretation of the model. This friendly independence is most evident in the second chorus, when pianist Basie and guitarist Freddie Green simultaneously make their separate ways through the bridge.

So much for easy-to-hear forms. I would have been remiss not to have slipped a reference to George Gershwin's *I Got Rhythm* into a discussion of jazz song forms, because this 34-bar *aaba'* tune, when regularized to 32 bars and *aaba* (leaving out the 2-bar tag at the end), is second only to the blues progression as the most frequently used model in jazz. By chance the song makes a fleeting appearance in one of the twenty-one selections of this book. In *Manteca,* one of its three composers (more likely Dizzy Gillespie or Gil Fuller than Chano Pozo) plugged the *a* section of *I Got Rhythm* into the accompaniment to Big Nick Nicholas's tenor sax solo. Here the least oblique reference to an element of Gershwin's song may be heard in Al McKibbon's walking bass line. Against this bass line, the arranged chords in the wind instruments operate at a considerable remove from Gershwin's original; and in bars 9–12 of his solo, Nicholas throws the listener off the scent by quoting the melody of *Blue Moon,* a song that happens to begin with the same chord progression that *I Got Rhythm* uses. Try to pick McKibbon's bass part out from under these other more prominent sounds, and compare it with the chord progression of the model, which appears above the staffs in example 23. To locate this example on the CD, just listen for the tenor saxophone. (Note that *Manteca* uses other forms as well, which are discussed later in the chapter.)

Example 23. A passage from *Manteca* in which Al McKibbon builds his bass line upon the chord progression of George Gershwin's *I Got Rhythm.* Track 8, 1:47.

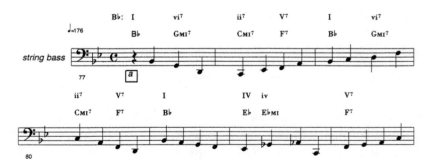

Extracting the Gershwin-inspired bass line from its surroundings should provide a good warm-up to the task of comprehending the form of Charlie Parker's *Koko*. An unscientific study of friends and acquaintances suggests that on first hearing, or perhaps even after several, this quintessential bop recording sounds incoherent: the better part of the trumpet and saxophone line skitters along at a rate of ten notes per second, sometimes accompanied by nothing more than a drumbeat; any contributions from the piano are sparse in content, irregular in rhythm, and not well recorded, thus obliquely suggesting rather than emphatically stating harmony; the steady walking string bass line provides the least complex element, but listeners accustomed to the high-fidelity sounds of digital-era electric bass guitars may have trouble picking out its softly stated details.

If the first experience of *Koko* results in a confusion of sounds, one might consider that the musicians are interpreting a radically revised version of a formal model, Ray Noble's popular song *Cherokee*. Although form in jazz is rarely an end in itself, learning the underlying form and harmony of *Koko* should help reveal the background—and hence the context—for one of the most relaxed (despite its lightning pace), beautifully crafted, tuneful alto saxophone improvisations ever preserved on a studio recording.

Koko has a lengthy, jittery, mysterious introduction and ending, and one should note the sequence of events in each before getting into the central song form. The 32-bar introduction has drum accompaniment only. The string bass is silent, as is the piano. At a tempo of 300 beats per minute Parker and Gillespie play in octaves; Gillespie improvises; Parker improvises; finally the two winds come together in parallel thirds and then in octaves again. The ending comprises Max Roach's drum solo (taken at an even faster tempo) and a reprise of the introduction, minus its last 3 bars. String bassist Curly Russell jumps in on the last beat.

Sandwiched between this newly invented material is Parker's improvisation on the 64-bar structure of *Cherokee*, in the pattern *aaba*, a structure sounded out on piano, bass, and drums.[3] Just as a jazz blues form tends to adhere to a strict metric scheme, frequently 12 bars long, while leaving open the possibility for dramatic transformation of the harmonic scheme (depending on individual and group styles), a jazz song form also tends to adhere to a strict metric scheme, frequently 32 bars long (*Cherokee*'s is twice that), while leaving open the same possibilities for transforming harmony. *Koko* provides, throughout its two rapid choruses, scores of examples of what jazz musicians can do to pop harmony. There is so much improvised freedom that any attempt to identify every harmonic and nonharmonic tone, every root and inversion, every functional relationship, must fail. It is better to think of this sort of jazz harmony as a pliable, living organism.

Each harmonic component of *Cherokee*, and of *Koko*, may fleetingly stick out little rhythmic feet, intruding on its neighbor's territories without disturbing the overall scheme. Lacking head or tail, each component spins freely, making nonsense of roots and inversions, but at the same time keeping a limited set of pitches trapped by the power of its harmonically functional essence. From one appearance to the next, each component changes shape by altering chordal elements, expands by extending into upper elements, contracts by eliminating elements, or mutates by substituting a related chord. From one instrument to the next, the same sorts of changes, expansions, contractions, and mutations may take place simultaneously. Consequently at any given point there need not be a strict relationship among (1) a chord appearing on Noble's copyrighted version of *Cherokee*; (2) the equivalent harmony in Charlie Barnet's hit version of *Cherokee*, recorded by his big band in 1938; (3) the manifestation of that harmony in Gillespie's piano chording on Parker's *Koko*; (4) the delineation of that harmony in Russell's string bass part; (5) the linear and melodic expression of that harmony in Parker's alto saxophone line; and (6) the expression of that harmony in Parker's other recorded versions of *Cherokee* and *Koko*, and in any of ten thousand other versions played by professional jazz musicians. This slippery, elusive aspect of jazz practice is a part of what makes the music strong and subtle. Searching for a definitive answer is like grasping a cloud firmly.

Conveniently underscoring this point, the original published sheet music to *Cherokee* itself undermines the idea of a definitive harmonic progression by offering conflicting progressions. On the top staff, intended for singers, is the melody, with lyrics directly below and two types of chord symbols above: fake-book notation and guitar tablature, the latter showing a guitarist where to press the strings to produce each chord. On the bottom staffs, for pianists, the melody is repeated, together with an accompaniment written out in full musical notation.

As is often the case with sheet music for popular songs, the fake-book symbols for this copy of *Cherokee* are casually and sloppily done. Some symbols disregard the harmonic implications of the melody, some fail to make good sense harmonically, and some disagree with the harmonies spelled out in the piano accompaniment. To make matters worse, symbols are missing altogether in bars 38–40.

The guitar tablature follows the fake-book symbols, replicating the same mistakes and omissions. Additionally, a couple of guitar notations that should indicate finger placement are missing. And there is one place where the sheet music gives three different instructions for the same chord: at the start of the bridge, the piano sounds an F$^\sharp$ dominant 13th chord, the simplified fake-book symbol asks for an F$^\sharp$ dominant ninth chord, and the further simplified guitar fingering forms an F$^\sharp$ dominant seventh.

Thus example 24 ignores the published chord symbols and instead gives, above the top staff, a roman numeral analysis of the first 48 bars of the piano part from the sheet music (that is, sections *aab* of the chorus). This piano accompaniment was prepared with greater care than were the symbols. The notation makes sense harmonically, and nothing seems to be missing. Using this seemingly correct version as a point of departure, one can then ask: How are the central choruses of *Koko* based on the harmonies of *Cherokee*? In what ways do these harmonies demonstrate the liberties a jazz musician might take?

The bottom three staffs of example 24 provide the basis for a partial, but detailed, answer. They present the piano and bass accompaniment of the first chorus, from the start of Parker's solo through the end of the bridge.[4] Along the top of these staffs is a roman numeral analysis of their general harmonic content.

Example 24. The first 48 bars of the piano arrangement of Ray Noble's *Cherokee*, as originally published in sheet music (upper two staffs); Thomas Owens's transcription of the piano chords and bass line during the first 48 bars of Charlie Parker's solo choruses on *Koko* (lower three staffs). Track 17, 0:25. Roman numeral analyses done by Barry Kernfeld.

Cherokee (Indian Love Song)
Ray Noble
Copyright © 1938 The Peter Maurice Music Co. Ltd., London
Shapiro, Bernstein and Co., Inc., New York.
International copyright secured.
Used by permission.

A few dissimilarities between this musical notation for *Cherokee* and *Koko* are immediately obvious. The registral placement and spread of piano chords (their "voicing") is not at all the same. In a couple of spots Gillespie alters chordal elements to make the harmonies of *Koko* sound a little less sweet than those of *Cherokee*: a minor ninth and augmented fifth at bar 62 ($V^{9}_{\flat 7}$ in place of V^{13}); an augmented 11th at bar 73 ($V^{13}_{\sharp 11}$ in place of

V^{13}). He consistently substitutes chords oriented toward minor and diminished intervals, in place of the augmented dominant ninth chords ($V^{\sharp 5}_{9}$) in *Cherokee* (bars 34, 48, 50, 80).

In *Koko*, the very nature of the bass line distinguishes its harmonic implications from those of *Cherokee*. By walking his line stepwise up and down, Curly Russell sounds numerous pitches that cannot be automatically dismissed as incidental nonharmonic tones, given the richness of the overall chordal palette. His walking line also breaks down distinctions between root position and inverted chords. Consequently chordal identity is obscure. How does one pin a label on a chord if its position, root, and extent are unclear?

A closer look reveals additional discrepancies between *Cherokee* and *Koko*, and within *Koko* itself. Were these discrepancies simply one-time musical eccentricities of Gillespie and Russell on that day in 1945, there would be no reason to examine these details. But as it turns out, the diverse paths that they take through the chord progression are not at all stylistically odd but instead illustrate characteristic ways in which jazz musicians manipulate harmony.

In bars 33–38 of the piece (the first measures of this chorus), Russell simplifies the version given in the sheet music. He walks the bass upward an octave and a half, from B♭ to E♭, and in doing so lays out a B♭ dominant thirteenth chord (B♭-D-F-A♭-C-E♭-G) with two chromatic passing tones thrown in along the way (B and C♯).

By contrast, Gillespie is interested in a more complicated approach to harmony. Independently he inserts chordal alterations and substitutions. The quiet chords in bars 34–35 might be labeled as extensions of a B♭ chord, with its bottom missing, or as A♭ chords (IV of IV); however one hears it, Gillespie alters the sheet music. In the next bar he makes his way to E♭ by means of a tritone substitution, in which a chord built on the pitch F♭ replaces a chord built on B♭ (the interval between F♭ and B♭ being a tritone). In this case, B♭ serves as a dominant, leaping down to E♭, and its replacement, F♭, achieves the same purpose but from an adjacent position, so that the harmony—rather than leaping down—slides a half step directly from F♭ to E♭. Specifically, Gillespie plays an extended ♭II chord (spelled F♭-A♭-C♭-E♭♭-G♭) in place of V^{13}/IV (spelled B♭-D-A♭-C-G in this bar of *Cherokee*), with the notes A♭ and E♭♭ (= D) linking the functionality of these differing routes to E♭. During the second *a* section of this chorus the same chordal substitution returns, now one bar earlier, with Russell giving his full support in bar 51 (the pitches A♭ and F♭) and with Russell suggesting something more along the lines of the sheet music in bar 52 (the pitches F and D, which could be called vii/IV or a rootless V/IV).

In the final bar of example 24, the dominant eleventh chord has a lowered ninth and fifth (F-A-C♭-E♭-G♭-B♭). Here it might be simpler to think of the two men playing independently, with Russell sounding the dominant while Gillespie slides down from ii to ♭II to I (C minor to C♭ to B♭).

To continue exploring this minute but vital aspect of jazz performance, interested readers might pursue *Koko* along yet another plane, by comparing the piano and bass parts to the harmonies implied by Parker's improvised solo (transcribed in chap, 6, ex. 47).[5]

Other song forms exist besides *aaba*. Instead, a chorus may split neatly in half, the first part leading to the dominant, the second ending on the tonic (for example, George Gershwin's *Summertime*). Often either half ends with a 2-bar break, as the accompanying chords and the beat momentarily drop away explicitly (though both continue implicitly). Louis Armstrong's *Hotter than That* focuses on this model, as indicated in the structural diagram that Gunther Schuller drew for his book *Early Jazz* (reproduced as ex. 25).[6] This song form may be heard in the sections that Schuller marks *A1, A2, A3, A4* (track 1, 0:08, 0:45, 1:21, and 2:18, respectively). (Up to this point, lowercase letters have identified subsections of single themes: *aab* lyrics, *aaba* form, the *a* section, and so forth. Here, in *Hotter than That*, and whenever appropriate in other pieces, uppercase letters distinguish individual themes.)

Example 25. The structure of Armstrong's *Hotter than That* (from Gunther Schuller, *Early Jazz* [New York: Oxford University Press, 1968], 111). Track 1.

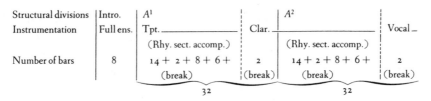

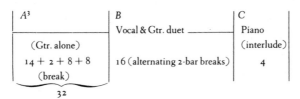

A^4		B			
Trombone (Rhy. sect. accomp.)	Tpt.	Full ens.	Stop-time	Full ens.	Gtr. alone
14 +	2 + (break)	8 +	4 +	2 +	2

32

Coda	
Tpt. (alone)	Gtr. (alone)
2	2

What about those other sections of *Hotter than That?* Armstrong and guitarist Lonnie Johnson (who was making a guest appearance as the sixth member of Armstrong's Hot Five that day in 1927) engage in a series of exchanges between out-of-tempo scat singing and in-tempo single-string picking (track 1, 1:54). (Schuller in his diagram labels this exchange "theme *B*.") Lil Armstrong pounds out a rocking piano interlude to get the engine revved up to speed (track 1, 2:14). And under the direction of Armstrong's majestic trumpeting, the ending steams along again in song form until it abruptly disintegrates (track 1, 2:53). Although none of this contrasting material seems substantial enough to constitute a theme, it does demonstrate that there need not be a firm boundary between song form and multithematic form. We are about to reencounter this same point, coming from the other direction.

Marches and Rags

The next most important formal model is the march and the rag, whose compositional approach inspired many performances in New Orleans jazz and revivals of the style. Marches and rags normally have two, three, or four themes, each 16 bars long; in moving from one theme to the next, there is sometimes a change of key. Jelly Roll Morton's *Black Bottom Stomp* was inspired by ragtime (in which Morton was fluent), and beneath its extraordinary originality, this formal tradition is evident. Example 26 summarizes the structure of *Black Bottom Stomp* as described by Schuller in his definitive analysis of the piece. Schuller notes that from the point of view of chord progressions, *Black Bottom Stomp* has two themes, but each statement of the first has a distinct melody; thus, from a melodic point of view the piece has four themes.

Example 26. The structure of Jelly Roll Morton's *Black Bottom Stomp* (Schuller, *Early Jazz*, 157). Track 15.

Intro.	A1	A2	A3	Modulation
8 bars	16	16	16	4
0:00	0:07	0:22	0:36	0:51

B	B	B	B	B	B	B	Coda
20	20	20	20	20	20	20	2
0:55	1:14	1:32	1:50	2:09	2:28	2:47	

In spite of the apparent differences, a ragtime-oriented piece such as *Black Bottom Stomp* shares essential features of song form, and it is not difficult to see how one tradition easily gave way to the other as jazz fashions changed during the 1920s. A typical march or rag theme is built on an antecedent and consequent structure paralleling that of the later 32-bar antecedent and consequent song form. Although some of these themes are constructed in a self-enclosed manner that ends neatly, others share with song form an energizing structural instability, whereby the strongest metric and harmonic events are out of sync with one another. Morton's part *A*, if anything, takes this idea further. As Schuller explains, its chord progression is the expected 16 bars long, but it avoids a root-position tonic chord (B♭) altogether. That chord arrives only after the three statements of *A* are finished, and then only fleetingly, as the piece modulates to E♭. Part *B* is closer to the norm, insofar as harmony is concerned, but Morton stretches out the consequent phrase to 12 bars rather than keep to the symmetry of 8 plus 8 bars. This treatment is unusual—one cannot overemphasize the importance of symmetrical phrase lengths in nonblues structures in jazz. But apart from this asymmetry, the form of the second section of *Black Bottom Stomp* is akin to the form of the main section of *Hotter than That*, and in several statements of this theme there is a similar provision for solo breaks at the last 2 bars of the antecedent phrase.

Like a song form, a march or rag theme may repeat—just as a chorus does—rather than move on to the next theme. In typical compositions, a 16-bar strain will almost invariably repeat once before moving on to the next strain. And in virtually all jazz interpretations of these scores, as well as in new jazz compositions inspired by these scores, there is likely to be more than a single repeat of at least one of the themes. Morton himself takes *Black Bottom Stomp* at a frenetic tempo that enables him to squeeze three statements of the first 16-bar theme and seven of the second 20-bar theme, plus an introduction, interlude, and ending, onto a 78 RPM record.

Because of the close relationship between marches and rags, and songs, and the flexibility inherent in jazz performance, it is not surprising that musicians sometimes treat a multipart form as if it were a chorus form. This is simply the next logical step, one that links the two approaches. *Panama*, written in 1911 by the ragtime composer William H. Tyers, quickly became a mainstay in the repertory of New Orleans bands. The form of *Panama*, as Tyers wrote it, is as follows:

Example 27. The form of William H. Tyers's ragtime piece *Panama*, as published in 1911 by Leo Feist in New York.

(F major)					(Trio: B♭)				(F)		
Intro.	*A*	*A*	*B*	*B*	*A*	*C*	*C*	*D*	*D*	Intro.	*A*	Ending
4 bars	16	16	16	16	16	16	16	16	16	4	16	8

When performing *Panama*, a jazz band may borrow several strains from Tyers's multithematic scheme. But not necessarily. For the version of *Panama* that his Creole Jazz Band recorded in mid-1959, Kid Thomas Valentine followed an approach heard in many jazz renditions of the piece: he discarded every strain but the last (theme *D*), a straightforward 16-bar progression that recurs throughout the recording. In effect Valentine made a chorus form out of a rag, while retaining the historical reference to an earlier tradition. For the sake of comparison, in example 28 Valentine's melodic paraphrase at the opening of the recording is aligned beneath Tyers's theme D. (The Creole Jazz Band's choruses are in B♭ and have the rhythmic feeling of $\frac{4}{4}$ time, but to facilitate the comparison, Valentine's part has been cast in Tyers's terms, that is, transposed up a whole step and compressed into 2 beats to the bar.)

Example 28. The melody of the fourth theme of William Tyers's *Panama* (upper staff) and that melody as paraphrased by trumpeter Kid Thomas Valentine on a recording from 1959 (lower staff). Track 20, beginning.

Static Forms

In addition to becoming multipart forms, song forms sometimes merge with static forms, which consist of little more than an instruction to play a brief pattern over and over again. Underlying that pattern will be a drone (a continuous single sound), or two chords, or a little succession of chords.

For many years Caribbean and South American dance patterns have served in this manner as a basis for jazz performances involving drones and ostinatos. Gillespie's *Manteca,* from 1947, has a static Afro-Cuban dance pattern that melds into and frames two song forms. During this static portion of the piece, band members play interlocking 2-bar patterns that sit on the tonic chord, I^{7} in the key of B♭. (See ad hoc forms, below, for a diagram of the relationship of the tonic drone to the song forms; for a notated example of the drone, see chap. 2, ex. 8b.)

Later, rock, soul, funk, disco, and rap provided a new source of inspiration for static forms in jazz. Ornette Coleman's *Honeymooners* begins by referring to this tradition, with Al MacDowell's electric bass guitar repeating a syncopated pattern (track 3), but something else emerges, as the potentially static form is filtered through Coleman's delightfully twisted vision of funky dance music. (Again, see below, ad hoc forms.)

Modal Jazz

Many static forms can be grouped under modal jazz, a term that is often hard to define. In theory, modal jazz explores scales found in ethnic or ecclesiastical music.

In ethnic borrowings, a scale is presumed to evoke an exotic flavor vaguely reminiscent of flamenco, Arabic, Oriental, African, Balinese, or other regional music. As part of the global expansion of jazz that began in the 1960s, this idea represents, in meaning rather than in sound, a return to the spirit that Ellington brought to the Cotton Club in the late 1920s, when he created a pseudo-African "jungle style."

Borrowings from ecclesiastical modes similarly take a nonspecialist approach to the subject, with none of the difficulty encountered upon trying to figure out what modality really means in medieval and Renaissance church music. In jazz, these revived ecclesiastical modes—dorian, phrygian, lydian, mixolydian, aeolian—simply represent diatonic scales. By comparison with the major scale, the lydian mode includes a raised fourth step; the mixolydian mode, a lowered seventh step; the dorian mode, a lowered third as well the lowered seventh; the aeolian, a lowered sixth as well as the lowered third and seventh; and the phrygian, additionally a lowered second. Any of these may be transposed freely. For example:

> D mixolydian (D E F♯ G A B C)
>
> E♭ mixolydian (E♭ F G A♭ B♭ C D♭)
>
> F mixolydian (F G A B♭ C D E♭)
>
> A dorian (A B C D E F♯ G)
>
> B♭ dorian (B♭ C D♭ E♭ F G A♭)
>
> D dorian (D E F G A B C)
>
> A aeolian (A B C D E F G)
>
> C♯ aeolian (C♯ D♯ E F♯ G♯ A B)

So much for theory. In practice, the key element of modal jazz is a single and, at the time, profound idea: slow harmonic rhythm. Harmonic rhythm is the rate at which chords change. This slower rate is achieved through the use of drones or of weakly functional successions (rather than strongly functional progressions) of two or more oscillating chords. In the sense that this slowing down involves the weakening of functionality, the resulting music might be called modal rather than tonal. On the whole, however, the label and the resultant theoretical emphasis, as understood in jazz, are quite misleading, because modal jazz turns out to have much more to do with harmony than with scales.

Regardless of definitions, the concept is an important one and owes its existence to Miles Davis. Until the late 1950s, the static harmonies of a piece like *Manteca* were unusual. In most jazz, chords changed once every one or two bars, and sometimes as fast as once every beat. Above this background, bop, cool jazz, and hard-bop soloists would create fast-moving and ever-changing lines, to accord with the changing harmonies. But Davis felt hemmed in by this approach. He wanted to play tuneful melodies. He was uninterested in early jazz or swing, both of which were predominantly tuneful styles, and instead sought to create a new stylistic environment. On the albums *Milestones* (1958), *Porgy and Bess* (1958), and *Kind of Blue* (1959) he took the first steps toward this goal, by playing tunes in which the harmonic rhythm moved slowly. This is modal jazz.

A somewhat later representation of modal jazz is *Maiden Voyage* (1965), written by Herbie Hancock while he was the pianist in Davis's quintet. The piece uses a 32-bar *aaba* structure, but a single harmony governs half of each 8-bar phrase (ex. 29):

Example 29. The form and harmony of Herbie Hancock's *Maiden Voyage*.

A$_{MI}$^{7}/D					C$_{MI}$^{7}/F				
A$_{MI}$^{7}/D					C$_{MI}$^{7}/F				
B♭$_{MI}$^{7}/E♭					C♯$_{MI}$^{9}				
A$_{MI}$^{7}/D					C$_{MI}$^{7}/F				

Hancock explained the harmony this way: "You start with a 7th chord with the 11th on the bottom—a 7th chord with a suspended 4th—and then that chord moves up a minor third. . . . It doesn't have any cadences; it just keeps moving around in a circle."[7] Thus in addition to a slow-paced harmonic rhythm, this composition features chords that individually and collectively avoid a strong sense of tonal function.

As Hancock explains it, the first sound of *Maiden Voyage* represents an A minor eleventh chord, with the eleventh (D) in the bass. Alternatively this same construction could be heard as representing some sort of D chord; but whether it is a D dominant eleventh or a D minor eleventh is ambiguous, because the third step (F♯ or F) is unspecified. This chord is then transferred up a minor third and back down again, the result conveying the abstract impression of a move between relative major and minor keys, though Hancock's cleverly ambiguous chords intentionally obscure the identity of that key. At the bridge the basic chord makes a weakly functional movement, being transposed a half step up. Then, in the second half of the bridge it seems (despite Hancock's explanation) that the character of that chord changes, from an ambiguous eleventh chord to an unambiguous C♯ minor ninth chord. In any event, this sonority does nothing to disturb the overall harmonic ambiguity, and Hancock's summary seems right on the mark: exemplifying modal jazz, the static chordal succession of *Maiden Voyage* "doesn't have any cadences; it just keeps moving around in a circle."[8]

Ad Hoc Forms

Major portions of jazz do not rest neatly in the lap of tradition but instead reflect an ad hoc approach to form. The majority leave aside references to conventional models. At one extreme is John Coltrane's orchestral improvisation *Ascension*, which offers a simple form: an alternation of ensemble and solo sections. In every other respect, however, this is a profound, gut-wrenching performance; there is no better example of a large-scale piece in which sophisticated form is completely irrelevant. At the other extreme among orchestral improvisations from *Ascension*, for improvised music, would be Sun Ra's *Outer Nothingness*, in which the players, through sensitive and spontaneous interaction, find their way to a unique form that does not lend itself to schematic representation. Among composed music, Joe Zawinul's *Birdland*, written for and recorded by Weather Report, is another example of unconventional form. A few details of its themes appeared in chapter 2. To illustrate its formal intricacy, the following examples offer an analysis of its shape (ex. 30a) and a key to the leading idea of each theme (exx. 30b–30g), with the exception of theme *A* (detailed in chap. 1, ex. 12) and theme *E* (which consists of a drone on the tonic and therefore requires no example).

Example 30a. The form of *Birdland*, as recorded by Weather Report in 1976.

Introd.	*A*	*B*	*C*	*C'*	*D*	*D'*	*E*	*F*
12 bars	16	8	24	18	16	8	20	14
0:00	0:18	0:43	0:55	1:31	1:59	2:24	2:36	3:07

Transition	*A*	*B*	*C*	*D*	*D'*
4	16	8	8	16	40 + fade
3:29	3:35	3:59	4:11	4:24	4:48

Example 30b. A cue to theme *B* of *Birdland*. Track 21, 0:43.

Example 30c. A cue to theme *C*, beginning at its fifth bar. Track 21, 1:02.

Example 30d. A cue to theme *C'*. Track 21, 1:31.

Example 30e. A cue to theme *D*. Track 21, 1:59.

Example 30f. A cue to theme *D'*. Track 21, 2:24.

Example 30g. A cue to theme *F*. Track 21, 3:07.

As might be expected in a performance in which improvisation dominates, the ad hoc form of Ornette Coleman's *Honeymooners* (track 3) is simpler than that of a carefully controlled composition like *Birdland*. The piece involves a "segment" and an "interlude" (labels chosen solely for this discussion) demarcated by changes in texture that are undergirded and linked by a fast and steady beat. Because the group's mastery of rhythmic disorientation makes it difficult to count blocks of measures, the following description is cast in terms of minutes and seconds.

0:00—Segment 1, featuring Al MacDowell, is a virtuosic, syncopated solo for electric bass guitar, accompanied by crisp electric guitar chords and drum rhythms (mainly ride cymbal, but also snare and bass drums).

0:37—The interlude is a dense polyrhythmic passage for the full ensemble.

0:46—In segment 2 the solo expands into a duo of contrasts, with Coleman's bluesy, moderately paced, lyrical alto saxophone set against MacDowell's rapid, snappy electric bass.

1:23—The interlude returns.

1:33—The first segment having been a solo, and the second a duo, in segment 3 the level of activity expands further, with the electric guitar moving out of the realm of accompaniment and into the realm of collective improvisation.

2:42—Without an interlude, segment 4 gets under way, as the texture recalls the first segment: solo electric bass guitar, crisp electric guitar chords, and drums.

3:20—The interlude returns for the third time. One notices that the volume of the drum rises abruptly here, indicating that the studio engineer as well as the musicians (all of whom were presumably under Coleman's direction) had a hand in articulating the ad hoc form of *Honeymooners*.

3:30—Segment 5 is marked by a heavier dance beat, by collective improvisation among guitars and bass guitars, and by Coleman's absence. The piece ends by fading out.

Less common among ad hoc forms are pieces that rework conventional models into new, unconventional shapes. *Manteca* represents one of the many types of stylistic fusions essential to jazz, namely, Afro-Cuban jazz. As the quintessential recording in that style, *Manteca* manages to bring together, or to juxtapose, elements of instrumentation, rhythm, improvisation, and form associated variously with Afro-Cuban dance music and jazz. In its multipart form, the aforementioned static Afro-Cuban dance pattern frames two song forms, while also melding into those song forms. At the opening, the static pattern builds instrument by instrument to Gillespie's trumpet solo, yields to a 2-bar chordal break, and then subsides. The first song form uses a 40-bar *aabb'a* pattern (with the bridge 16, not 8, bars long), and the first 6 bars of each of its *a* sections are on the same static pattern, thus enabling the song form to emerge and recede seamlessly. The second song form is a variant of the first, with the insertion of *I Got Rhythm*.

Example 31. The form of *Manteca*, as recorded by Dizzy Gillespie in 1947. Track 8.

Opening (0:00)

22 bars	+ 2	+ 4
drone	chords	drone

Chorus 1 (0:38)

a		*a*		*b*	*b'*	*a*	
6	+ 2	6	+ 2	8	8	6	+ 2
drone	chords	drone	chords	chords	chords	drone	chords

Interlude (1:33)

10

drone

Chorus 2 (1:47)

c	*c*		*b*	*b'*	*a*	
8	8		8	8	6	+ 2
chords	(*I Got Rhythm*)		chords	chords	drone	chords

Ending (2:42)
16
drone

Like *Manteca*, Charles Mingus's *Fables of Faubus* offers a complex
dressing up of *aaba* song form, which by 1959 was otherwise getting rather stale, having already served for three decades, alongside blues, as the central basis for jazz performance. In the theme, each segment of song form subdivides further into its own little form, with this result:

Example 32. The form of the theme of Charles Mingus's *Fables of Faubus*, as recorded in 1959. Track 13.

a (0:00)				*a'* (0:37)			*b* (1:14)				*a'* (1:45)		
19 bars				18			16				18		
c	*c*	*d*	Intro.	*c*	*c*	*d'*	*e*	*e*	*f*	*g*	*c*	*c*	*d'*
4 + 4 + 9 + 2				4 + 4 + 10			4 + 4 + 4 + 4				4 + 4 + 10		

Mingus's composition represents a rare example of the successful introduction of a moderate amount of sophistication into jazz forms, but as with all compositions in new styles of the past few decades, *Fables of Faubus* was an isolated experiment of no consequence for formal models. And whatever its level of structural sophistication, no one would mistake Mingus's achievement for the heady architecture of Mozart and Beethoven. Indeed the comparison is spurious, though not uncommon. In the search for alternatives to blues, popular-song, rag, and march forms, there have been many failed attempts to move toward the elaborate formal constructions of classical music, as if their absence in jazz were somehow a weakness. Advocates of such changes (who are often motivated not by genuinely musical considerations but by a desire to equalize the unequal sociocultural status of jazz and classical music) may suffer from a misunderstanding of the relative weight of the building blocks of jazz and hence a fundamental inability to judge jazz on its own (profound) merits.[9]

Jazz forms are simple and, in a way, unimportant. Of course familiarity with these forms helps a listener to hear what is going on, and that after all is the purpose of this chapter. Once a form is identified, a listener's attention turns elsewhere. Forms are the least significant building blocks of jazz. They are the molds into which jazz is poured. What matters is how these molds are filled.

4 ARRANGEMENT

I started writing just to avoid arguments. Smoke Richardson was musical director, and we used to make head arrangements, but they'd give out the harmony all ass-backwards, and it was hard to remember.
—Sy Oliver

Listeners are often curious about how jazz is made. Is a performance arranged, composed, or improvised? In this chapter on arrangement and in the chapters that follow, the aim is to continue with the approach taken for rhythm and forms: to endeavor to give a practical, commonsense explanation of how these concepts work in jazz, with clear examples drawn from a set of great recordings. But there are other aims as well. These three chapters compare related pieces (using additional musical selections) and interpret the comparisons in terms of the creative procedure. With this background, the listener may be able to figure out how a performance has been put together. Much more important—because after all we are interested in the results, not the process—it should also become apparent that particular techniques have a particular sound. In the following discussion, four important areas of arrangement will be analyzed: the note-for-note reinstrumentation of an existing piece; the elaboration of form; orchestration for big bands; and finally (and deceptively) arrangement as a term used in jazz to describe pieces that are not arrangements of anything, but instead entirely new compositions.

Given the diversity of these aspects of arrangement and the conceptually imprecise possibility that arrangement might actually mean composition, readers should not be surprised to discover in these next three chapters that distinctions among arrangement, composition, and improvisation are often not clear-cut. In many cases the process of music making simply cannot be known; or the process seems irrelevant to the resulting sound; or more than one process is involved. Thus a different aim in listening, quite at odds with the preceding one, is to recognize areas of uncertainty and overlap.

Hand in hand with a curiosity about how music is made comes an interest in knowing who makes it. Identification of a musician (a passionate topic among jazz fans) seems virtually a component of sound—along with melody, harmony, rhythm, timbre, form, and the like—and commonly serves as a shorthand for stylistic description: "He sounds like Louis." After detailing diverse areas of jazz arrangement, the present chapter introduces the topic by examining how questions of memory, documentation, and royalties can cloud the identification of an arranger.

Note-for-Note Arrangement

In its most restrictive sense, arrangement involves the note-for-note reinstrumentation of an existing piece. Although there is no example of this sort of arrangement among the twenty-one music selections, we need not stray far to find one. In the years immediately following his session of September 1926 (which produced *Black Bottom Stomp*), Jelly Roll Morton and his Red Hot Peppers made new recordings of a number of his compositions that he had recorded as an unaccompanied pianist in 1923–24. In jazz, there is usually nothing special about the practice of a leader making a new recording of a piece, but this specific instance is special—from the point of view of note-for-note arrangement—because of the precise and literal ways Morton transfers details of the piano versions of 1923–24 to the equivalent band settings of 1926–28. Examples include *Grandpa's Spells*, recorded in 1923 and 1926, and *Kansas City Stomps*, from 1923 and 1928. Above all, Morton's handling of *The Pearls* (1923 and 1927) exemplifies a traditional arrangement. Whereas normal practice in expanding a jazz performance from piano to band might give the instrumentalists considerable artistic license, in *The Pearls* Morton carefully arranges the instrumental parts, so that, for example, a syncopated, twinkling piano break is re-created exactly but is now played by the clarinet.[1]

Note-for-note arrangements such as these fill a small niche in jazz. They are found in multithematic pieces, because the very fact of having more than one theme gives the arranger something substantial to arrange; examples can be heard in New Orleans jazz or in jazz fusion. And they are sometimes used in renditions of classical music (referred to as "jazzin' the classics"), usually with disastrous results. Occasional masterpieces do result, however, as with Gil Evans's arrangement of Rodrigo's *Concierto de Aranjuez* on Miles Davis's album *Sketches of Spain.*

But in many performances of multithematic pieces, note-for-note arrangement may be evident only in a trivial, technical sense. The emphasis may be on soloing instead, as in Sidney Bechet's breakneck romp through Scott Joplin's *Maple Leaf Rag,* which Bechet recorded for Victor as a member of the New Orleans Feetwarmers in 1932.[2] But at least the possibility of a note-for-note arrangement existed for Bechet, because the existing piece has a substantial form and detailed themes that might have been preserved in the reworking.

In chorus forms—the most common structure heard in jazz arrangement —the potential for making a note-for-note arrangement diminishes. What makes the chorus form a perfect vehicle for jazz performance is its elegant, pliable simplicity, unburdened by formal and thematic detail. This very quality leaves little material to arrange: perhaps merely a melody and chord progression, or perhaps a chord progression alone.

Duke Ellington's recording of *Trumpet No End,* based on Irving Berlin's *Blue Skies,* represents what can be done with a chorus form. Characteristically for jazz arrangement, the performance is by a big band, which for Ellington in 1946 meant five trumpets, three trombones, five saxophones, and a three-piece rhythm section. The last serves as any swing-style rhythm section might in a popular song: piano and bass make their way through the borrowed chord progression, while the drums play swing rhythms. All the rest—eight brass and five reeds—need to be coordinated in a more restrictive way, since (to use an anachronistic comparison) the freedom of the wind players on Coltrane's *Ascension* would have been ridiculous in this stylistic context. One way to meet that need—though certainly not the only one—is to have the players deliver an arranged version of Berlin's song.

The arranger and pianist Mary Lou Williams did just this in the portion that she contributed to Ellington in 1943, at a time when her husband, Shorty Baker, was playing trumpet in the band.[3] The song shines through in several ways. Cat Anderson, a specialist in high notes, sings out a lightly ornamented version of Berlin's melody in the *a* section (ex. 33a) at the start of the fourth and final 32-bar chorus (ex. 33d); and the trumpet section presents in unison a syncopated version of Berlin's melody for the *b* section (ex. 33b) during the bridge of the first chorus (ex. 33c, bars 17–24). Although Anderson's contribution is spectacular from the point of view of trumpet playing, neither of these segments of melody offers a spectacular demonstration of arranging abilities. Instead, the point to note is Williams's approach to arranging the *a* sections of the first chorus. In these three 8-bar phrases, she disguises the song. Berlin's melody serves as an accompaniment to a trumpet solo melodically unrelated to *Blue Skies*, and Williams takes care to alter that accompaniment at each new phrase by introducing a variety of syncopations (ex. 33c, bars 1–8, 9–15, 25–32). Also, at the start the saxophone section sounds out in held tones the most colorful notes of Berlin's chord progression. Otherwise Williams's harmonic concerns focus on a presentation of Berlin's tune in densely chromatic block chords, an approach that allows her to stretch out the idea of note-for-note arrangement as far as possible. (For the sake of comparison, exx. 33a and 33b have been transposed from Berlin's key, G, to Williams's, B♭.)

Example 33a. The melody in the first *a* section of Irving Berlin's *Blue Skies.*

Example 33b. The melody in the first half of the bridge of *Blue Skies.*

Example 33c. The first chorus of Mary Lou Williams's arrangement of *Blue Skies* for Duke Ellington's orchestra (from the archives of the Smithsonian Museum of American History). Track 7, 0:08.

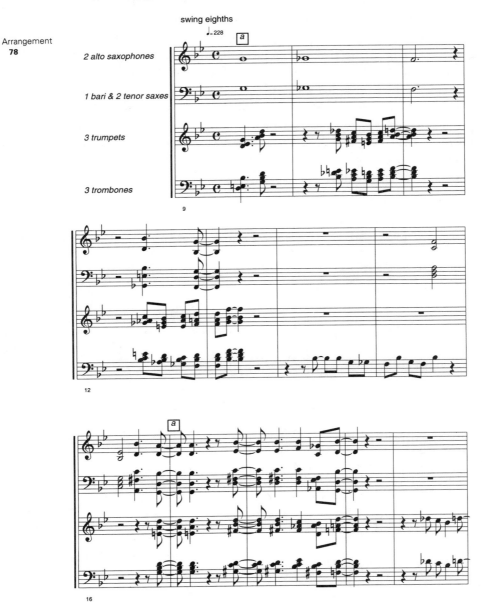

Arrangement
80

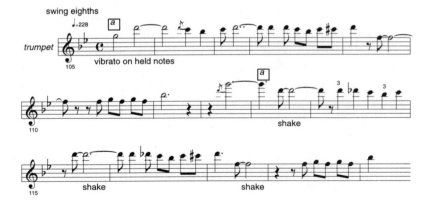

Example 33d. Cat Anderson's solo trumpet paraphrase of a portion of Berlin's melody during the fourth chorus of Ellington's *Trumpet No End*, recorded in 1946. Track 7, 1:50.

When a jazz musician works with a skeletal chorus form, a note-for-note arrangement is likely to disappear altogether. A typical example would be Charlie Parker's *Koko*, which in this respect is only distantly related to Ray Noble's *Cherokee*. Parker's combo discarded Noble's melody entirely, with Parker inventing a completely new melody over a highly embellished version of Noble's chords and the group adding material entirely foreign to Noble's conception: Parker and Gillespie's slippery melodies in the half-composed, half-improvised introduction and ending; and Max Roach's hurried snare drum solo.

The Elaboration of Form

These modifications to *Cherokee* introduce a second area of arranging, one that allows the arranger greater creativity: the elaboration of an existing form. *'Round Midnight*, as performed by Miles Davis in 1956, offers an especially fine example of this aspect of arrangement because of its relationship to a number of earlier recordings. By comparing these versions, one begins to see how Davis's rendition of Thelonious Monk's composition gained its structural appendages.

In chapter 2 three versions of Monk's melody were introduced: one from the first recording of *'Round Midnight*, which Cootie Williams's big band made in 1944; and two from recordings for Columbia and Prestige that the Miles Davis quintet made a dozen years later. In the latter two the arrangement proceeds as follows:

Segment 1: 8-bar introduction featuring Davis (track 5, 0:00)

Segment 2: 32-bar *aaba* chorus featuring Davis (0:30)

Segment 3: 3-bar fanfare for the whole ensemble (2:39)

Segment 4: 32-bar *aaba* chorus featuring John Coltrane (2:56)

Segment 5: 8-bar ending featuring Davis (5:07)

Hence Monk's composition, heard in segments 2 and 4, has been framed and linked by an introduction, fanfare, and ending. How might these segments—1, 3, and 5—have developed? Davis's rendition of this arrangement of *'Round Midnight* does not have its roots in the original recorded version. Williams's arrangement—with its abrupt 3-chord introduction, inappropriately cheery 8-bar interlude, and pleasant but forgettable ending—was of no interest to Davis. Instead he used a much more substantial and memorable arrangement, which Dizzy Gillespie is believed to have written in the years following Williams's session, at least on the evidence of surviving recordings. Given the extent to which Theolonius Monk and Gillespie played together informally during the war years, Monk may also have had a hand in this creative process early on.

The most stable element of the arrangement is the ending (segment 5), which was already present when Gillespie first recorded the piece with his sextet in February 1946. Subsequently Gillespie adapted this ending for use with his big band.

In January 1953, Davis recorded the tune.[4] Like several of Gillespie's versions, the performance appeared under its alternative title, *'Round about Midnight*. By this time Davis had adopted Gillespie's approach intact (ex. 34, upper staff) and continued to stick with it, as evidenced three years later in the sessions at a Columbia studio in September (ex. 34, lower staff) and again at Prestige in November.

Example 34. Davis's versions of Dizzy Gillespie's melody for the ending to *'Round Midnight,* as recorded in versions for Prestige in 1953 (upper staff) and for Columbia in 1956 (lower staff). Track 5, 5:07.

The fanfare (segment 3) makes its appearance on recordings by Gillespie's big band. At a concert recorded in Paris in February 1948, his *'Round about Midnight* has an interlude that separates the second and third 32-bar choruses. It consists of a brief but jumbled piano solo and the fortissimo fanfare. For a concert recorded in Pasadena the following July, Gillespie abridged the performance and used the big-band fanfare as an introduction, in place of the original one (segment 1).

Davis followed the Parisian model. He (or Gil Evans?) pared Gillespie's fanfare down to the bone, to suit a quintet. One uncomfortable result was that in playing a little sawtooth-shaped line of swing sixteenth notes, Paul Chambers found himself trying to make the string bass take the place of several saxophones.

But there were other changes as well, and these made the interlude more striking than Gillespie's original. In 1956, at the Columbia and Prestige sessions, the arranger reduced the piano solo to a reiterated octave leap, played quietly. This 1-bar break heightened the contrast in dynamics between the first chorus and the fanfare and set the table for a subtle play with double time, as described in chapter 2, where a transcription of this passage appears (ex. 2; track 5, 2:39). The result was one of the purplest of purple patches in all of jazz. Davis's intensely quiet, muted, middle-register sound gives way to the softest possible tinkling piano notes and then to a repeated, ecstatically swinging block chord shouted out by the whole ensemble, with Davis unmuted and in his highest range. The group seems to be tightening a giant spring, which then uncoils in a sudden burst as Coltrane begins his solo.

The introduction (segment 1) has a slightly more complicated history, beginning with a version of *I Can't Get Started* recorded by Gillespie in 1945. At the end of the song, Gillespie plays the first 4 bars of what was to become, the following year, the introduction to *'Round Midnight*, as recorded by his sextet. At this point in 1946 the sequentially descending melody and chord progression have been stretched out from 4 to 6 bars, leading to a 2-bar-long break (ex. 35, upper staff); the breathing spaces at the second half of bars 2, 4, and 6 are filled out by a double-time figure.

For the session in 1953, Davis adopted all of these features, in addition to extending the double-time figures into the 2-bar break. In the sessions with Coltrane a new element entered the arrangement. Still intact were the borrowed chord progression and the double-time figures, but now, in 1956, Davis supplied an entirely new melody, the essence of which he carried through from the session for Columbia into the session for Prestige (ex. 35, middle and lower staffs). Thus the introductory harmony and accompanying rhythms had been codified permanently, but the melody had undergone a process of metamorphosis, Gillespie's line giving way to Davis's new one, with no guarantee of permanence. In this little snippet, arrangement presents itself as a renewable, flexible process within a tradition of improvised performance.

Example 35. Gillespie's melody in the introduction to *'Round Midnight*, from a version recorded with his sextet in 1946 (top staff); Davis's melody in the introduction on his versions for Columbia (middle staff) and Prestige (bottom staff), recorded in 1956 (transcribed by Franz Kerschbaumer). Track 5, beginning.

Arrangement as Orchestration

Nearly all of the renowned jazz arrangers were celebrated for their ability to orchestrate for big bands. The attempt to understand this activity presents an odd mix of the obvious and the impenetrable. Although basic principles of organization recur with great regularity, the art of big-band orchestration is anything but obvious. The beauty of orchestration may lie in fine details, the exact register in which a particular instrument lies, how it is pitted against or joined with another. Furthermore, the principles and details, whether formulaic or idiosyncratic, exist for the public mainly on recordings, not on paper. The need to depend on one's ear, without assistance from a notated score, makes the task of appreciation all the more difficult. Sometimes, because of the number of instruments playing simultaneously, a carefully controlled swath of big-band sound can be as difficult to pin down as the wildest moment of free collective improvisation. Sophisticated touches of orchestration may sound garbled or pass by unnoticed. Although this book does not hold the key to such mysteries, it does enumerate the basic principles.

Foremost among the principles is a strong tendency to exploit natural timbral contrasts among instruments by orchestrating along sectional lines: the brass section, subdivided into trumpets and trombones; the reed section, mainly saxophones, though reed players doubled on the clarinet during the heyday of the big bands and in later years often doubled on the flute; and the rhythm section, some combination of chordal, bass, and percussion instruments. Count Basie's *Jumpin' at the Woodside* offers a systematic example of divisions along sectional lines (ex. 36). As testimony to Basie's preference for timbral contrast, a solo instrument is never accompanied by that same instrument.

Example 36. An outline of orchestral groupings in Count Basie's *Jumpin' at the Woodside.* Track 2.

Intro (0:00) rhythm section (continuing throughout the piece)

Chorus 1 (0:07)

a	*a*	*a*	unison sax riff, chordal brass riff
		b	alto sax solo, chordal brass riff

Chorus 2 (0:39)

a	*a*	*a*	unison sax riff, chordal brass riff, piano solo and riff
		b	piano solo

Chorus 3 (1:11)

a	*a*	*a*	trumpet solo, chordal sax riff, unison trombone riff
		b	trumpet solo, sax chords

Chorus 4 (1:44)

a	*a*	*a*	tenor sax solo, chordal brass riff
		b	tenor sax solo

Ending (2:17)

a		clarinet and trombone duo and riffs
a		clarinet solo, unison sax riff, chordal brass riff
a	*a*	clarinet solo, unison sax riff, chordal brass riff, unison trombone riff
a	*a*	clarinet solo, unison sax riff, trombone riff

Duke Ellington's *Ko-Ko* is as rigorously sectional as *Jumpin' at the Woodside.* The only noteworthy exception occurs in the introduction to *Ko-Ko* and again at the end, when Harry Carney's baritone saxophone functions neither as part of the saxophone section nor as a melodic voice; offering instead an independent low voice, it fills a niche that would later be taken over by the electric bass guitar. Carney's biting, nasal drone is paired with Sonny Greer's tom-tom drumming (in the introduction, not at the end) and set against Jimmy Blanton's deeper, smooth-toned walking bass (ex. 37).

Example 37. Use of the baritone saxophone as a member of the rhythm section in the introduction to Ellington's *Ko-Ko* (from the score prepared by Dave Berger). Track 6, beginning.

Arrangement
87

Ko-Ko
Duke Ellington

Manteca, too, has many strictly organized sections, but in this orchestration from 1947 for Dizzy Gillespie, Gil Fuller, the arranger and co-composer, worked a portion of the piece along different lines. As the introduction unfolds, four interlocking ostinatos build up on top of one another with little regard for conventional sections (see chap. 2, ex. 8b; track 8, beginning). The first two ostinatos sound in rhythm instruments, namely Chano Pozo's conga drum and Al McKibbon's string bass; Kenny Clarke, on drums, roughly doubles the rhythm of the conga drum. The third ostinato begins with the baritone saxophone of Cecil Payne functioning as part of the rhythm section, just as Harry Carney does at the beginning and ending of *Ko-Ko*. Then, a variety of instruments double Payne's line: trombone; other saxophones, an octave higher; and finally trumpets, also an octave above the baritone sax. Against all of this, other members of the trombone section enter with the fourth and last ostinato, and Gillespie plays a trumpet solo.

When the material from this introduction returns as an interlude between the two 40-bar choruses of the piece (see the diagram in chap. 3, ex. 31), Fuller orchestrates it with a clever twist: the string bass and the trombones have traded material. The ostinato belonging to the bass is in the trombones, and the trombone's is in the bass, though now it sounds through every measure rather than in alternate segments of 2 bars of sound and 2 of silence (track 8, 1:33). (For rhythmic, not orchestral, reasons, the string bass could not possibly have dropped out for 2 measures at a time in a driving piece such as this.)

Whether an arrangement organizes instruments along sectional lines or in an ad hoc manner, pitches must somehow relate to one another within each grouping, as dictated by the traditional notions of melody and harmony. One solution, obviously, is to play a line in unison or (if necessary to accommodate differences in range) in octaves. Alternatively, if a group of instruments plays in harmony, three interwoven principles apply widely.

One principle is classic: individual lines should move in an economical fashion rather than leap about. Thus, in the first chorus of *Jumpin' at the Woodside*, the brass outline the underlying progression as concisely as possible. At the change of harmony (see below, bar 13 of ex. 40a) the chord remains constant, except for one note, which moves up half a step.

Operating along with this economical movement are two principles characteristic of much twentieth-century music. One is active, the other passive, but both have the effect of complicating the harmonic works. The active principle allows any grouping of instruments to slide along in parallel or (with adjustments to accommodate the underlying harmony) similar motion. In effect a blanket of quickly moving block chords covers a fundamental structure. Examples in *Ko-Ko* include two passages of sliding chromaticism (exx. 38a–38b), as well as a moment in which ascending diatonic chords pile up, one on top of the other, section by section (ex. 38c). Further examples of parallel and similar motion are also heard in the *a* sections of the first chorus of Ellington's *Trumpet No End* (see above, ex. 33c), as Mary Lou Williams presents Irving Berlin's melody in thick block chords.

Example 38a. Block chords descending chromatically in parallel motion during the introduction to Ellington's *Ko-Ko*. Track 6, beginning.

Example 38b. Chromatically colored block chords descending in parallel and similar motion at the start of the first blues chorus of *Ko-Ko.* Track 6, 0:13.

Example 38c. Diatonic block chords ascending in parallel motion in preparation for the first solo string bass break in *Ko-Ko.* Track 6, 1:44. (All three examples are from the score prepared by Dave Berger.)

Ko-Ko
Duke Ellington
Copyright © 1940, renewed 1968 Robbins Music Corporation.
Rights assigned to EMI Catalogue Partnership.
All rights controlled and administered by EMI Robbins Catalog Inc.
All rights reserved. International copyright secured.
Used by permission.

The passive principle gives soloists and the rhythm section greater freedom, allowing them to be guided by stylistic convention rather than by specific instruction. An arranger may sometimes indicate when solos occur and use fake-book notation to lay out the accompanying chord progression, but a professional band may not require such cues. On paper, Williams's arrangement of *Trumpet No End* survives as eleven orchestral parts—for three trumpets, three trombones, and five saxophones. Chord symbols and indications of when to solo are not indicated. A soloist was simply expected to be familiar with the harmonies of *Blue Skies* and to know where his solo was situated in the arrangement. The only exception occurs in the introduction, where the second tenor saxophonist is given a 2-bar notice to lay down his instrument and pick up a clarinet for a 10-beat-long solo break (no chord symbols supplied).

As a consequence of this nonintervention, improvisation remains a possibility, under circumstances that are otherwise tightly controlled. In *Trumpet No End* the opportunities are extensive: the glorious trumpet solos and the swinging accompaniment of the rhythm section are at least as important as the orchestrated parts.

A footnote to this activity, arrangement as orchestration, provides a fascinating insight into a commonplace phenomenon in jazz, namely that practical considerations almost always take precedence over theoretical ones. According to Dave Berger, a renowned expert in Ellington's music, *Ko-Ko* was written in 1939, at a time when Ellington's orchestra had four reed players. The parts written for those instrumentalists—two alto saxophonists, one tenor saxophonist (doubling on clarinet), one baritone saxophonist—are complete in themselves. The acclaimed recording was made the following year, after Ben Webster, a tenor saxophonist, joined the band; for this fifth reed Ellington himself wrote a custom-made part that dances about, weaving between or doubling individual reed or brass parts, without showing strict allegiance to a section or to parallel movement yet without disturbing the overall effect of the sectional groupings or the sliding block chords.

Arrangement as Composition

The distinction between arranging and composing has always been cloudy. At some point an arranger goes beyond existing material and supplies new ideas that sit squarely in the domain of composition. This area of arranging embraces, for example, all the portions of Williams's *Trumpet No End* that are neither arrangements of *Blue Skies* nor improvisations but new accompaniments and ensemble melodies. In jazz, all of this new invention is considered a part of Williams's arrangement. Hence references to a band's arrangements may often pertain as much to new composition as to the arrangement of an existing piece.

Within this domain of arrangement as composition is the head arrangement, a piece that a group organizes orally (and aurally) and memorizes.

The idea of arrangement as unnotated composition sometimes elicits special musical qualities: for some bands, the deliberate avoidance of notation has stimulated creativity and encouraged flexibility. The repertory of Count Basie's band in the late 1930s epitomizes this approach. As Basie explained: "With most of our arrangements, one of the boys or I will get an idea for a tune, like *Every Tub* for instance, and at rehearsal we just sorta start it off and the others fall in. First thing you know, we've got it. We don't use paper on a lot of our standards. In that way, we all have more freedom for improvisations."[5]

The lasting result of this process was a group of recordings for Decca that form, along with Ellington's work, the standard against which all big-band jazz is measured. The key to the Basie orchestra's head arrangements is the intricate use of a simple device, the riff, a catchy, strongly rhythmic fragment of melody or harmony that is repeated. This sort of rhythmic motive is widespread in African-American music, and it is often impossible to determine whether a riff has been newly coined or borrowed. Swing riffs of the 1930s traveled from band to band and were molded into diverse musical settings.

In the case of *Jumpin' at the Woodside*, recorded in 1938, Chris Sheridan traces the pair of interlocking riffs that start off the first chorus (see below, ex. 40a) back to *Jammin' for the Jackpot*, which the Mills Blue Rhythm Band recorded in 1937 (ex. 39), and from there further back to *I Gotta Swing* (a version of Jelly Roll Morton's *King Porter Stomp*), which Blanche Calloway's big band recorded in 1935.[6] In the liner notes to the album *Jammin' for the Jackpot: Big Bands and Territory Bands of the Thirties*, J. R. Taylor points out that the Mills Blue Rhythm Band included Harry Edison, "who probably carried the *Jammin'* riff into the Basie band" when he joined in 1938. As further evidence of lineage, Eli Robinson, credited as the arranger of *Jammin' for the Jackpot*, had played trombone on Calloway's disc.[7]

Example 39. A pair of interlocking riffs from the Mills Blue Rhythm Band's recording of *Jammin' for the Jackpot* (1937).

In spite of these musical interrelationships, *Jumpin' at the Woodside* should not be construed as a true arrangement of the earlier pieces. Anyone who listens to the track by the Mills Blue Rhythm Band will discover that *Jumpin' at the Woodside* borrows nothing more than the initial saxophone riff (now played in unison rather than harmonized) and the rhythmic placement of answering chords from the brass (now with different pitches and briefer duration). Otherwise, Basie's track offers a less convoluted form, a more swinging rhythm, and vastly superior riffs and soloists.

In Basie's band, outstanding head arrangements were always new compositions based on blues and song forms. The form of *Jumpin' at the Woodside* is easy to grasp. Basie plays a 2-bar walking bass pattern, which gets the rhythm churning. After the rest of the rhythm section joins in, the introduction gives way to song form, four 32-bar *aaba* choruses. At the end of the piece, the bridge drops away, and the *a* section is restated just short of six times. Underlying this form is the straightforward harmonic progression noted in the previous chapter (ex. 22): the tonic and dominant in the *a* section and two secondary dominants in the bridge.

Across this structure the band overlays a network of riffs that function either as themes or as accompanimental material for soloists. The riffs have an immediate accessibility that characterizes Basie's style, but beneath the smooth surface lies considerable musical thought, expressed through the varying and interconnected riffs. Because virtually a complete score would be required to illustrate this complexity, examples 40a–40i should be considered merely a summary of the riffs in this head arrangement.[8]

In listening, note what happens to the two borrowed riffs that serve as the theme of the first chorus (ex. 40a). As the chorus ends, the held note in the sax riff gives way to a repetition of the riff's eighth notes (ex. 40b); the *a* phrases of the second chorus continue to end in this manner. Of greater interest, that same held note discreetly pulsates during the second chorus, as the saxophones stagger their entrances (ex. 40c). Meanwhile the initial syncopated rhythm played by the brass (ex. 40a) has been extended by one note (ex. 40c).

As a background for Buck Clayton's trumpet solo and Lester Young's tenor saxophone solo, new riffs fill the *a* sections of choruses three and four (exx. 40f and 40g). In the clarinet line that starts off the bridgeless segment of the piece (ex. 40h), the opening sax riff returns, though clipped and two octaves higher. At this point what will become an improvisation begins as a duet of riffs for clarinet and trombone, in a blurring of the line between

Example 40b. The varied saxophone riff at the end of chorus 1. Track 2, 0:37. (Examples 40b–40i transcribed by Dave Berger.)

Example 40c. Riffs in chorus 2. Track 2, 0:39.

Arrangement
94

Example 40d. A second rifflike figure in Basie's piano part during the second *a* section of chorus 2. Track 2, 0:47.

Example 40e. Basie again, playing a third rifflike figure during the third *a* section of chorus 2. Track 2, 1:04.

Example 40f. Riffs in chorus 3. Track 2, 1:11.

Example 40g. Riffs in chorus 4. Track 2, 1:44.

Example 40h. Solo riffs for clarinet and trombone in the first *a* section following chorus 4. Track 2, 2:17.

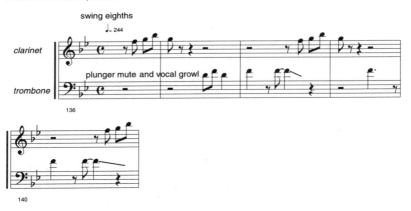

Example 40i. Riffs in the third *a* section following chorus 4. Track 2, 2:33.

Jumpin' at the Woodside
Count Basie
Copyright © 1938 WB Music Corp. (renewed).

improvising and riffing. While Herschel Evans's clarinet solo develops, the saxes take back the riff, this time ornamenting it (ex. 40i shows this same line, 8 bars later). At the climax of the piece the brass join in; their chords again recall the opening chords, but they are now inverted, harmonically denser, positioned one full beat earlier than before, and partially obscured by ascending glissandos in the trombones (ex. 40i).

All of this variety occurs among the choruses. Within the *a* sections of each chorus, the riffs remain steady, except where minor adjustments are required to avoid clashes with the underlying harmony (compare the trumpets in bars 1–4 and 5–6 of ex. 40a). Such repetition is, after all, essential to the idea of a riff and is to be expected in a head arrangement.

There is, however, a significant exception to the repetition of the riff: Basie's piano playing during the second chorus. In general, jazz distinguishes between a solo, which features an individual, and a riff, which democratically unites members of the ensemble. But Basie softened distinctions between soloing and riffing, thereby creating an understated, highly original, and widely imitated personal style. On *Jumpin' at the Woodside* he starts with a sparkling riff that sets off the brass and reeds by means of contrasting register and accents (ex. 40c). After one repetition of the riff, he disengages and momentarily improvises a continuously changing line, which in turn changes the texture of the music. Here Basie temporarily emerges as a soloist, and the reed and brass riffs serve as accompaniment rather than as leading ideas. In the next phrase, Basie begins even more ambiguously. His descending figure is rifflike in its repeated contour, but its speed intensifies (ex. 40d). Again the texture shifts to that of soloist and accompanists, as Basie leaves the rifflike ideas aside in favor of a changing line. After the bridge, Basie returns with a new riff to finish the chorus (ex. 40e).

Often we cannot know how a body of jazz came into being. Perhaps the musicians never explained how they went about making their music. If a piece was written down, perhaps the scores, parts, or sketches of melodies and chords ("lead sheets" in jazz parlance) no longer survive. Even when these details are known, they may not matter, because there may be no clear connection between the process and the result. For Count Basie, however, we know, and appreciate, the process. His use of head arrangements in the late 1930s greatly influenced his band's sound. Given the strengths of this group, head arrangements provided a compositional and organizational method perfectly balanced between swing combos (a forum for soloists) and big bands (a forum for groups of instruments) and between dance music (toe-tapping rhythm and catchy riffs) and art music (subtly interlocked and interrelated riffs).

Who Arranged What?

Although the work of many fine jazz arrangers has been properly attributed, a comprehensive identification of arrangers and arrangements seems impossible to hope for. Apart from blatant misinformation or disinformation, there may simply be a lack of information, for practical reasons. Because arrangers earned no royalties, recording companies had no need to keep a tune-by-tune log of an arranger's work. Scores and parts that might testify to the arranger's hand are frequently in private hands or long lost. For arrangements existing independent of notation, identification depends on someone's memory; oral history teaches that such events are sometimes remembered only vaguely.

'Round Midnight offers a perfect example of such obfuscation. On a reissue of 1973, album notes identify Gil Evans as the arranger.[9] As we have seen, this claim seems doubtful. On the strength of the recorded evidence, credit would seem to be due to Dizzy Gillespie, if anyone. And according to George Avakian, the producer of the Columbia recording,

Evans was not at the session.[10] But perhaps Evans and Davis collaborated on this title at some other time. Perhaps it was Evans who had a hand in creating the small details that make Davis's performance so memorable: the gradually intensifying interaction of time and double-time, the sudden contrast in dynamics, the orchestration of the fanfare. It seems unlikely that we will ever know the whole story.

Consequently, listening to jazz arrangement may involve the detective work of searching for relationships among performances, analyzing style, and surmising the identity of the arranger. Making identifications along these lines is a popular listening game and an activity open to all. Nonetheless, many a great arranger—and arrangement—is destined to remain anonymous.

5 COMPOSITION

I usually start with the bass line. . . . Then I try to figure out where it gets boring. . . . Should there be rhythmic changes, changes in density, harmony colors? . . . Where should there be melody? . . . Should it be played strictly or can it be played in a skeletal way so that the person who's playing it will have more freedom to create his own part? . . . How far should I go? That's always the big question.

I think that the best single composition I ever wrote was *Maiden Voyage.*

—Herbie Hancock

Newcomers to jazz often ask: Is it true that jazz is all improvised? Somehow the casual and romantic notion that jazz is generated in an entirely spontaneous manner has become deeply rooted in our society. Presumably this book will have dispelled that notion by now. With the addition of this chapter devoted to jazz composition, newcomers should begin listening to jazz, and thinking about what they hear, in a different way. Readers already well familiar with nonspontaneous aspects of jazz will forgive me for offering a warning that they did not need to hear.

The main aim in this chapter is not simply to establish that there is composition in jazz but to explain some of the ways it works. In chapter 2, the tour through forms described the borrowing of composed themes from other genres—blues, brass band music, ragtime, American popular songs, African-American gospel music, rock, soul music, disco, Brazilian samba, West Indian calypso, and the like. The concern here is with composition as a process within jazz. As Herbie Hancock explained in describing his own compositional method, the key issue is control: what to compose and what to leave open. The chapter surveys types of material that might be composed for jazz: a theme, or perhaps just a little idea, that serves as a framework for improvisation and underlies that improvisation; a high level of detail that controls an ensemble's performance; or a preset contour that shapes the direction of a solo.

The chapter ends by taking up the question of identification, with special attention paid to the issue of composer royalties: who wrote what, and who got the money? Its purpose is to suggest that owing to practical circumstances of copyright law and the jazz life, and to the fundamental nature of jazz performance, the relative status of jazz composition and of the jazz composer is necessarily uneven; far greater attention is often paid to the composition than to the person.

Types of Jazz Composition

In a sense the discussion of head arrangements in chapter 4 has already introduced the subject of jazz composition. There the focus was on Count Basie, who, by avoiding notated compositions, encouraged a particular style of playing that stressed riffs and solos. Here the perspective is different, and the method of transmitting ideas (whether orally or on paper) is of no concern. Instead, the discussion focuses on the vague, isolated, detailed, or pervasive ways that composition controls an ensemble's performance.

The sandwich approach to jazz composition involves taking an existing form, creating a melody that fits that form, and placing this "composition" on either side of a series of solos that depend on the borrowed form, not on the new melody. That melody might be a single line or a harmonized version, but in either case the underlying, borrowed progression always controls it. Sometimes the melody has genuine character, and its style matches the improvisations that it frames. But too often this type of theme is unmemorable, and any genuinely musical justification takes a back seat to other considerations: money and pretension. Writing a skeletal theme is the simplest way to stake a claim to royalties and the simplest way for a performer to become a composer—and thus to acquire the status that that label carries in our society.

Thelonious Monk's *Misterioso* (track 14) is a piece that pokes fun at the sandwich approach by exaggerating the contrast between the solos and the surrounding theme. Overlaid on a standard blues progression, the theme imitates a warm-up exercise from a beginner's music lesson. Monk, on piano, Milt Jackson, on vibraphone, and John Simmons, on string bass, offer, in harmony, a strict succession of alternating leaps and steps. To differentiate the theme from the solos even more, the three men present Monk's mock etude in ploddingly straight eighth notes rather than in swing eighths. The joke works. Because the theme is so drastically isolated from the contour and rhythm of the solos, or for that matter from the general contours and rhythms of this style (a blend of swing and bop), it is, paradoxically, full of character and as memorable as any jazz composition.

From this type, an isolated, nonstructural idea having little or no influence beyond its framing statements, jazz composition opens up into areas of greater substance. Some pieces retain the sandwich of theme-solo-theme but unify the segments, and some discard the sandwich. Among the former are Monk's *'Round Midnight*, Hancock's *Maiden Voyage*, and Charles Mingus's *Fables of Faubus*.

'Round Midnight and *Maiden Voyage* borrow one familiar thematic convention—a 32-bar *aaba* structure—but upon this skeleton Monk and Hancock have constructed not just a new melody but a new chord progression as well. At the risk of stating the obvious, this means that as the 32-bar choruses cycle again and again through a performance of *'Round Midnight*, Monk's chord progression (rather than a borrowed chord progression) governs the solos, leaving his compositional mark on the whole piece, whether or not a performer chooses to stick close to Monk's handsome melody. The same is true for Hancock's *Maiden Voyage* (the chord progression of which is given in chap. 3, ex. 29); in this case a rhythmic ostinato (chap. 2, ex. 10) stamps a further mark upon the whole.

Fables of Faubus, in the version that Mingus's Jazz Workshop recorded in 1959, takes this idea yet another step. In addition to a new melody and chord progression, Mingus has constructed lines of accompaniment and a new form (though that form uses an *aaba* pattern as a point of departure). Also, in this version of *Fables of Faubus*, Mingus's conception has spilled over into the rhythm section (in which Mingus himself is the bass player) in a more specific and detailed way than that of the rhythmic ostinato underlying Hancock's *Maiden Voyage*.

Normally, a jazz composition allows the rhythm section considerable freedom in the voicing of chords, the selection of bass notes (unless the piece is built on a rigid ostinato), and the placement of drum accents. A composition may supply rhythmic cues at points where the rhythm section supports some unified action in the rest of the ensemble. Otherwise, through familiarity with the tradition that lies behind a piece, members find their own way, either by ear or with the help of chord symbols. In this area, composition is left behind, and in its place stylistic convention takes over. But a number of rhythmically coordinated phrases in *Fables of*

Faubus reveal that Mingus has given out rather specific instructions. As a guide to the manner of controlling his performance, example 41a repeats the diagram that appeared in chapter 2; example 41b is a transcription of the theme.

Example 41a. The form of the theme of *Fables of Faubus*.

a (0:00)				*a′* (0:37)			*b* (1:14)				*a′* (1:45)		
19 bars				18			16				18		
c	*c*	*d*	Intro.	*c*	*c*	*d′*	*e*	*e*	*f*	*g*	*c*	*c*	*d′*
4 + 4 + 9 + 2				4 + 4 + 10			4 + 4 + 4 + 4				4 + 4 + 10		

Example 41b. The theme. Track 13, beginning.

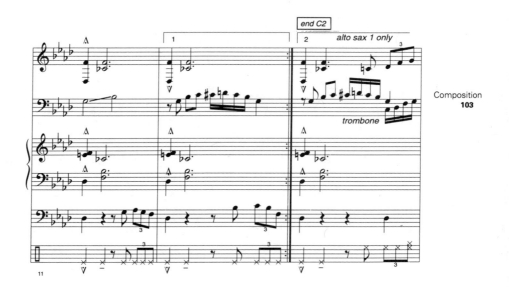

Composition
105

Composition
106

doubletime (swing 16ths)
alto sax 1 only

alto sax 2

Fables of Faubus, by Charles Mingus. Used by permission of The Charles Mingus Institute.

In subsection *c* (first heard in bars 9–12, following the 8-bar introduction) Mingus coordinates pianist Horace Parlan's chords with alto saxophonist John Handy's melody and trombonist Jimmy Knepper's accompanying line (track 13, 0:00). Meanwhile Mingus alternates between a two-beat rhythm and a descending triplet figure that lands on the down-beat. Within this rather tight compass, Mingus allows himself improvisa-tory discretion in the selection of pitches, the exact details of which change slightly through the introduction and through repetitions of subsection c. By tapping along with both the melody and the triplet figure, drummer Dannie Richmond adds another part coordinated rhythmically within the ensemble.

In segment d (first heard in bars 17–26) Richmond goes into a conven-tional swing rhythm, but bar by bar he interrupts or accentuates the pattern in a manner that directly coincides with Parlan's chords (track 13, 0:15). Parlan in turn supports the melody in the winds (trombone and three saxophones). Within this phrase there is also a different type of coordination, involving dynamics rather than rhythm: a piano chord and a drumbeat sound at the exact moment of the winds' sforzando accent (first heard in bar 22; track 13, 0:24). In exploiting dynamic contrasts in this manner, Mingus pursues a compositional path generally underexplored in jazz.

At the end of segment d' (bars 44–47) the two alto saxophone parts split into octaves, while the rest of the band repeatedly accents a block chord (track 13, 1:06). As another nice and unusual touch, Mingus ties this segment of the theme to the end of the bridge (bars 60–63), by having the rhythm section reiterate a block chord in exactly the same syncopated pattern (track 13, 1:37).

At the bridge (comprising subsections e, e, f, and g), Mingus loosens the reins, as is apparent from a comparison of bars 48–63 with that same section at the end of the piece.[1] Apart from the syncopated pattern in the rhythm section (bars 60–63), sharply defined elements of the bridge in-clude two alto saxophone parts: Shafi Hadi's melody (most of which tenor saxophonist Booker Ervin doubles when the bridge returns at the end) and Handy's moans (first heard in bars 50–55). More general agreements in-clude the flamencolike point of departure for Knepper's improvised coun-termelody; Parlan's chord progression; Mingus's leap from a rocking two-beat to a double-time walking line; Richmond's move from swing rhythm to double-time swing rhythm; and in the pyramid of sound that ends the bridge, Hadi's long-short swing eighths, pulsating out of phase with Handy's "backward" short-long swing eighths (bars 62–63). In all of this, Handy, Knepper, and the rhythm section exhibit some freedom in their choice and placement of notes, and Handy's double-time solo (bars 56–59) is improvised anew when it returns at the end.

For the solos that follow the theme, Mingus retains the unusual 71-bar form rather than regularizing it to 64 bars; in doing so he runs the risk of disrupting improvisation by forcing the musicians to concentrate on an odd structure in phrasing. Mingus the composer also keeps his hand in by rearranging the position of the double-time passage. During the theme it sounds in bars 9–12 of the 16-bar bridge (segment *f*). During the solos, segment *f* is in regular time, and the double time is shifted ahead and split into two parts, heard during bars 3–4 and 7–8 of the bridge (the second half of each statement of segment *e*). As interesting and unusual as this might be from the point of view of jazz composition, the scrambling of double-time phrases would probably have been somewhat distracting to an improviser. These factors might help explain why the solos on this version of *Fables of Faubus* are not especially brilliant.

All in all, this version of *Fables of Faubus* exemplifies a jazz performance in which the composed theme is vastly more interesting than the improvised solos. In listening, one should remember that for Mingus *Fables of Faubus* was, like all his pieces, a work in progress and that we are speaking of but one recording of it here. A comparison of versions made over the next two decades would quickly quash any search for a definitive version of this composition: over the years, his group, and his ideas about the piece, and the circumstances of recording continually changed. Nonetheless, such flexibility does not diminish the interest and importance of his specific, detailed sense of jazz composition in this particular performance of 1959.

A different approach spreads compositional detail throughout a piece, instead of concentrating it into thematic statements at the beginning and end, with improvisation sandwiched in between. This approach may entail nothing more than a sprinkling of such detail, with composition having no special place among the elements that explain the creation and inform the character of a performance. An example is Ornette Coleman's *Honeymooners* (track 3), in which the compositional decisions seem to be the textural contrasts among segments and interludes (as described in the section on ad hoc forms in chap. 3), as well as the electric bass guitar pattern at the opening and the heavy drum rhythm at the end (each weighted more toward dance music than toward originality). But the essence of *Honeymooners* is improvisation on these ideas, not the ideas themselves.

At the other extreme, composition may permeate an entire piece. A perfect example is Ellington's *Ko-Ko,* for which there exists a master take

(take 2), which has been issued many times; a full score of the master take, transcribed by Dave Berger and Alan Campbell for the National Jazz Ensemble in the mid-1970s and then revised by Berger after he examined the surviving parts in the archives of the Smithsonian Museum of American History; and an alternate take (take 1), which appeared in the 1980s in the *Jazz Tribune* series issued initially by the French branch of RCA (for full details, see appendix 2). A reading of the full score against the recordings of both takes reveals how much of the piece remains intact from one take to the next. Because a recording of take 1 may prove difficult to locate, listeners may have to accept on faith the following description of the elements that differ between the two takes.[2]

As mentioned in the discussion of big-band orchestration and again in the description of *Fables of Faubus*, writing note-by-note parts for the rhythm section is not standard practice. This approach, however, does not necessarily mean that musical detail will change radically from one version of a piece to the next. Indeed, in *Ko-Ko*, Sonny Greer's drumming changes scarcely at all. The most noticeable difference between the two takes—and it is a tiny refinement indeed—is his addition of offbeat accents before beat 4 of bars 10, 12, 14, and 16 of take 2.

Ellington the composer writes his piano out of the introduction, first chorus, and ending. During the intervening choruses, he plays nothing more than single offbeat chords between composed riffs, with two exceptions. After the trombone solo of Tricky Sam Nanton, when the du-wah brass riff—consisting of notes alternately muted (the "du") and unmuted (the "wah")—compresses from six notes down to two, Ellington fills the empty space between riffs with improvised variations on fast, sweeping whole-tone scales; and on both takes he ends this chorus in a similar (but not identical) manner, with leaping, syncopated chordal punctuations.

Jimmy Blanton, on string bass, carries the principal responsibility for marking the beat, which scarcely allows him room for improvisation. His selection of pitches varies somewhat from one take to the next, but this too is controlled by the simplicity of the underlying progression (in this case, a three-chord blues progression) and the contribution of the bass to the tone colors of the piece: there are only a limited number of ways that Blanton might have improvised a walking bass line without disturbing harmony or straying into an unacceptably high range (thus undermining his timbral role). These limitations—or to put in another light, these compositional decisions—extend to his three solo breaks, in which he remains wedded to walking patterns on the fundamental harmonies (ex. 42).

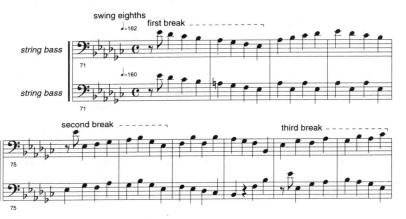

Example 42. String bassist Jimmy Blanton's solo breaks on take 1 (upper staff) and take 2 (lower staff, from the score prepared by Dave Berger) of Ellington's *Ko-Ko*. Track 6, 1:48.

Among the brass and reeds, only Nanton is allowed some improvisatory discretion, during a solo that fills the second and third blues choruses of each take. Evidently Ellington's composition restricted the limits of Nanton's solos, which are aligned in example 43. Using his ya-ya technique (which involves opening and closing the plunger mute in quick succession), as well as a tightly muted sound in several bars, Nanton plays mainly two pitches (B♭ and A♭), plus a gesture that trails off at the end of phrases. The phrases separate into 2-bar segments designed to coincide with the sound and silence of the other brass and to alternate with the moving line in the riff played by the saxophone section. Improvisation enters into the solo only in Nanton's choice of B♭ or A♭; in his microscopic placement of notes in relation to the beat; and in the occasional, slight reordering of ideas (compare bar 37 of each take), though even here he draws from previously stated material. In no way does his improvised variation involve the invention of new material from one take to the next.

Composition
112

Example 43. Tricky Sam Nanton's solo on take 1 (upper staff) and take 2 (lower staff, from the score prepared by Dave Berger) of Ellington's *Ko-Ko*. Track 6, 0:32.

Ko-Ko
Duke Ellington.

What do these nuances in detail reveal about the interaction of improvisation and composition in *Ko-Ko*? To answer that question, one might call up another moment in jazz. Near the end of 1957 Billie Holiday appeared with the pianist Mal Waldron and a group of jazz all-stars on the television show *The Sound of Jazz*. Now widely available on film and video (see appendix 2), the show contains a wondrous demonstration of improvisation, when Lester Young outshines all his distinguished colleagues by beginning his solo with a little blues phrase of unbelievable beauty and depth. His message: wonderful improvisation need not require more than a note or two.

Is this what happens in Ellington's *Ko-Ko*? Are the members of the rhythm section offering improvisations of great substance, however slight the detail might be? Is Nanton doing the same? I think not. To be sure, some improvisatory freedom may be heard in *Ko-Ko*, but none of it sounds terribly important. Instead, a two-stage process seems to be taking place, which is quite normal in jazz: each performer takes up his task with a framework in mind and then improvises within that framework.[3] In *Ko-Ko*, the improvisatory process seems uncomplicated, because the framework, being highly detailed, overwhelms opportunities for significant variation.

In short, *Ko-Ko* is extensively composed and minimally improvised. In this brilliantly paced, moody, churning tone painting, Ellington melds the aesthetic poles of jazz in a manner that summarizes what is arguably the best of this music. At one extreme he imbues the piece with earthiness, in the form of a relaxed swing, an explicit pulse laid out in the bass line, tuneful riffs, a three-chord blues form, growling and vocalized timbres, and an overall structure that moves straight from a soft, low-pitched introduction to a loud, high-pitched climax; at the other, he deals in high art, through the creation of an entirely original set of composed blues variations, unlike any heard before in music; a sliding chromaticism and his whole-tone runs on the piano, superimposed upon the seemingly simple chordal underpinning; and most important, wondrous instrumental combinations and voicings that could be only guessed at before the original parts were donated to the Smithsonian Institution. This is obviously musical composition in the classic sense of the term. As such, *Ko-Ko* stands in contrast not only to *Honeymooners*, with its sprinkling of compositional detail, but also to Hancock's *Maiden Voyage*: Hancock opts for democracy, in endeavoring to draw a perfect balance between compositional shape and improvisatory freedom; Ellington is the dictator, impressing a detailed musical vision upon an entire ensemble.

The Status of Composers

In a privately taped interview from the 1950s the trumpeter Roy Eldridge and Ray Spencer reminisce about recordings of the song *Squeeze Me*. Spencer asks if Eldridge is referring to Fats Waller's composition of that name or to some other song called *Squeeze Me*, and Eldridge replies, "This is one thing you got me tied up on. I don't know who wrote what." Why would Eldridge, a talented and knowledgeable jazzman, make such a comment?

The creative processes of jazz focus on performance. Interpretation is the essence of the music, and although a player such as Eldridge would have had to be intimately familiar with thousands of titles, many of them cherished favorites and all of them a part of his daily work, he would have been less obliged to pay close attention to the names associated with those titles. Scott Joplin, George Gershwin, Cole Porter, Jerome Kern, these men supplied the fodder for jazz musicians, even though they were not a part of jazz performance themselves. As an example of the remoteness of a composer from the jazz process, the violinist Eddie South recorded his *Improvisation sur le premier mouvement du concerto en ré mineur de Jean-Sébastien Bach* in Paris in 1937, two centuries after the piece was composed. As another example of such remoteness, in 1957 Thelonious Monk—in his characteristically eccentric and wry manner—arranged the hymn *Abide with Me* as a playful tribute to its nineteenth-century English composer, his namesake William Henry Monk. The arrangement, a little under a minute long, was for a quartet of trumpet, alto sax, and two tenor saxes (played by Coleman Hawkins and John Coltrane). William Henry might have found the results somewhat pleasing.

Whatever large portion of jazz is given over to borrowed themes, the music nonetheless reflects a substantial contribution from within. Even among jazzmen, however, recognition often tips toward performers and away from composers, and for the same reason—benign neglect. The identification of a jazz composer might be available but go unnoticed because listeners have directed their attention elsewhere (as Eldridge did with *Squeeze Me*).

Historical, musical, and financial considerations as well have traditionally undercut the status of jazz composers. Each of these issues is bound up with the problem of identification. Sometimes the circumstances of creation can be entirely casual. In an innocent way, no one pays attention, because at the moment it does not seem to matter. Did Charlie Parker compose *Ornithology*, a modestly popular bop melody set to the chord progression of *How High the Moon*, or was it written by Little Benny Harris, a trumpeter? During the late 1930s, who contributed which details to the renowned head arrangements of the Count Basie orchestra? Over the decades, who brought which ideas into Duke Ellington's big band, and regardless of the contributor or the idea, to what extent did Ellington's personal genius shape the results? In untold situations such as these, either the composer cannot be identified or—more radically—there is no composer, in spite of the existence of a distinct composition.

Another explanation, not the least bit innocent, involves money. The tie between composing and royalties (which existed before jazz began to be spread by means of recordings) accounts for the widespread practice of false attributions. A stake in a hit recording can earn a tidy sum, even in the modest world of jazz finance. There is considerable motivation for managers, hangers-on, and the musicians themselves to take credit for creating something that is not their own.

For the musicians themselves, it works both ways: some give up material, others appropriate it. Those who give it up might trade the copyright for a fee or for some type of service rendered. Probably the best-known instance of this involves Fats Waller, who is reputed to have sold songs for hamburgers (perhaps a legend, perhaps true); in any event, he certainly lost a fortune by selling great songs for very little. Alternatively, a creator might give up a percentage of prospective earnings, with the result that two or three names appear in the credits, when there ought to be only one. This practice was so commonplace that it became known, cynically, as the "cut-in." Conveniently, the quintessential jazz composition *'Round Midnight* is a perfect example of the cut-in. According to oral tradition, the piece belongs to Thelonious Monk. Legally, from the time of its first recording and in its separate existence as sheet music, the tune belongs to Monk, Cootie Williams, and Bernie Hanighen. Williams evidently was taking a cut-in as the bandleader at the recording session in 1944. Hanighen has a much more legitimate claim to the piece, in that he wrote the lyrics most frequently associated with Monk's melody. In this capacity he acquired a share of the profits dating all the way back to that first recorded version, by Williams's big band. It might be noted, though, that Hanighen received his cut even though this particular version has no lyrics. Most subsequent versions leave the lyrics out as well.

Those musicians who appropriate material, instead of giving it away (or having it taken forcibly), simply put their own names on borrowed ideas and hope that no one challenges the claim, even if the truth were recognized. Such a practice might seem outrageous at first, and sometimes it is. But sometimes such behavior is just a fact of the jazz life. Musicians do whatever they must to survive in this rough world. And sometimes the practice of appropriation seems entirely justified, for a rather higher-minded reason that offers further explanation why composers often have a diminished status in jazz. An innovative jazz performance can effect such a radical transformation of an existing theme—new melody, rhythm, instrumentation, and timbre, together with a reharmonization of a borrowed progression—that it seems fair to call the result new. But even under such circumstances, copyright law assigns the monetary reward for creation to a composer, however small that composer's contribution to the finished performance may be. The law, for all its stages of evolution, has a long way to go before it will be able to deal intelligently with the problems specific to jazz, which is first and foremost a performer's music, not a composer's. Hence the act of appropriation, substituting illegal justice for outmoded law. Might jazz musicians be forgiven for blatantly staking a claim to a little bit of music that is not their own, in order to earn something for the large amount of music that is truly theirs? To whom are we attributing what?

For all these disclaimers, jazz has its known composers, some of whom are great. Charles Mingus was one such musician, and in an extreme way he put a stamp on the fact by taking firm control of most productions of his music. A handful of his compositions circulates in fake books but only one, *Goodbye Pork-Pie Hat*, has had a substantial life outside of Mingus's Jazz Workshop, his memorial band Mingus Dynasty (populated mainly by former sidemen from the Workshop), and occasional performances by those sidemen in other contexts. More than any of the great jazz composers, Mingus represents one whose creations are inextricably bound up with his own playing and directing.

Unlike Mingus, Thelonious Monk composed in a more expansive and conventional way. He played his own pieces, but so did many others. He eventually became so strongly associated with his compositions that Monk the composer became separate from Monk the performer. If this sort of widespread knowledge of a composer's work were typical, rather than rare, the subject of jazz composition would be less frustrating, for listener and musician alike.

6 IMPROVISATION

Mingus listens for a long time to Dr. Leary's anarchic approach to spontaneous art, Mingus's art, improvisation. "You can't improvise on nothin', man," Mingus says at last. "You gotta improvise on somethin'."
—Janet Coleman and Al Young, *Mingus/Mingus*

Improvisation—the spontaneous creation of music—is the element of jazz that many listeners find most fascinating and mysterious. How do musicians organize their collaborations during an improvisation? What methods do individual improvisers use? Taking as its inspiration Charles Mingus's instruction in his succinct put-down of thoughtless, unprepared improvisation—"You gotta improvise on somethin'"—this last of three chapters on procedures provides insights into that "somethin'" from the points of view of group organization and individual method.

One way to understand improvisation in jazz is to explore the relative prominence of members of an ensemble: several members may engage in collective improvisation, or one member may deliver a solo. Both processes are at work in John Coltrane's *Ascension*, which for almost its full forty minutes presents (with one exception) a strict alternation of collective and solo improvisation, as follows: the whole group; Coltrane, on tenor saxophone, with the rhythm section; the whole group; Dewey Jackson, on trumpet, with the rhythm section; the whole again; Pharoah Sanders, on tenor saxophone, with rhythm; the whole; and so on, until finally the pattern breaks as the piano solo of McCoy Tyner blends directly into an improvised duo for string bass. *Ascension* ends as it begins, with the whole group engaged in improvisation.

This differentiation of instrumental roles seems clear-cut at first glance, but on closer examination it proves to be somewhat murky. Because solo and collective improvisation often blend, it is important to spell out circumstances where one might be confused for the other.

Solo improvisation is such a standard event in jazz that it requires no special comment, except to say that a focus on soloing does not preclude improvising among the accompanists. It may well be the nature of an improvisation—the freedom of invention, the virtuosity, and the ornamental elaboration allowed a soloist—and not the fact of improvising that distinguishes that soloist from the accompanists. This is certainly the case in *Ascension*; the discussion of rhythmic interplay during Coltrane's solo revealed the extent to which Coltrane's three accompanists are improvising (see chap. 2). It is also the case during Parker's solo on *Koko*, in which the bass and piano parts exemplify this very point (chap. 3, ex. 24).

The term *collective improvisation*, which one might expect to apply to the extemporaneous interplay among soloists and accompanists described above, is instead reserved mainly for two stylistic contexts: improvisation among wind instruments playing in the New Orleans style and its various derivatives, as in the first and last choruses of the New Orleans Rhythm Kings' dixieland classic *Tin Roof Blues*; and improvisation among any or all members of an ensemble playing in a free-jazz style, as in Coltrane's *Ascension*, Sun Ra's *Outer Nothingness*, and Coleman's *Honeymooners*.

Collective improvisation may also be used to describe what might more properly be called "duo improvisation," namely a pair of soloists engaging in an improvised musical dialogue. This practice is characteristic of some performances in the substyles of bop known as cool jazz and West Coast jazz. Among well-known jazz groups, the principal exponents are Gerry Mulligan and Chet Baker, in Mulligan's quartet; Dave Brubeck and Paul Desmond, in Brubeck's quartet; and John Lewis and Milt Jackson, in the Modern Jazz Quartet.[1]

New Orleans collective improvisation involves a combination of wind players known as the *front line*, stereotypically comprising trumpet (or cornet), clarinet, and trombone. Most often the trumpeter (or cornetist) presents the melody. A clarinetist weaves an improvised line, characteristically more ornate and higher pitched than that melody. Meanwhile a trombonist contributes a characteristically simpler and lower counterline, one that dances between two functions, spelling out harmony and making counterpoint; a good deal of splatted glissandos (that is, harsh-toned slides from note to note, known as "tailgate" trombone playing) often go along with this type of improvising.

Listeners should be forewarned that in some quarters the classic formation of trumpet (or cornet), clarinet, and trombone developed into an unyielding cliché. Historical styles admitted saxophonists into the front line with some regularity; if the saxophonist were Sidney Bechet, he might grab the melody away from the high brass, thus altering the presumed roles of the instruments. Early on in the history of this music, the front line often included a violinist, who carried the melody around which the collective improvisation swirled.

Tin Roof Blues, a widely admired early model that inspired much imitation, exemplifies the classic formation. The piece survives in three versions, all recorded on March 13, 1923: an unlabeled take (hereafter called "take 0"), as well as take A and take B. All three were widely available on LP, the most accessible issue being a double LP on the Milestone label. That Milestone collection has been reissued on compact disc, but unfortunately, because of current limitations in the playing time of a CD, only take B has been used. Consequently, listeners may have to search to find the variant versions transcribed below in examples 44 and 45. (For discographical details, see appendix 2.)

The first 12-bar blues chorus of *Tin Roof Blues*, following the piano introduction, appears in example 44. Here, the three versions have been compressed into a 7-staff score. In the middle is cornetist Paul Mares's part, given only once, because he plays a composed melody in the same fashion on all three versions, except for a slightly different turn of phrase in the last 9 beats of take A. Surrounding Mares's line are the improvisations of clarinetist Leon Roppolo and trombonist George Brunies from take B (staffs 3 and 5, respectively). Above and below these are their clarinet and trombone improvisations from take A (Roppolo on the second staff, Brunies on the sixth) and take 0 (Roppolo on the top staff, Brunies at the bottom). This format should facilitate a comparison of a complete collective improvisation (the three lines from take B at the center of the example) with its improvised variants.

The final chorus of each of these three recordings (exx. 45a-c) could not be compressed into a single system, because at the end of the piece Mares joins in on the collective improvising by varying his melody line from take to take instead of repeating it literally. Thus within these examples of collective improvisation, the thematic component shifts from composition toward improvisation.

Example 44. The opening chorus of *Tin Roof Blues*, from three takes recorded by the New Orleans Rhythm Kings in 1923. Track 16, 0:08.

Improvisation
122

Example 45a. The last chorus of take 0 of *Tin Roof Blues*.

Improvisation
124

Example 45b. Take A of *Tin Roof Blues.*

Example 45c. Take B of *Tin Roof Blues*. Track 16, 2:24.

Improvisation
126

Tin Roof Blues

Lyric by Walter Melrose.

Music by New Orleans Rhythm Kings.

Copyright © 1923 (renewed) Edwin H. Morris and Company, a division of MPL
Communications, Inc.

A comparison of these six separate blues choruses confirms that Roppolo and Brunies are truly improvising. For convenient identification, the smaller sections discussed here are bracketed and labeled (*a* through *i*) in examples 44 and 45.

On all three takes Roppolo has a set way of getting into the opening

chorus, by sounding a note that slides up into the third degree (D) of the tonic scale (B♭)—this sliding effect is called a blue note. And on each take he gets out of that note in a similar but not identical way (segment *a*). On take 0 and take A, he also sounds a blue note to get into the subdominant (E♭), by sliding up to the third degree (G) of that chord (segment *b*), but this idea does not recur in take B.

At the same metric position in four of these choruses, Roppolo repeats an eighth-note figure in which two chromatic neighbors (involving the notes A-G♯-A and F-E♮-F) interrupt a descent (segment *c*). Alternatively in the opening chorus of take B and the ending of take 0, at this ninth bar of the blues progression (bars 13 and 73 of the piece), he repeats a different, higher-pitched figure (segment *d*). On this tune at least, something about this particular measure of the blues brought forth from Roppolo less imagination than he shows elsewhere.

All six choruses end on the same note (D). It is preceded by variations on a chromatic motion up from and back down to that pitch in the ending choruses and in the opening of take B (segment *e*), with that motion having been implied at the start of the master take (segment *e′*).

Roppolo also ties together his line in the last chorus at the end of take 0, by repeating an eighth-note triplet figure (F-G-F) in bars 67, 71, 74, and 76 (segment *f*). The idea returns once in take A, but then he abandons it.

Otherwise, Roppolo's choruses are not obviously dependent upon one another. Sometimes the marvel is that he is able to remain inventive within the tight restrictions of the early dixieland style. This is especially true at the subdominant (E♭) measures of the blues (bars 9–10 and 69–70 of the piece), where he manages to rearrange his line every time, while playing nothing but the notes of an E♭ triad. Sometimes the marvel is the sophistication of his invention, most evident in an elaborately ornamental series of blue notes as his clarinet line swoops downward in bar 8 of take B.

The trombonist is somewhat less active than the clarinetist, with Brunies sticking more closely to basic materials. This is especially true in the opening chorus of take A, in which the trombone part comprises nothing but chordal arpeggiation, except for a single chromatic passing tone (G♭) at the end. In spite of this seeming simplicity, Brunies improvises continuously. The only evidence of his having a set plan for getting through some part of the chorus is his use of a B♭ chordal arpeggiation ascending up a tenth (to D) and then settling down a whole step (to C; segments g in 5 choruses and a fragment, segment g', at the end of take A), and his use of a couple of flexible formulas for finishing off the first chorus (segment h) and for ending the piece (segment i). Even this material is varied on each appearance.

The other principal forum for collective improvisation is the free-jazz style, which emerged a half century after the birth of New Orleans jazz. This return to collective interplay, after a protracted emphasis on soloists, was a landmark in the history of jazz.

The collectively improvised sections of *Ascension* are completely egalitarian. No one monopolizes the spotlight. Instead, each man subordinates his personal identity to the creation of pulsating masses of sound, as the band works together into a froth of impassioned, screaming emotion. Some of these passages can be heard in relation to small and distinct collections of pitches (the pentatonic scale F♯ A B C♯ E, for example), but clusters and chromaticism operate to an extent that overwhelms any sustained sense of modality or tonality. The jazz writer Ekkehard Jost has aptly named these collectively improvised passages "sound fields."[2]

It seems useful to say something about the character of *Ascension*, for if its methodology is straightforward—egalitarian collective improvisations alternating with improvised solos and accompaniments—the resulting sound is certainly not. For many listeners this sort of playing represents the most inaccessible stylistic area of jazz.

Colleagues organizing a freshman music seminar once asked me to suggest a jazz recording that might be played with other types of radical music as a point of departure for asking the questions: What is noise, and what is music? I suggested *Ascension*. Not having listened to the piece for about four years, I cued it up on the record player and found it to be perfectly coherent, emotionally powerful, and in its own way beautiful. In those four years I had gained such a better understanding of jazz that *Ascension* now seemed to be a poor choice for the seminar, because it was obviously music and hence did not raise significant questions about boundaries between music and noise. That same day, my colleagues came to say that they had decided not to use *Ascension*, because it was clearly noise, not music! "It sounds like a band warming up before a performance."

There is a lesson in this story: people hear noise before they hear music. Just as those who dismiss hard rock as noise may hear first and above all timbral distortions coming out of amplifiers and the arrhythmic mixing of percussive timbres, and those of us who love hard rock hear these elements of noise in a musical context and indeed find the distorted timbral mixes to be an essential and even beautiful component of that music, so those who dismiss aggressive, collectively improvised free jazz as noise probably hear timbral distortion, arrhythmic combinations, and untuned pitch, while those of us who love this style have come to understand how these so-called noise elements fit into a musical context.

How can one learn to appreciate *Ascension* and perhaps even discover its beauty? One key is to listen more than once and to listen to the entire forty-minute piece. Although a four-minute excerpt serves well enough to demonstrate several facets of jazz discussed here, it does not reveal the overall structure and coherence of *Ascension*, which depend upon, and reveal themselves through, the cumulative effect of an alternation of ensemble and solo passages. The second key—which might take months or years, not just several forty-minute listening sessions—is to hear *Ascension* in its context by listening to many of Coltrane's recordings from the 1960s and to recordings by his contemporaries in this style. Because the present book is not the place for a stylistic survey of free jazz, suffice it to say—without supporting argument—that in this case familiarity with the musical context ought to bring about a recognition of the musicality of *Ascension*.[3] Listeners who are initially put off by the piece might even come so far as to find it rather tame by comparison with some of Coltrane's last work (for example, his duets with the drummer Rashied Ali) or with the hectic and even more radically aggressive approaches to free jazz subsequently popular in Europe (for example, saxophonist Peter Brötzmann's album *Machine Gun*, recorded in 1968, a year after Coltrane's death).

The employment of collective improvisation in free jazz by no means dictates that everyone ought to be playing continuously, as in the portions of *Ascension* featuring the full ensemble. Indeed *Outer Nothingness* presents an altogether different sort of collective improvising, in which solos, duos, and various small combinations emerge from within Sun Ra's Arkestra and the traditional distinctions between melodic and accompanying instruments are called into question, with contributions coming equally from all quarters. Again Jost provides a key idea: he suggests that the title serves as a programmatic instruction to the improvisers: "The 'emptiness' of space is translated into a musical context by coupling two expressive ideas: a strong emphasis on the low instrumental register, and tonal and rhythmic indeterminacy" (188). There are static moments (Sun Ra's rumblings on bass marimba) and moments of clear direction (John Gilmore's deliberate heightening of range and intensity during his tenor saxophone solo; see ex. 50). There are also large-scale alternations of relaxation and tension (for details, see chap. 7, ex. 57). The result is a piece in which the sequence and duration of musical events seem original, unpredictable, and in their own strange way memorable.

Sun Ra did not record another version of *Outer Nothingness* (to which comparisons might be made), and neither he nor his sidemen were inclined to offer an analytical account of their creative processes. As far as anyone knows, *Outer Nothingness*, in all its fine detail, was improvised, sensitively, flexibly, and collectively, on the spot.

Once having been established within the domain of the free-jazz style, techniques of free collective improvisation could be transferred into any other style. As if to test the possibilities, the trio Air, composed of reed, bass, and drum, recorded an album of ragtime and early jazz compositions in 1979;[4] and the Art Ensemble of Chicago, operating under the banner of "Great Black Music—Ancient to Modern," has made a career of interpreting everything from ragtime to reggae. In these groups, however, stylistic borrowings are clearly subordinate to the aesthetics of free jazz. A different and more balanced approach is heard in Ornette Coleman's group Prime Time, devoted to the marriage of free collective improvisation and contemporary African-American dance music; *Honeymooners* (track 3) is representative.

Another way to understand improvisation in jazz is to explore methods for creating individual lines. Although no two jazz improvisations evolve in exactly the same way, three basic methods are common or even standard. Paraphrase improvisation is the recognizable ornamentation of an existing theme. Formulaic improvisation is the building of new material from a diverse body of fragmentary ideas (either in response to a theme or independently). And motivic improvisation is the building of new material through the recognizable development of no more than a few fragmentary ideas.

This is not to say that a soloist deliberates about the method to be used as the moment arrives. A professional jazz musician's improvisatory methods develop over years of practice and experience on stage, eventually becoming second nature, a matter of reflex. Occasionally one hears a player working out an idea, but often the whole process is unconscious. Cannonball Adderley put it this way: "To tell you the truth, I never really thought about what you think about when you're playing. I imagine if I really went into it, I notice sometimes—like you say you've heard me play different ways sometimes—I have the ability to put my mind completely out of what I'm doing. I can play a solo and play 20 choruses and not even think of the fact that I'm playing. Then I realize, Wow, I played a long time, and I stop, because my mind is on some woman uptown."[5]

Why should these methods matter to a listener? Because regardless of whether an improviser is conscious of, or even cares about, method, there are frequently characteristic links between a method of jazz improvisation and the resulting sound. In considering the broad categories discussed here, listeners might ask these questions of a particular performance: How much material does the improviser borrow from existing music? How much is newly invented? How much of this material changes from moment to moment? How much of it recurs with variations?

Paraphrase Improvisation

The label "paraphrase improvisation" was coined by writer André Hodeir in the 1950s.[6] Paraphrase—the recognizable ornamentation of an existing theme—is a crucial procedure in jazz and quite likely one of the techniques that gave birth to the music at the beginning of the twentieth century (when someone presumably took a march or rag and "jazzed it up"). One hears paraphrasing in just about any piece based on a tuneful theme, because after all, only the rare and dull jazz musician can stand to play a tune entirely straight, without fiddling with some detail. This restless, creative urge to keep altering things (however slight such alterations may be) has a great deal to do with what jazz is all about.

The paraphrasing of a melody may be no more complex than the introduction of a few ornamental flourishes into an otherwise faithful repetition of the original tune. But at its most inventive it may involve a highly imaginative reworking of that melody. In discussions of other topics, examples of paraphrase improvisation have already appeared: to illustrate microscopic rhythmic nuances, Miles Davis's paraphrase of *'Round Midnight* (chap. 2, ex. 11); to illustrate the melodic delineation of form, Earl Hines's paraphrase of *Sweet Sue—Just You* (chap. 3, ex. 21); and to illustrate how a multipart form might be made into a chorus form, Kid Thomas Valentine's paraphrase of the melody of *Panama* (chap. 3, ex. 28). What remains to be analyzed is a special example for drums, in which a procedure normally associated with conventional melodic ornamentation is translated into the domain of drum and cymbal pitches and timbres.

This special type of paraphrase fills roughly the first half of Max Roach's drum solo on Sonny Rollins's *St. Thomas*, recorded in 1956. In example 46 the first three of Roach's unaccompanied 16-bar choruses are aligned beneath the opening melody.[7] What is striking about Roach's solo is the extent to which he kept the tune in mind instead of launching into some sort of technical display disassociated from the rest of the piece.[8] Remarkably, Roach invented a way to paraphrase the tune, even though the drum kit he was playing did not have the capacity to convey the melodic contour of *St. Thomas*. He accomplished the task by translating standard melodic and harmonic qualities into segments differentiated by the tuning and timbre of various components of his drum kit as well as by rhythmic figures. Through these devices he retained a strong enough connection to the phrasing of *St. Thomas* that a sense of paraphrase comes shining through.

Example 46. The melody of Rollins's *St. Thomas* (upper staff) and the first three of drummer Max Roach's five solo choruses (lower staffs). Track 18, 0:17 and 2:28, respectively.

Improvisation
134

begin swing eighths

snare mechanism on

This relationship between existing tune and improvised drum solo is far simpler to understand in sound than in words. The most straightforward explanation to be offered is this: hum the melody while you play the recorded drum solo, and listen to how the two coincide, phrase by phrase. Some listeners may find the relationship self-evident on first hearing; others may benefit from the following detailed description of that coincidence.

Roach begins by marking time with the calypso rhythm that began the piece. A fanfare on a tom-tom drum (the one pitched roughly to A♭) announces the start of the creative portion of his solo (bars 7–8). The oblique paraphrase begins at bar 9. By analogy with the melody, which in bars 9–12 consists of three notes up and a pause, then three down and a pause, Roach plays three syncopated accents, each preceded by a grace note, in bars 9 and 11, while following this figure with an alternately low (pitched to C) and high (on A♭) pattern on the tom-tom, in bars 10 and 12. The melody in bar 13 echoes that of bars 9 and 11 but continues in a different manner, bringing the tune to a close; similarly Roach in bars 13–14 continues the syncopated accents and starts his pattern on the low tom-tom but continues in a different manner, bringing his first chorus to a close. He plays a single offbeat accent (once again with a grace note attached) and then returns to the opening calypso pattern.

In the first half of his second solo chorus, Roach transfers the span of the melody, its areas of activity and silence, into an alternation of a rapid explosion of accents (bars 1–3 and 5–7) and fragments of the calypso beat (bars 4 and 8). When at bar 9 the melody changes in character, Roach changes along with it by initiating a series of new rhythmic figures. He keeps to the syncopated pattern of accents heard in his first solo chorus, but this time through he matches the repeated melodic pattern of three notes and a rest to his own repeated figure, emphasizing a burst of sixteenth notes, with accents falling on the fifth in each group of 6 sixteenth notes. To end this chorus, he relaxes into 2 bars of the now-familiar calypso pattern and then plays another fanfare (bars 15–16), which has nothing to do with paraphrase: at this juncture between choruses, he converts the rhythmic feeling from duple subdivisions of the beat to swing (as discussed in chap. 2). To underscore the moment of change, he turns on the snare drum mechanism, thereby supplementing the thud of tom-tom drums with the characteristic crackle of a snare.

Up to this point, Roach has anchored his playing with a steady, rocking alternation of his feet, the right playing a two-beat on the bass drum pedal, the left a backbeat on the hi-hat cymbal pedal. For the first half of his third chorus he breaks into a freer, four-limbed dance, with a nearly continuous line of eighth-note accents scattered unpredictably throughout the drums and hi-hat (bars 1–8). Then, at the upbeat to bar 9, he turns to an as-yet-unheard component of his drum kit, the ride cymbal, to deliver an overt rhythmic paraphrase of the melody, which he transfers into a series of simultaneous cymbal crashes and bass drum thumps.

Over the next chorus and a half, Roach leaves aside the sense of paraphrase (which is why this passage is not transcribed in ex. 46). But to end his fifth and last chorus, he once again overtly refers to the melody by playing the same series of simultaneous crashes and thumps. Prepared by this signal, Rollins jumps back into his own improvisation on tenor saxophone without skipping a beat, after having been interrupted by Roach's magnificent 80-bar solo. It is true that any good drummer should always be aware of structure (regardless of whether structure influences the making of a drum solo) and that any other good jazz musician should always be aware of what the drummer is doing (including making changes in rhythmic feeling, as in this example). From this perspective, Rollins's clean and swinging reentry is of no special importance, given Roach's rigorous adherence to the 16-bar pattern, his rather substantial paraphrase of details of that pattern, and his formidable sense of swing. But on *St. Thomas* Roach's preparation to close is so elegant and Rollins's reentrance so immediate and propulsive that together they produce another of those magical moments in jazz that impress the listener time after time.

When the paraphrase of an existing theme is not at work, jazz musicians build new lines from fragments, which are usually distinguished by rhythmic and intervallic shape. Far less often they may exploit some aspect of timbre (for example, singer Eddie "Cleanhead" Vinson's characteristic rising, broken squeak or Stanley Turrentine's hollow whoop at the top of the normal range of his tenor saxophone). Seldom could the fragments be described as melodic in a tuneful sense, although they provide the material on which most performers improvise new melodies. In analysis and description, the fragments may be called, variously and often interchangeably, "ideas," "figures," "gestures," "formulas," "motives," and so forth. In jazz parlance they are often referred to as "licks" and in New Orleans jazz specifically as "hot licks."

In the process of improvisation, the substantial differences lie not in the structure or character of the fragments as they stand alone but rather in the ways they are combined and manipulated. What matters is the environment in which a fragment operates. In the same way, the label applied to an isolated fragment is of little consequence. What matters is the context. Here below, for the sake of clarity, the word *formula* is used in the discussion of formulaic improvisation, and *motive* in the discussion of motivic improvisation. The need to maintain such a rigid literary separation should diminish once a listener learns how to distinguish the sounds of one process from the other.

Formulaic Improvisation

The principal manifestation of the fragmentary idea in jazz is in formulaic improvisation, the most common kind of improvisation in jazz, spanning all styles. In formulaic improvisation many diverse formulas intertwine and combine within continuous lines. Milman Parry and Albert Lord developed this concept after Parry recognized in the late 1920s that recurring phrases in the *Iliad* and *Odyssey* might be evidence of oral composition. The two men studied a living poetry, Yugoslavian epics, and applied their findings to the Homeric poems. By extension, Leo Treitler adapted the concept to early Western ecclesiastical chant as a means of explaining how an elaborate, sophisticated music might flourish through time and place in the form of oral tradition, independent of music notation.[9] By further extension, the idea seems appropriate to a good deal of improvised jazz. Particular musicians and groups often create a repertory of formulas (their licks), which they use again and again in their music.

The essence of this type of improvisation is the artful weaving of formulas, through variation, into ever-changing, continuous lines. Like paraphrase improvisation, formulaic improvisation may be based on a theme, the rhythmic and harmonic structure of which remains inviolate in terms of meter, phrase lengths, tonal relationships, and principal harmonic goals. A theme, however, is treated with greater freedom than in paraphrase improvisation. Its melody need not remain recognizable. Instead, against repetitions of an existing structure, a new melody emerges.

The greatest formulaic improviser in jazz was Charlie Parker. Those who have closely studied the hundreds of recordings Parker made testify that he seems never to have repeated a solo. This is a staggering thought, given the consistent quality of his work. How did he do it? Without offering the key to his genius (there are, after all, both great and lousy formulaic improvisers), the concept of formulaic improvisation illuminates a technique for responding instantaneously to the intense requirements of his preferred style, bop. Influenced far more by the generalities of key and tempo and by the specifics of moment-by-moment harmonic progression than by the particular tune that he happened to be playing, Parker brought to any musical situation a well-rehearsed body of formulas, which he then embedded into his lines in a fluid and frighteningly effortless manner.

The two solo choruses on *Koko* constitute probably the greatest improvisation of Parker's studio recordings. Many of the formulas used in the piece are presented in example 47. Lettered brackets below the staff indicate the surprising amount of formulaic material that recurs within the solo; given the great speed of Parker's improvised melody and the artful way that he reuses material, the repetitions are hardly noticeable. (The letters, alphabetical in order of appearance, have no special significance beyond this example.) Lettered and numbered brackets above the staff indicate the formulas that Thomas Owens has identified as belonging to Parker's central repertory of about one hundred fragments, which Parker worked and reworked with astonishing facility, inventiveness, and musicality throughout his career.[10]

Example 47. Recurring formulas in Charlie Parker's solo choruses on *Koko* (transcribed by John Mehegan). Track 17, 0:25.

Improvisation
140

It is one thing to recognize that formulaic improvisation is the normal means of operating for jazz musicians and quite another to identify an entire repertory of formulas, as Owens has done. Ordinarily such catalogs do not exist for a given performer, and perhaps should not, because no one wants formulas to get in the way of enjoying music. Establishing the link between formulas and personal musical identity (that is, learning a musician's favorite or most original licks) may be important, but at the same time formulaic fragments should not stick out gracelessly above a sense of continuous line. When constituent parts become more prominent than the whole, the term *formula* takes on another meaning, involving predictable, thoughtless, clichéd, fragmentary playing rather than the artful and subtle interweaving of fragments.

Motivic Improvisation

In motivic improvisation one or more motives (but never more than a few) form the basis for a section of a piece. The performer varies—in musical parlance, develops—a motive through such processes as ornamentation (adding notes within and around the motive), transposition (restating the motive at a higher or lower pitch), rhythmic displacement (beginning it at a different point within the measure), expansion (stretching out its contour with larger leaps between notes), compression (flattening that contour with smaller leaps), augmentation (slowing down the speed of its individual notes), diminution (speeding up these notes), and inversion (turning the contour of the motive upside down). In the course of this motivic development, the improviser aims to make the motive stand out, so that a listener may recognize it and follow its transformation. To be successful, the musician must strike a delicate balance between the trivial and the complex, avoiding literal restatement (the motive is easy to follow, but the resulting improvisation is dull) and also avoiding overly elaborate variations that effectively obscure the motive (in which case the improvisation may be quite engaging, but we are no longer talking about motivic development, because the motive has lost its identity).

Motivic improvisation was fairly unimportant during the first half-century of jazz, for this reason: until the advent of modal jazz and free jazz in the late 1950s, an improvisation was always expected to accord somehow with its theme; the theme was usually based on a harmonic scheme that changed chords at every bar or two (and sometimes every beat or two); and the improvisation itself often moved along quickly. Given these conditions—which are vital to New Orleans jazz, swing, bop, and their assorted substyles—it would take a superhuman talent to improvise the systematic development of a motive without stumbling. One thinks first of Beethoven and his painfully protracted struggles to compose perfect motivic developments (which he did). Imagine trying to imitate his achievement not at leisure but in a matter of seconds, with the chords changing every measure or half-measure and the measures moving at over 200 beats per minute.

Sonny Rollins took on exactly these conditions at the start of *St. Thomas* and came as close as anyone to achieving this feat, although he could not sustain a motivic improvisation for long and soon moved into his regular improvisatory style, involving a wonderfully flexible formulaic technique that rivaled Parker's. Still, it is remarkable that he pulled it off at all. Rollins's opening chorus, transcribed by Charles Blancq (ex. 48), explores inversions, transpositions, intervallic extensions, and ornamentations of the opening notes of the melody (cited in ex. 46).

Example 48. Motivic development at the start of Sonny Rollins's solo on *St. Thomas* (transcribed by Charles Blancq). Track 18, 0:55.

Elsewhere within the New Orleans, swing, and bop styles, one needs to look long and hard to find reasonably fast-paced examples of motivic development, as heard on *St. Thomas.* A few prominent musicians found success playing sparsely, the liberal space between each motivic statement allowing time to prepare the next. Leading practitioners included Count Basie, Thelonious Monk, John Lewis, Benny Carter, and Paul Desmond. The comparatively lesser known Kid Thomas Valentine also favored this approach. On the version of *Panama* that his band recorded in 1959, in the chorus following the piano solo, Valentine shows how his improvisatory style, founded on electrifying bursts of sound, might lend itself to a motivic approach (ex. 49). The whole chorus consists of repetitions of a blue note, variously shaded by the use of rhythmic displacement, wa-wa effects (created by opening and closing a plunger mute), and a throat growl.

Example 49. Motivic work in Kid Thomas Valentine's trumpet playing during the ninth chorus of *Panama*, recorded in 1959. Track 20, 2:24.

When modal jazz and free jazz began to open up alternatives to conventional harmony—either by focusing on static accompaniments or by rejecting the need for an improviser to accord with the accompaniment—motivic improvisation began to take on a much greater currency. Some players were thrilled to be freed from what they perceived as a harmonic straitjacket: the chord progressions of standard jazz themes. But that straitjacket had provided a guarantee of coherence: however rambling an improvisation might be, the underlying theme might nonetheless hold the listener's interest. Now, instead, the improviser took on the full burden of organizing ideas coherently. Motivic development provided a means toward achieving this goal. Saxophonist John Coltrane supplied its fullest realization in his breathtaking motivic improvisations of the early to mid-1960s. By the time of *Ascension* (1965), his attention was turning toward the exploration of extreme timbres and registers, but even in this example listeners may be able to hear passages of motivic development (track 4).

John Gilmore's tenor saxophone solo on Sun Ra's *Outer Nothingness* (ex. 50) provides a clear example of how an instrumentalist might use motivic improvisation to tie together a portion of a free-jazz performance in which there is neither thematic melody nor thematic harmony to guide the improviser and to shape the piece. Gilmore's motivic work should require little explanation: he starts with a three-note motive, which he repeats, transposes upward and downward, compresses, inverts, and augments. (Some listeners might question whether Gilmore is playing bass clarinet rather than tenor sax; this possibility will be taken up in chapter 7, in the section on instrumentation and timbre.)

Example 50. Motivic development in John Gilmore's tenor saxophone solo on Sun Ra's *Outer Nothingness*. Track 19, 1:09.

Modal Improvisation

Before completing this survey of opportunities for motivic improvisation, the related question of modal improvisation must be discussed; its connection to motivic improvisation will soon become evident. Improvisation can sometimes be described strictly in terms of pitch—which pitches are selected more than how they are put together—and indeed much of the conceptual discussion of improvisation in the realm of jazz education has been directed toward this issue. The key concept is "chord-scale," which means, in short: given chord X, improvise using scale Y. For the most part the present chapter concentrates on an understanding of improvisation in which the selection of pitch is but one component of a larger conception that considers contour, repetition, rhythm, and coherence, all functioning either in relation to the paraphrasing of existing lines or in relation to the invention of new ones. However, one category of chord-scale playing, modal improvisation, is sufficiently distinctive to warrant a separate discussion.

Modal jazz was mentioned in chapter 3 as a type of static form. There it was argued that the label can be rather misleading, because modal jazz has much more to do with harmony—specifically the slowing of harmonic rhythm and the weakening of chordal interrelationships—than with scales construed as representing a jazz version of ethnic or ecclesiastical modes. For modal improvisation, additional cautions are in order: this label can be misleading because modal improvisation often unfolds in a flexible and unsystematic way that undermines the identity of specific ethnic or ecclesiastical modes and because normally the modal quality of a piece will center around a static accompaniment that allows only limited opportunity for improvisation. For example, on a number of John Coltrane's recordings from the early 1960s, there are modal elements, but the improvisations are highly chromatic. At the extreme edge would be *Ascension*, portions of which are said to be based on four scales that Coltrane gave to his sidemen.[11] It should be obvious from listening that these scales had only the smallest influence on the resulting collectively improvised, dense sound fields. Less extreme and better known would be those versions of *My Favorite Things* for which pianist McCoy Tyner supplied the modal element: chordal ostinatos that sound over and over again beneath Coltrane's freely chromatic improvisations. Hence in "modal improvisation" it is often the accompaniment, not the improvisation, that is modal.

There are, however, performances in which the formal basis of modal jazz—slow moving, weakly functional harmony—determines an improviser's selection of pitches. Representative of this approach is Freddie Hubbard's trumpet solo on Herbie Hancock's *Maiden Voyage* (ex. 51).

Example 51. Freddie Hubbard's solo on *Maiden Voyage*. Track 9, 0:07.

Improvisation
148

Hubbard occasionally inserts a chromatic neighbor note (in this instance, a note located a half step away from an element of the modal scale) or a chromatic passing tone (a move by half step between two adjacent elements of the modal scale), as for example in the fleeting appearances of the pitch C$\sharp$ in bars 108 to 116. Otherwise he takes only the liberties that Hancock's harmonically ambiguous composition allows. At the opening, the trumpeter avoids the pitches F and F$\sharp$ (bars 73–76 and 81–84), neither of which is specified by the first chord (A minor seventh with a D in the bass); when that chord returns at the end of the first chorus, he selects F (bars 97–100); in the second chorus, he plays F$\sharp$ (bars 113–16 and 129–32). To ponder whether the resulting collections of pitches might represent the modes A aeolian, A dorian, D dorian, or D mixolydian is perhaps to miss the point of modal improvisation, which involves selecting pitches in a deliberate manner that accords closely with Hancock's static harmonies.

A restrictive approach to pitch selection says something about the sound of Hubbard's solo, but it is of scarcely any use in explaining why this is such a magnificently creative improvisation. A more satisfying explanation results from a broader view: the examination of Hubbard's use of motivic improvisation as a tool for creating coherence within an improvised melody of widely varying character.

As is often the case in modal jazz and related forms, static harmony affords an opportunity for an improviser to state and vary motives, a task that (as mentioned earlier) is not easily taken up in the context of conventional jazz harmony. Over the course of his solo Hubbard develops motives in batches lasting anywhere from three to eleven measures. Within and among these segments of the solo, the trumpeter creatively combines and contrasts aspects of expression, tempo, rhythmic subdivision, dynamics, and timbre.

Through much of the first of Hubbard's two 32-bar choruses, his improvised melody is moderately paced and lyrical. He begins softly, with a gentle tone, but upon repeating the shape of the opening motive at bar 81 (D - E - D), his lyricism—now one octave higher, loud, and brassy in tone—becomes majestic. He lets the line fall off to a whisper, with a "half-valve" timbral effect sounding along the way. (Pushing the trumpet valve down half-way produces a squeezed, muffled timbre.)

Tunefulness and softness continue through bar 100, but bars 89–96 feature swing rhythm, and accordingly the subdued formality of his melody is replaced by something with a greater bite. At bar 101, a sixteenth-note run serves as preparation for an increase in volume, a return to brassiness, and a move into double-time. This begins in earnest at the start of Hubbard's second 32-bar chorus (bar 105), where he develops a syncopated motive that skitters up to and then dances around a high B.

Lyrical, then pointedly rhythmic, his solo now—in contrast to both of these approaches—explores rapid scalar fragments in a style freed from the beat (bars 109–11); the rhythms defy exact transcription. Hubbard introduces a different sort of contrast during a brief return to rhythmic regularity and tunefulness, when he presents a measure of loud brassy sound (bar 116); here he associates loudness and brassiness with the low range of the trumpet, whereas earlier these qualities were associated with notes an octave or so higher. He then breaks away from the beat once again to return to the rapid scalar fragments, which develop into sustained swirling patterns (bars 117–27).

To wind down the solo, Hubbard recalls the gentleness and lyricism of the opening in the general character of his melody, but its specific content evolves directly from the preceding motive: he transforms the three-note scalar motive into a sweet and tuneful idea (stepping down a third and then back up); as this motive ascends, Hubbard broadens its rhythm (bars 128– 34). Finally, rather than let the solo fade away gently in this manner, he suddenly punctuates the ending by shouting out a double-time figure (bars 135–36) in which all but the last two notes are differentiated by timbre (same note, alternate fingerings) rather than by pitch. It is a brilliant ending to a vividly imaginative improvisation that juxtaposes melodic segments of widely diverse character, joining them by motivic means.

Essential differences distinguish the three basic improvisatory methods. Paraphrase involves the recognizable, bar-by-bar embellishment of preexisting material. In this sense it stands in opposition to formulaic and motivic improvisation, either of which involves the creation of new ideas. Paraphrase and motivic improvisations involve the constant development of a specific theme and a motive, either of which gives a piece a particular identity; the theme or the motive must remain recognizable if the improvisation is to achieve its intended effect, but at the same time the player must be inventive enough to create ever-new variations. In this sense paraphrase and motivic improvisations stand in opposition to formulaic improvisation, which generates ever-changing lines by means of the ingenious interweaving of fragments from a general repertory that is common to many pieces.

Such distinctions do not mean that the improvisatory methods are mutually exclusive. In practice a performer may follow or overlay one with another within a single improvisation and may even reuse new material in later work; thus an improvisation that was originally generated by motivic or formulaic procedures may be adopted as a preexisting theme and subjected to paraphrase in its turn. Moreover, all of these procedures intertwine with others in the realms of arrangement and composition. To illuminate such interworkings, this survey of jazz procedures ends with a close look at Billie Holiday's interpretation of *Georgia on My Mind*, by songwriter Hoagy Carmichael and lyricist Stuart Gorrell.

Nearly all of Holiday's early recordings were made with ad hoc collections of the leading swing musicians. On March 21, 1941, she recorded four versions of *Georgia on My Mind* with an eight-piece group. The master take

(take 1) has appeared on a nearly continuous succession of reissues. One of the other versions (take 2) has been distributed far less frequently and widely, though nonetheless internationally, on the double album *God Bless the Child*. (Details appear in appendix 2.) By comparing these two takes with the original song, it is possible to gain some insight into Holiday's approach to music making.

These recordings were made in New York for the OKeh label, which in 1938 had become a subsidiary of Columbia. No one seems to know whether OKeh at the time was assigning take numbers by sequence or by preference. Not knowing whether take 1 of the four was the first or the best, or the first and the best, one must shy away from drawing conclusions about the relationship of recording chronology to Holiday's method—though of course in instances where the chronology is known, that subject is well worth pursuing.

The arrangement used that day was unmemorable, spare, and conventional, except for a catchy piano introduction, which Eddie Heywood repeats verbatim on both takes. A trumpeter and three saxophonists play soft chords and a few moving lines in the background. The four men play the second half of each chorus the same way, and they might well have repeated all 32 bars, were it not for the variation introduced by the minimalist method of having them remain silent during Heywood's piano solo. This arrangement, such as it is, is the sort that would have been thrown together in the recording studio at the last minute. It assures that the winds provide a quiet, mellow cushion for Holiday's singing, without any of the chance discord that would have occurred had a trumpeter and three saxophonists been allowed to improvise their accompaniment.

This modest arrangement serves as a foil for Holiday's solos, each a highlight of her career in the recording studio. In example 52, the 32-bar *aaba* chorus of Carmichael's melody (shown in the upper staff) is aligned with each of Holiday's opening choruses from takes 1 and 2 (the two lower staffs). The upper staff has been transposed from Carmichael's key, F, to Holiday's, B♭, to facilitate the comparison between his melody and hers.

Example 52. The opening chorus of *Georgia on My Mind,* as published (upper staff), and two versions recorded by Billie Holiday in 1941 (lower staffs). Track 12, 0:09.

Georgia on My Mind

Hoagy Carmichael and Stuart Gorrell

It is important to note that she does not change or add a single word. There are no scat-singing syllables, no whispered asides, no interjected exclamations. This wonderful and deceptive ploy is of course available only to singers, not to instrumentalists. The trick is to disassociate at least some portion of the lyric from the melody. Thus casual listeners are treated to a continuously familiar verse, while devoted listeners recognize that they have been handed a new sound. With the right skills, the jazz singer is able to make this new sound worthy of the original. These are daunting tasks when dealing with a melody as familiar and beautifully crafted as *Georgia on My Mind*, but Holiday was up to the challenge.

At the opening words "Georgia, Georgia, the whole day through" (bars 1–4) and in the midst of the bridge, at the words "other eyes smile tenderly, still in peaceful dreams I see" (bars 19–22), Holiday clearly paraphrases Carmichael's material on both takes. On repetitions of the opening melodic phrase she continues to paraphrase, in part: at appropriate spots on both takes, at the words "a song of you" (bars 11–12) and "no peace I find" (bars 27–28), she recalls the second half of that melodic fragment, set to the words "the whole day through" (bars 3–4). But for repetitions of the first part of that same phrase, "Georgia, Georgia," she discards Carmichael's melody in favor of a stabbing cry that descends through a tritone in a gesture littered with blue notes; this figure sounds twice on each take (bars 9–10 and 25–26).

At bar 5 of both takes she recalls nothing more than a couple of pitches from the original song, fittingly on the words "song keeps." Otherwise she replaces the sweep of Carmichael's line with an intonation centered on a single pitch, at the words "just an old sweet song." This manner of flattening out a melody, a formulaic device that Holiday used often, returns at equivalent spots in repetitions of the opening phrase on both takes, at the words "comes as sweet and clear as" (bars 12–13) and also on take 1 at the repetition of that same lyric, "just an old sweet song" (bars 28–30). But at bars 28–30 of take 2, in lieu of the flattened-out melody, Holiday delivers a variant of a line heard at the end of the second chorus of take 1 (not transcribed here). Thus she presents an alternative route though this segment of the melody, and the idea, unrelated to Carmichael's original, recurs from one take to the next in a closely related paraphrase.

In the first half of each chorus, at the words "Georgia on my mind" (bars 6–7) and "moonlight through the pines" (bars 14–15), Holiday paraphrases a melody that differs yet again from Carmichael's. By contrast, at the words "Other arms reach out to me" (bars 17–18), she approaches each version in a different manner, on take 1 departing entirely from Carmichael's melody but on take 2 singing something roughly related to the original.

If one considers all these details together, the most striking thing about these three versions of *Georgia on My Mind* is that Holiday's two are much closer to each other than to the original. Holiday, like many other jazz musicians, uses an integrated, two-stage process of creation. First she composes in considerable detail a theme, made in part from Carmichael's original theme but in greater part from her own ideas. Although this private theme is neither fully polished nor rigidly fixed, it is something much more substantial than a mere outline for improvisation. Whether she composed this theme at the moment of recording her first take on that day in 1941 or long in advance of that day cannot be known. The point is that two successive takes are built from the same general melodic conception; one might therefore conclude that she prepared at least one take, and perhaps both, ahead of time.

In the second stage of this process, improvisation, Holiday's rhythmic imagination is hard at work. At the normal level of quarter notes, swing eighths, and the like, she freely moves phrases ahead or back. Only occasionally do the basic rhythms coincide on the two recordings. At the microscopic level of rhythmic placement, of the sort discussed in chapter 2 in relationship to Miles Davis's paraphrase of *'Round Midnight*, she improvises with abandon. It is extremely difficult to hear just when notes enter or just how long notes last, and her use of leaping grace notes and sliding blue notes further heightens the mystery of precise rhythmic placement.

At the same time, she brings together aspects of paraphrase and formulaic improvisation by paraphrasing a small network of melodic phrases keyed to the text of *Georgia on My Mind* and by occasionally substituting one phrase for another. Thus, in this improvisation she not only paraphrases her private theme, derived from Carmichael's ideas and her own, but also reconstructs portions of it. In a situation such as this—and such a situation is commonplace in jazz—composition and improvisation come together to create a performance that is simultaneously fixed and fluid, premeditated and spontaneous. A great strength of jazz is that it provides the forum for bringing these opposing qualities together.

Years later, Teddy Wilson recalled Holiday's approach: "On the recording sessions Billie did a lot of composers favors. I remember one particular experience. We had gone through a couple of numbers that were accepted, when in walked a man who had composed one of these tunes. He heard the playback of his composition, then said, 'That's a nice job, but it isn't my tune.' Billie said, 'That's the way I've done it. If you don't like it we'll just cancel it. We have several tunes here we could do instead.' The man said 'Oh, no, oh, no.' I can't remember what the tune was, but it turned out to be one of Billie's hit songs."[12]

In 1941 Hoagy Carmichael was an established star who needed no favors from Billie Holiday, but she approached his song with the same independent jazz-minded spirit that she brought to any of her material. One hopes that Carmichael was impressed with the results.

7 SOUND

H

e would borrow a horn, anybody's horn, and it would always come out his sound.
—Bill Graham, saxophonist, speaking of Charlie Parker

A pliable set of sounds is at the heart of jazz. The main ingredients are a collection of principal instruments, in which an emphasis on percussion is virtually indispensable, and a personalized approach to the production of timbre and vibrato. In many cases these sounds have been developed within jazz by its musicians, as a consequence of their experimental spirit.

A lesser ingredient is the type of tuning system used. Although tuning does not necessarily have a special identity or origin in jazz, it too affects the instantaneous impression that the music makes, its sound.

Before trying to describe the sound of jazz, it seems imperative to address a technological issue having a great deal to do with sound in general, namely, recording fidelity. The best live jazz is unbeatable, but practical considerations dictate that much of what we hear will have been recorded, including all the music selections upon which this book is based. Which recordings capture the sound of a performance with reasonable accuracy, and which distort it?

Fidelity

Fidelity—the accuracy with which recorded sound reproduces instruments and voices—has varied wildly in jazz of all eras, owing to the vagaries of available equipment and the uneven skills of recording engineers. Nevertheless, it is safe to say that the first three decades of jazz recording produced low-fidelity sound, by comparison with the hi-fi sound that became common in the 1950s, after tape mastering and microgroove recording were adopted as standard practice in the industry. Subsequently, there was a sudden improvement in the ability to differentiate sounds spatially (using stereophonic techniques); a sudden reduction in extraneous noise (with the advent of digital recording); steady progress in the precision of two weak links in the chain, the microphone and the loudspeaker; and an increased dependence on electric, electronic, and synthesized music, with a concomitant breakdown in distinctions between recorded sound on the one hand and real instruments and voices on the other. A side effect of this remarkable progress in recording fidelity is that people brought up on glossy, clean sound find it harder and harder to enjoy classic jazz recordings. Many such listeners claim that although in principle they would like to learn to appreciate this repertory, they cannot tolerate such low-fidelity sound. Surface noise, a lack of balance, exaggerated treble and inadequate bass, all get in the way of the music.

Some enthusiasts have looked to technology for an answer to this problem. To date, the most fashionable solution is to be found on a series of reissues that recording engineer Robert Parker began to produce in the 1980s for Australian Broadcasting Company compact discs. These discs offer classic jazz recordings remastered in digital stereo, with improvements in balance, clarity, fullness, and separation. Yet whatever one's preferences with regard to early or later styles, whatever one's feelings about Parker's controversial tinkering with the original recorded documents, one could hardly assert that anything in this series approaches Weather Report's sensuous high-fidelity sound on *Birdland*. To achieve truly hi-fi classic jazz is a vain hope.

Thus, rather than point toward some magical technological solution, the purpose of raising this issue is, first, simply to acknowledge that it exists and, second, to issue a caveat concerning not only recording fidelity but also many other areas of the music. The caution is that jazz is an inherently imperfect music, and in significant ways a desire for perfection clashes with aesthetics peculiar to jazz. Some imperfections should merely be disregarded. The fumbled stop-time chorus on Morton's *Black Bottom Stomp* does not prevent this piece from being on everyone's short list of the greatest jazz recordings. Nor do failed takes and an intermittently squeaky saxophone (repaired before the recording of Parker's *Koko*) prevent the entire session of November 26, 1945, from being regarded as *the* central event in Parker's career.

Other flaws actually enhance the music. Grating clashes are essential to the gruff sound of several styles of collectively improvised jazz; without such clashes, the music might sound sterile. Audience involvement, with all its noisy elements—people dancing, clapping for a good solo, shouting encouragement, talking irreverently, clinking glasses, ringing (nowadays beeping) cash registers—can, under the right circumstances, spur musicians on to an ecstatic level of performance unmatched at the sort of jazz concert where everyone must sit in perfect silence.

From this perspective, low-fidelity sound should be regarded as just another category of imperfection, something the listener should try to work around. Before turning to the subject of tuning systems, and then to instrumentation, timbre, and vibrato, listen again to *Trumpet No End* and *Tin Roof Blues*, perfect examples of the marriage of horrid fidelity and great music (tracks 7 and 16). Recognize that these are being heard, in effect, through an opaque, scratchy filter, and try to imagine what each might have sounded like in the studio. Then listen again, for what they really are, not for what they might have been. Forget about low fidelity, and enjoy the strength of the playing.

Tuning Systems

Take a swath of jazz sound. Is it in tune? In some contexts, the question lends itself to a straightforward answer, because there is a clear standard against which that sound can be judged—the system of equal temperament that developed in classical music more than two and a half centuries ago. At other times the question is a controversial one, and perhaps an irrelevant one (in tune to *what?*), for reasons that seem to involve individual attitudes toward listening as much as any absolute standard for producing pitch.

In equal temperament, the octave is divided into twelve uniform semitones, the equidistant chromatic notes that everyone tries to learn in beginning music lessons. In jazz the direct adoption of this time-honored classical system of intonation is in part simply a matter of accepting the tuning system that came along with the many instruments of European origin. It applies most readily to instruments in which pitch is fixed externally or mechanically (the piano, organ, and vibraphone, for example) rather than to those in which precise pitch depends upon the willingness and ability of the musician to put fingers (as in the case of the violin and fretless bass), lips (any wind instrument), or voice in the correct position.

But equal temperament has not come into jazz merely as some sort of passive, accidental adjunct to instrumentation. Many musicians have embraced it wholeheartedly. For example, Earl Hines performs *Sweet Sue* on a well-tuned piano, without using any technical gimmicks that might alter pitch. If *Sweet Sue* sounds out of tune on some LP issues (it is far better on the new CD issue), wobbles introduced at some stage in the record-making process are to blame. The distortion has nothing to do with Hines's ear or with his conception of jazz piano playing. Without a doubt he would always have been happy to play on the most well-tuned instrument and to record in the most well-equipped studio. As testimony to that, see Hines's exuberant account of his being given a magnificent Steinway grand piano in 1969.[1] Count Basie's orchestra, as another example, was staffed by bandsmen who could keep pitch focused and in tune. On *Jumpin' at the Woodside*, the saxophone section is rock steady in its expression and repetition of the riff that sews together the *a* sections of the first two 32-bar choruses (track 2, 0:07–1:09). Muted brass punches accompany this riff, and within them the lead trumpeter is just as steady in doubling the note G an octave above the saxes. During the second chorus, that same note remains steady even as the saxophones break up their attacks to create a pulsating effect. (Transcriptions of these fragments of music appear in chap. 4, ex. 40.) Such precision of pitch, with each note expressed in ensemble passages as a pinpoint, rather than as a cloud, contributed greatly to the rhythmic precision for which Basie's big band was always renowned.

Equal temperament also occurs in instrumental circumstances far removed from its European roots. One need look no further than the opening moment of *Manteca*, in which Chano Pozo produces pitches on his Afro-Cuban conga drum to accord with the prevailing ostinato (transcribed in chap. 2, ex. 8b).

Equal temperament presumes that if the music is to be perceived as being in tune, a note will remain steady in pitch (except for the undulation known as vibrato) and the interval between a given pair of notes will remain fixed in pitch. Individual moments of jazz often depart from this European-based notion and instead take up an African-American idea, that the pitch of a note may move in a subtle, oblique manner. Such a sound, which can be described as a continuum of pitches in motion, is called a blue note. Traditionally the blue note operates in the vicinity of the third and seventh of whatever chord happens to be in operation at the moment. But this is a flexible concept that also works well in other harmonic positions.

The blue note has already been indicated as a harmonic component of blues tonality in the New Orleans Rhythm Kings' *Tin Roof Blues* (chap. 3, ex. 20) and as a rhythmic component of Billie Holiday's melody on *Georgia on My Mind* (chap. 6, ex. 52). These examples stand as representatives of the device, without further comment, except to say that listeners should probably not miss the moaning alto sax in the bridge of the theme of Mingus's *Fables of Faubus* (chap. 5, ex. 41b). What might be added are a reference to the simulation of blue notes and a discussion of how blue notes can meld with equal temperament.

If we ignore, for the purpose of argument, the countless detuned, untuned, never-tuned, beaten, miserable pianos on which jazz musicians have had to work over the years, and if we reject any romantic, primitivist notion that a great pianist might enjoy playing a lousy instrument, then it may be claimed (at least in theory) that the piano in jazz is a machine with rigid steel strings that are fixed (or that ought to have been fixed) in equal temperament. Consequently the piano does not readily lend itself to the bluing of pitch that might be achieved with a delicate motion of the fingers, lips, or throat on any number of other instruments (including of course the voice). To convey at least the impression of this effect, which is an integral part of the character of the music, pianists since the early years of jazz have used the technique of crushing adjacent notes and then releasing one, so that the pitch moves, blurring and then crystallizing. One of the best at this, because of his hammerlike touch, was Thelonious Monk. While in the process of articulating the bare essentials of a blues progression during his accompaniment to Milt Jackson's vibraphone solo on *Misterioso*, Monk simulates the effect of blue notes with a slide up to the minor seventh of each of the three chords, B♭, E♭, and F (ex. 53a). During the piano solo that follows, his simulated blue notes slide down to the minor third of B♭ (spelled in ex. 53b as an augmented ninth, C♯, rather than as a minor third, D♭, for ease of notation).

Example 53a. Simulated blue notes in Thelonious Monk's accompaniment to Milt Jackson's vibraphone solo on *Misterioso*. Track 14, 0:46.

Example 53b. Simulated blue notes in Monk's solo on *Misterioso*. Track 14, 1:30.

Sound
164

Blue notes often operate within the context of equal temperament. Along this line, it is instructive to read what the clarinetist Barney Bigard—who was fully in control of the blue note idiom—had to say about a New Orleans revival group, the Yerba Buena Jazz Band: "I never cared for their kind of music at all. I hate to say it but in that style it seems that everyone plays out of key. I mean the clarinet player I heard with them seemed to know his horn but was so out of tune the whole time. What kind of ears do they have? He must hear that he is out of tune."[2]

A comparison of Bigard's attitude with the music that he played (with King Oliver, Louis Armstrong, and Duke Ellington) reveals that, from his point of view, blue notes can be assimilated into the system of equal temperament. The presence of their ambiguous pitch has no effect on the larger question of whether an entire performance is in tune, or not, in the traditional sense of the phrase. Many share this view.

What, then, should be made of performances in which equal temperament is thrown out the window? Is such a performance simply out of tune, with all that that critique implies (technical incompetence, bad music), or might another conception of tuning be at work?

Arguments over conceptions of tuning raged when Ornette Coleman, a pioneer of free jazz, came on the scene in the late 1950s. Claims that he was unable to play in tune were pitted against a perspective best summarized by Coleman himself, in this frequently quoted statement: "You can play flat in tune and sharp in tune."[3] Time quickly settled this dispute in Coleman's favor, as he demonstrated his mastery of a conception of pitch in which, in effect, any and every note could be a blue note—as beautifully illustrated in his improvisations on *Honeymooners*. Perhaps the most obvious moment of unconventional intonation occurs in segment 3, where he varies a motive by sliding its highest pitch up and down (track 3, 2:11). (For an account of the segments and interludes in *Honeymooners,* see the section on ad hoc forms in chap. 3.)

Ironically, only a few of the people who have learned to appreciate Coleman have noticed the close connection between his conception of intonation and that of some exponents of the New Orleans jazz revival. In this area the question of tuning remains controversial, even fifty or more years after the revival. Fans of Kid Thomas Valentine's music will not be pleased by the idea of putting his band in the same category as the Yerba Buena Jazz Band, but insofar as tuning is concerned, Valentine's *Panama* presents exactly the sort of playing that Bigard was describing. Is "out of tune" a fair label? One camp might say yes and dismiss the music altogether. Another might appeal to the group's folklike, semiprofessional character and then point (with apologies for the faulty intonation) to the great strengths of the music, Valentine's unique tone quality and melodic conception. And another might make no apology whatsoever, because—after a wide sampling of revivalist sounds—it becomes apparent that alongside the equal temperament heard in Armstrong and Bigard's school of New Orleans jazz is a school made up of leading bands, including Valentine's, that show no such respect for the European tradition. Instead, rancid intonation is an crucial part of their style, contributing—along with collective improvisation—to the sharp edge that gives the music its life. Listeners who appreciate a swath of unequal temperament pulsating across a transparent triadic underpinning—as in some of the earliest punk rock—are advised to seek out the session recorded in 1946 by the Original Zenith Brass Band (for the issue on CD, see appendix 2). These recordings are the most wonderful example of warped tuning in the New Orleans revivalist style.

Tuning systems in jazz also extend into an area that is often disregarded by listeners, the tuning of the drum set. The basic set of drums and cymbals offers a combination of pitched and unpitched sounds, depending on which members of the set (typically, bass drum, tom-tom drums, snare drum, paired hi-hat cymbals, and other individual cymbals) happen to be sounding at the moment and how they are struck. Whatever the details, the main contribution of these percussion instruments is rhythmic and coloristic. For rhythm, tuning is irrelevant. For tone color, tuning may be a consideration, as in the effort to make cymbals ring (rather than sound like garbage can lids) and lower-pitched drums boom (rather than sound like oatmeal cartons), but the specific pitch is not an end in itself.

Some drummers play the drum set just as they find it, without bothering
to tighten or loosen drum heads; others pay close attention to tuning for
timbral effects. In either case, a drum set gives off spongy pitches that
listeners might strive to hear, insofar as these pitches support or undermine other tuning systems in operation in a performance. By chance, there
is a fascinating example of drum tuning at the recording session that produced Sonny Rollins's *St. Thomas.* Max Roach is known for being particularly sensitive to melodic and timbral aspects of drumming. At this session
with Rollins, Roach evidently retuned his drum set track by track. The
titles, keys, and prominent drum pitches of four of the selections recorded
that day are listed in example 54.

Example 54. Max Roach's drum tunings at Sonny Rollins's recording session of
June 22, 1956.

Title	Key	Bass drum	Tom-toms			Snare
St. Thomas	C major	E♭	C	E	A♭	B♭
Strode Rode	F minor	D	D		A♭	
Blue Seven	B♭ blues	D♭	D♭	G♭	A	
Moritat	B♭ major	D	D♭		A	

None of these recordings demonstrate a strong relationship between the
key and the drum pitches. It would be interesting to know if this disparity
was intentional. When asked about this in 1993, Roach remembered some
aspects of the recording process, such as the placement of the drum set and
the microphone, but he could not recall anything about drum tuning—and
why should he, after thirty-seven years![4] The point is that, intentional or
accidental, drum tunings are a part of the sound of jazz. Their presence
may color, and perhaps subtly disrupt, conventional harmony. Although
undoubtedly resulting from rhythmic and timbral considerations, drum
sounds, when heard from the perspective of pitch, add to jazz a subtle
tension that has nothing to do with rhythm or timbre, and everything to do
with tuning.

The Instrumentarium of Jazz

From the beginning of jazz, sometime during the first decade of the
twentieth century, to the early 1960s, its creators focused on developing a
personal sound within what might be called an instrumentarium, that is, a

tightly circumscribed body of instruments: the trumpet, cornet, trombone, clarinet, piano, guitar, banjo, string bass, tuba, drum set, and voice. To be sure, there were important innovators on other instruments: the violin, vibraphone, and conga drum. But such examples are rare by comparison with the legions of significant players and singers who followed the creators, building a music in which possibilities for varied instrumentation remained limited but possibilities for individual expression on these instruments were expansive and previously unimagined.

From the mid-1960s this creative principle of trying to find a personal sound on a standard jazz instrument coexisted with a new and drastically different principle—that of trying to make a jazz sound on an instrument new to jazz. In the course of about one decade, the instrumentarium expanded enormously. The main sources of inspiration were Third World music (especially percussion from Brazil, Africa, and India) and rock (with its explorations of amplified and synthesized sound); at the same time some players carved out an idiomatic niche for those orchestral winds and strings that had earlier seemed ill suited to jazz, such as the flute, bass clarinet, french horn, and cello. Meanwhile, the central instruments remained central, with the exception of the clarinet, and new approaches developed for the trombone, saxophone, piano, guitar, string bass, and drums.[5] The first principle, personal sound, continued and continues to be a prime consideration.

To understand the most important component of personal sound, timbre, there is no better introduction than Louis Armstrong's scat singing on *Hotter than That*. Reexamine that passage, this time not for its rhythm but for its phonetics. As with any instrument, the inherent (in this case God-given) construction of Armstrong's voice defines a basic area of sound. Alive with noise elements, this instrument is raspy, perfectly suited to the African-American conception of sound upon which jazz timbre is founded. Within the boundaries of this instrument, Armstrong's inventiveness is astonishing. His manipulation of timbre, with details of the grittiness continually changing, is as subtle as the rhythmic play. These profound trains of musical thought run beneath the outpouring of an irresistibly joyful private language:

Example 55. Ever-changing timbres in the "text" of Louis Armstrong's scat-singing duet with guitarist Lonnie Johnson on *Hotter than That*. Track 1, 1:18.

Dip deh doop da, doe doe doe doe.

Dah dew dah doot doot dew, da dee dee doot, daw bee do bee dup baw lahp baw.

Bah bee boop, buh dee bee doop bee, hew law bah de bohm, bah bah bah bough.

Wah bee bah bee bee, low bah dah-oh-ah, lah dah bee bop bah deep bah feh.

Dah to dit dit dew dup, dee duh doe.

Rip dee duh duh dew dah daw-ee-ya doe doe dip dip, baw buh bah bah baw beep bah beep baw bah baw bah bah beep bah beep thiz dit duh duh.

Reap dew dit done, dah nah naw naw deep dah dee, dah done dah dew.

Bah bah dah beep bew.

Bah bee dut zuh bow.

Wah-oh dove dew, duh boop bee dew the boop, wah-oo-lough. (guitar solo)

Zwee boo bee dew um-wow dah-dah-wow. (guitar solo)

Oooooo dah-dum-wah um-mough hmaf hwow. (guitar solo)

Reap deh diddle dee tih duh, boo wuh buh bow.

Reading scat-singing syllables may be a good way to introduce the idea of timbre, but in moving from the voice to other instruments, different rules of analysis apply. The galaxy of instrumental tone colors can still be written down on paper, but only as representations of the frequency spectrum of instants of sound. These graphs and numerical samples, essential to physics and acoustics and to the development of synthesizers, are not particularly helpful for critical description, beyond establishing a few general observations, such as whether a note is fairly pure or loaded with overtones, and what it looks like at moments of attack and release.

In evaluating timbre in instruments, the only alternative to mathematical analysis is vague analogy: tone quality can be described as gritty, raspy, nasal, bright, cutting, round, full, deep, thin, dry, warm, cool, and the like. Such a vocabulary, lacking the precision of vocabularies for rhythm, form, harmony, and melody, quickly wears thin. All one is left with is a directly musical approach: listening carefully to an instrumentalist, remembering his or her personal sound, and then comparing that sound to other personal sounds, until through experience one begins to recognize timbral identities and interrelationships even without being able to express these identities and interrelationships in words (apart from stating the name of the performer and a few characteristic adjectives of the sort listed above).

Conceptually simpler and less versatile than timbre, but nonetheless a prominent element of personal sound, is vibrato. Its speed, spread, intensity, or steadiness, or its absence altogether, is sometimes a factor in the following examples. The first examination of selections involving personal sound quickly surveys the tenor saxophone. The second, involving categories of trumpet sounds, is more elaborate.

Before investigating these examples, it must be said that there are a lot more musicians than individual sounds. Personal sound is the most coveted possession in jazz, a virtual prerequisite for—though no guarantee of—being counted among the giants of the music. Occasionally it is inimitable (as in the case of Billie Holiday's singing), but usually one person discovers a new sound, and others, sometimes many others, follow. For easily reproducible sounds, a labyrinthine procession of direct imitators and modifiers, and imitators of the modifiers, descends from the top of the mountain, emulating the tones of Armstrong's cornet, trumpet, and voice in the 1920s, the sound of Parker's alto saxophone in the 1940s, Coltrane's tenor saxophone in the 1960s, or Pat Metheny's electric guitar in the 1980s.

Because of the high value attached to personal sound—the creators elevated, the modifiers appreciated perhaps in a qualified way, the imitators sometimes dismissed or even disdained—many listeners seem to engage in a considerable amount of self-deception (and many musicians and managers in a considerable amount of false promotion). Jazz fans find (or claim to find) personal sound in the tiniest details, while ignoring, first, the impossibility of everyone having a personal sound and, second, the importance of preexisting style, role playing, and ritual as factors that counteract individuality in jazz.

The situation is by no means clear-cut. At the most ethereal level of appreciation, one subscribes to this search for ever-new personal sound and the value system that comes along with it. It seems important, necessary, laudable, and a part of what makes the greatest jazz great. For performances that are "merely" excellent, professional, and memorable, and for the many performances that fall short of that high standard, the search may be unrealistic, its overemphasis leading to a strained effort to find a new personal sound within a borrowed one. Such self-deception gets in the way of listening.

In any event, this issue is not problematic for players of such stunning individuality as John Coltrane, Coleman Hawkins, Sonny Rollins, and Lester Young. To learn the personal sounds of these tenor saxophonists, begin by comparing Young on *Jumpin' at the Woodside* (track 2, 1:42) with Rollins on *St. Thomas* (track 18, 0:17). Except for the du-wah effect that starts off Young's solo (which is discussed below), both men keep to a single conception of timbre. Young's tone is veiled and silky smooth, Rollins's hollow and dry, with a bright, hard edge. Both avoid vibrato.

In contrast to these focused approaches, the sounds of Coleman Hawkins and John Coltrane are expansive. Hawkins begins *The Man I Love* with soft, smooth, vibratoless held tones, in a line descending beneath Eddie Heywood's piano solo during the *a* sections of the first chorus (track 10, 0:09). Hawkins picks up this thread at the end of Oscar Pettiford's string bass solo, becoming louder (now he is the soloist) and introducing a pronounced, steady, rapidly undulating vibrato, but just as gently as in the beginning (track 10, 2:35). In the second of his two choruses (the last chorus of the piece), his tone grows grittier. He adds vocalized growls to intensify it further, and finally his vibrato slows and widens on held notes. The whole creates the effect of a straightforward progression from detachment to passion.

Coltrane's expansiveness on *Ascension* is, by contrast, a multilayered presentation (track 4, 1:00). In the lowest register he blares out harsh notes; some are multiphonics, that is, smeared conglomerates of sound in which two or three high overtones become so pronounced that they take on their own identity as separate pitches rather than just being hidden contributors to the tone color of the low-pitched fundamental note. In the highest register, above what was originally the normal range of the instrument, he produces a strained, squeezed, nasal sound. (John Gilmore's solo on Sun Ra's *Outer Nothingness* offers in its squeals and honks a less subtle version of these two areas of timbre; track 19, 1:42.) In between the extreme registers, Coltrane has the same steely sound that was characteristic of his earlier years (including Davis's recording of *'Round Midnight* from 1956; track 5, 2:55). During his solo on *Ascension*, Coltrane moves among the three areas of timbre, the manipulation of which thus becomes, in itself, a structural element in the improvisation, just as it is for Hawkins.

The most blatant differences in jazz trumpet playing have to do with whether the bell of the instrument is open (unmuted), closed (muted), or opening and closing (for du-wah, wa-wa, and other onomatopoeic effects). Each of these possibilities defines a realm within the world of jazz sound. To some extent, the distinctions involve dynamics (loudness), especially for those types of mute that most tightly block the bell. But despite the misleading term *mute*, the main reason for placing such a device into or against the end of the instrument is not to diminish volume but to alter timbre.

Within the realm of open sounds, the selections in this book range from the polite to the rough-hewn. In beginning with a comparison between George Mitchell, the cornetist on Morton's *Black Bottom Stomp*, and Louis Armstrong, the trumpeter on *Hotter than That*, mild apologies are in order for the imprecise but convenient classification of these instrumental cousins together under the heading "trumpet." Sometimes in jazz discography no one can distinguish which of the two instruments is being played. In this case the distinctions are clear and classic: Mitchell's cornet is pretty and gentle (track 15, 0:22 and 0:51), Armstrong's trumpet bright and buzzing (track 1, 0:00 and 2:33). Both men shape their tones carefully, neatly clipping notes off at the corners.

Other open sounds involve trumpet alone. On three brief solos in *Manteca*, Dizzy Gillespie's tone varies with the speed of his ideas. At the most relaxed pace, during the bridge of the first chorus, he produces a sumptuous, romantic sound, with a broad, warm vibrato on held notes (track 8, 1:10). Earlier, during the phrases that conclude the opening ostinato, and later, during the bridge of the second chorus, he works his way from a medium pace, with a comparatively dry tone, up to a fast pace, in which— unlike Mitchell and Armstrong's work—the quick succession of notes have little tonal quality apart from their attack, which overwhelms the rest of the sound (track 8, 0:18 and 2:19).

Miles Davis produces a small, pinched sound in a brief but dramatic moment of open playing during the fanfare that serves as a transition to the tenor saxophone solo on *'Round Midnight* (chap. 2, ex. 2; track 5, 2:42). Like Coltrane on *Ascension*, Davis strains to produce sound in what is, for him, a high register, and he uses that strain for expressive effect, to convey tense emotion. By contrast, Armstrong in his succession of high notes is sending a different message: "Look how effortless this is—for me."

All these open tones seem smooth by comparison with Kid Thomas Valentine's trumpeting on *Panama* (track 20, beginning). His playing is the furthest removed from a classical conception. White hot and burred, it spreads out, like a sound from an overdriven amplifier. On top of this, he and Emanuel Paul, his saxophonist, use a heavy, fast vibrato, continuing a tradition among some New Orleans musicians; this same style of vibrato can also be heard much earlier, in the playing of Leon Roppolo on *Tin Roof Blues*. Just as clarity of pitch is an underappreciated component of the Basie orchestra's rhythmic precision, so a purposefully dense tone, together with purposefully imprecise pitch (resulting from an extreme approach to vibrato, from blue notes, and from an "out-of-tune" conception), contributes to the essential sludge in the sound of bands like Valentine's.

Sound
172

Jazz trumpeters and other jazz brass use mutes of diverse origin, ranging from found objects (perhaps a beer glass or felt beret) to formal accessories (a cup mute, straight mute, and harmon mute, among others). Types may sometimes blend: the toilet plunger, once available only as plumbing hardware, became the plunger mute (handle not included). The assortment of available materials and geometric shapes, and the varying degrees to which mutes cover the bell, allow a vast spectrum of tone colors.

While greatly supplementing the possibilities for trumpet sounds, some mutes paradoxically depersonalize the sound for the simple reason that the creation of timbre shifts from the person (through the use of diaphragm, throat, teeth, and lips) to the device (the mute). Thus on Basie's *Jumpin' at the Woodside* and Parker's *Koko*, the mute evens out timbral differences between the trumpeting of Buck Clayton and Dizzy Gillespie. For both, the sound is crisp, nasal, and distant. Distinctions seem to have more to do with vibrato than with timbre. Clayton uses a vibrato that begins subtly, widens on held notes during the bridge of his chorus, and then widens further in his last phrase (track 2, 1:11). Gillespie, together and in alternation with Parker, plays at such great speed that he eliminates any need for, or possibility of, vibrato (track 17, 0:06).

On the other hand, muted playing can be just as personal as any open sound. The most extreme example would be Miles Davis's use of the stemless harmon mute, heard on *'Round Midnight*, as recorded in 1956 (track 5, beginning). Two years earlier Davis had discovered this sound—which is breathy, intimate, buzzing, squeezed, metallic, hard-edged—and he made it his own. Whenever anyone else uses a stemless harmon mute to play a sensitive melody, that trumpeter evokes Davis's name.

The third area of trumpet sounds involves mutes manipulated by the left hand. This motion makes possible the conversational and animal sounds that contribute to the notion of jazz telling a story and that sometimes are a source of humor.

Beginning at the second 12-bar blues chorus of Duke Ellington's *Ko-Ko* and continuing through three choruses, the brass instruments play du-wah chords, a series of alternately closed and open plunger-muted notes (ex. 56). For two choruses these serve as an accompaniment to Tricky Sam Nanton's ya-ya solo, in which, as mentioned earlier (chap. 5, ex. 43), the plunger instantaneously opens and closes note by note.

Example 56. A du-wah figure in Ellington's *Ko-Ko* (from the score prepared by Dave Berger). Track 6, 0:32.

Sound
173

There is also a du-wah effect in the startling break that begins Lester Young's tenor saxophone solo on *Jumpin' at the Woodside* (track 2, 1:42). Although it is impossible to mute the bell of a saxophone unless all or nearly all the keys are closed (because a portion of the unmuted sound would escape through any keys that remain open), Young came up with two fingerings for the same pitch, which forced the sound out of different areas of the instrument, thus changing its timbre. His personalized adaptation of a trumpeter's du wah was convincing and widely copied.

In between the distinct open and closed positions of a du wah on alternate notes, and the instantaneous movement of a ya-ya on each note, are any number of gradual openings and closings under the general label wa-wa. Within the selections chosen for this book, these can be heard in several guises. Cornetist Mitchell uses wa-wa effects for his solo during the stop-time chorus in *Black Bottom Stomp* (just before the banjo solo; track 15, 1:50). Trumpeter Clayton, before pushing the mute in tightly, begins his solo on *Jumpin' at the Woodside* with a thrice-repeated figure that introduces a wa-wa on a sighing blue note (track 2, 1:09). Trumpeter Valentine, when he reenters after the piano solo on *Panama*, intensifies his already extraordinary tone with eccentric, plunger-muted wa-wa whinnying and neighing (track 20, 2:24). And Armstrong, while leaving the bell of his trumpet open on *Hotter than That*, sings seven different shades of wa-wa during the final phrases of his solo: wah-oh, wah-oo-lough, um-wow, dah-dah-wow, dah-dum-wah, um-mough, hmaf mwow (see ex. 55; this portion of the solo starts at track 1, 1:54).

As a supplement to the search for new personal sounds, the realm of possibilities has been expanded using instruments new to (or at least unfamiliar in) jazz. The introduction to this area includes two points of view. The first perspective traces the history of a single new instrument: it summarizes circumstances leading up to the emergence of the electric bass guitar as a replacement for string bass in big bands, as a member of the rhythm section in fusion bands, and as a vehicle for soloing. For several decades the story of the electric bass guitar was largely one of survival, not of any high-minded search for new timbres; eventually, however, as the fusion style matured in the 1970s, the electric bass guitar revealed its advantage. The second perspective studies a single performance, Sun Ra's *Outer Nothingness*, to show how unusual combinations of instruments and timbres might be used, in and of themselves, to create jazz.

Oral history and surviving photographs document the importance of the string bass in early New Orleans jazz, but in the mid-1920s, when big bands began to develop and to record, a tuba was likely to be heard beneath brass and reed sections. In less than a decade the stringed instrument returned to favor, as musicians discovered its capacity to produce the perfect underpinning for swing, owing to its smooth, rounded notes. In this context the tuba was rendered obsolete, but its replacement by string bass led to a problem of balance, because the latter instrument had little carrying power and thus could be easily overwhelmed by the volume of the other members of a big band. In the studio, skillful engineers made adjustments to compensate for the instrument's softness, as on Ellington's *Ko-Ko*, a recording that captures string bassist Jimmy Blanton's sound wonderfully (track 6). Other recordings, though, testify to the challenge that the instrument faced in providing a foundation for the sound of a big band. Listen, for example, to how Walter Page's contribution is reduced to a distant, indistinct boom on Basie's *Jumpin' at the Woodside* (track 2); the rhythm is marvelous, the pitch unclear.

By the 1950s a system of amplification had developed, involving a "pickup" (or microphone) attached to the instrument, and during the 1960s the fidelity of bass amplifiers improved dramatically, resulting in a sound that was true to the bass's quietly roaring tone and permanently suitable to what came to be known as "acoustic" ensembles (bands using no more than a modest amount of amplification or perhaps none at all). But the amplified double bass was no match for other instruments in those big bands that participated in the spiraling decibel inflation that swept through popular music from the mid-1960s on. With a microphone on every reed and brass, perhaps even on every element of the drum set, the string bass player had little choice but to discard his deep-toned instrument for the thinner-toned but louder and more cutting electric bass guitar. The new instrumental combination, an electric bass guitar beneath reed and brass sections, playing in a context oriented toward swing rhythm, became one of the crassest sounds in jazz.

Much more satisfying developments took place in jazz fusion groups. Following the lead of innovative electric guitarists in rock, jazz guitarists finally broke away from their adherence to the monochromatic timbre that had been prevalent in jazz since the late 1930s, when Charlie Christian made his mark. After numerous efforts to find a louder replacement for the piano, an array of new timbres—generally soothing rather than cutting— emerged on amplified electric, electronic, and synthesized keyboards. The synthesizer bass could speak as loudly as necessary, and when functioning in place of stringed instruments, it provided a sound that could roar in the true bass range, as Joe Zawinul's synthesizer does in the introduction to Weather Report's *Birdland* (track 21). Brazilian percussionists—above all Airto Moreira and Nana Vasconcelos—brought an array of new percussion sounds into fusion styles. And, in complete contrast to its incongruous blend with swing-oriented big bands, the electric bass guitar fit in with these timbres perfectly, better in fact than did the string bass. Thus, Jaco Pastorius's incisive twang on *Birdland* provides a foil for the rounded timbres of the keyboard, tenor saxophone, and voices (track 21, 1:45 and 1:59).[6]

Sound
176

A different set of problems faced the string bass when it began to be used as a solo instrument, generally from the 1940s on. (Isolated examples of string bass solos survive on recordings from earlier years.) The challenge of projecting over a band could be overcome by having the other instruments remain silent, except perhaps for a subdued drum accompaniment and some delicate chording from a piano or a guitar. Projecting pitches in a manner that clearly differentiated the contour of a fast moving melody was not a simple matter, however, for in doing so the instrumentalist was fighting against the very smoothness that had made the plucked string bass perfect for swing. In this respect distinctions between studio and live performances are often marked. There are many fine recordings of string bass solos. On Coleman Hawkins's *The Man I Love*, for example, the tunefulness of Oscar Pettiford's nimble improvisation comes through clearly; listeners may note that the producer, Bob Thiele, astutely turned up the volume of the microphone just before Pettiford began his solo (track 10, 1:53). But in live performance, the vagaries of amplification, acoustics, and background noise tend to overwhelm a soloist. Even in an era of high-fidelity public address systems, one still routinely encounters string bass solos in which fast-moving melody is reduced to a succession of booms and the solo becomes more of a visual than an aural experience.

The electric bass guitar provided an alternative. Following the lead of Pastorius and Stanley Clarke in the 1970s, many electric bass guitarists developed cutting timbres that enabled the instrument to outdo its predecessor as a vehicle for virtuosic soloing, at least from the perspective of clarity. The centerpiece of Ornette Coleman's *Honeymooners*, Al Mac-Dowell's virtuosic electric bass guitar solo, demonstrates this advantage well: every note pops out clearly (track 3). The point is underscored further during the last segment of the piece (about half a minute before the end). Coleman's group Prime Time includes two electric bass guitarists, and here, when McDowell and Chris Walker improvise at once, their dancing and stuttering lines remain easy to distinguish (track 12, 3:47).[7]

Other sorts of experiments with the instrumentarium took place in free jazz, as part of its questioning of the status quo. In some cases these experiments became the focus of a performance: if the piece were to have no familiar rhythm or form, then the manipulation of sound could serve as a structural principle, organizing the players' improvised interaction. Sun Ra's *Outer Nothingness* is such a piece.

The instruments are not unusual per se. All of them have ties to European orchestral and band music, including the bass marimba (even though it is of African origin). In addition, half belong to the long-standing central instrumentarium of jazz: tenor sax, trombone, bass trombone (heard in brass sections of some big bands), string bass, cymbals, and drums. By the time of this recording (1965), the flute had joined the central collection, and another instrument, the bass clarinet, was in the process of being added, owing to the innovations of Eric Dolphy earlier in the decade. Thus on *Outer Nothingness*, only the timpani and bass marimba stood completely outside the inner circle of instruments. Even these two were not completely foreign, the timpani having popped up from time to time as a novelty instrument in jazz, most regularly in dixieland recordings made by Vic Berton with cornetist Red Nichols in New York in the late 1920s, and the marimba having appeared occasionally (in its regular size rather than as a bass), notably on titles recorded by Red Norvo in 1933.

But the whole sound of *Outer Nothingness* is much more than the sum of the names of its instruments. Whether individually central to jazz or not, all these instruments participate through collective improvisation in the creation of uncommon combinations of timbre. The following graph of instrumental activity (ex. 57) serves as a visual aid toward hearing how they are deployed.

It should be noted that this graph, however accurately it may identify instrumental combinations on *Outer Nothingness*, does not match the general list of musicians and instrumentation on the album cover. For example, no trumpet can be heard. In the thick passages it is not easy to separate trombone from bass trombone, and squealing reed instruments obscure the sound of a piccolo. Perhaps the piccolo is imagined, in an attempt to account for what Sun Ra's veteran sideman Marshall Allen might be doing on this piece; nor is it clear what baritone saxophonist and percussionist Pat Patrick is doing. Owing to the leader's casual and otherworldly attitude toward documentation, the graph might be quite accurate.

Example 57. A graph of instrumental activity in Sun Ra's *Outer Nothingness*. Track 19.

```
         (time)  0:  15  30  45  1:  15  30  45  2:  15  30  45
piccolo
flute                            x
tenor sax                   xxx       ??????????????????xxxxxxxxxxxxxxxxxxxx
bass clarinet        xxxxxxx       ??????????????          xxxxxxxx
trombone             xxx                    xxxxxxxxxxxx      xxxx
bass trombone        xxxxxxx                            xxxxxxxx
string bass                          xxx
bass marimba                 xxxxxxxxxxxxxxxxxxxxxxxxxxxx
cymbals                         xxxxxxxxxxxxxxxxxxxxxx
drums             xxxxxxxxxxxxxxxxxxxxxxxxxxxxxxxxxxxxxxxxxxxxxxxxx
timpani      xxx

         (time)  3:  15  30  45  4:  15  30  45  5:  15  30  45
piccolo                               xxxxxx
flute                    x
tenor sax            x                xxxxxx
bass clarinet  xxxxxxxxxxx  x
trombone             x                xxxxxx
bass trombone        x                xxxxxx
string bass             xxxx  xxxxxxx
bass marimba         xxxxxx             xxxxxxxxxxxxxxxxxxx
cymbals                  x             xxxxxxxxxxx
drums                    x             xxxxxxxxxxx
timpani
```

On top of this, a mystery surrounds the solo that begins one minute into the piece. What instrument is playing, a tenor saxophone or a bass clarinet? Is it played by John Gilmore? By comparison with other passages on the album, which is entitled *The Heliocentric Worlds of Sun Ra, Volume 1: "Other Worlds,"* the timbre of the mystery instrument sounds more like that of Robert Cummings's bass clarinet than of Gilmore's tenor sax; but as the line continues for another minute and leads into a duet with the trombone, there are honking sounds that could have been made only on a tenor sax, not on a bass clarinet. Ekkehard Jost, who published a transcription of the solo, offers this opinion: "I just listened to the example some 20 times and I am now quite sure that this is a tenor solo (though sounding somehow strange) played by John Gilmore, judging on the basis of what I know his playing is like on other pieces."[8] Is Gilmore making an otherworldly sound on the sax, in keeping with the spirit of outer nothingness? Is he doubling instruments, beginning the solo on bass clarinet and then at some unidentifiable point picking up his tenor sax? The answer is not clear.

So much for disclaimers and mysteries. For the purpose at hand, the graph of *Outer Nothingness* serves to illustrate the main point of this piece: the improvised exploration of extreme timbres, especially low-pitched timbres. Timpani set the stage. When twelve seconds later Sun Ra lays down his timpani mallets to turn to the bass marimba, the baton passes to the drummer, who maintains a low, indistinctly pitched boom; to begin, the drummer avoids the cymbals, and thus the area of ringing and sizzling higher sounds remains empty. The rumbling starts to build toward one of the most unforgettable sounds in jazz: the boom of drums and bass marimba set against the blare of four kinds of low-pitched wind instrument: bass trombone, trombone, bass clarinet, and tenor sax, the last honking away in its lowest register. A reprise of this sound recurs twice, just before Cummings's bass clarinet solo and again, briefly, after it, in what seems to be an ending to roughly the first half of the piece. These remarkable moments frame less dense passages that concentrate in other ways on extreme registers, with a concomitant juxtaposition of fresh tone colors. Gilmore's tenor saxophone solo methodically ascends into the highest register of the instrument, with squeals and multiphonic outbursts providing the greatest possible timbral contrast to the continued rumblings of the bass marimba and drums; here the drummer uses cymbals as well, supporting Gilmore's thinner, higher-pitched area of sound.

The opposition of boom and blare presents itself from yet another angle during Cummings's solo. On the heels of the blare, and in comparison to the raspy middle and high registers of the bass clarinet, Cummings's low notes sound gentle; but when the bass marimba reenters with its exceedingly mellow tone colors, that same low range of the bass clarinet seems, reinterpreted in retrospect, edgy.

The last few minutes of *Outer Nothingness* are not as extraordinary as the first. Perhaps inconsistency is a price that must be paid in what is ostensibly a completely spontaneous collective improvisation devoted to the exploration of unusual sounds.

At the start of the book, it was suggested that whereas *Trumpet No End* is awash in exciting music and a great piece to listen to passively it might also reward a thoughtful, precise, analytical hearing. Now, looking back on concepts of jazz rhythm, forms, arrangement, composition, improvisation, fidelity, tuning, instrumentation, timbre, and vibrato, some of the paths to that type of active listening should be apparent, and the introductory paragraphs may have taken on a greater meaning. By way of conclusion, this same *Trumpet No End* serves as a model for tracing an additional and more difficult path along the road to appreciating the sound of jazz.

In the first stage of a tour through instruments, timbres, and their sometime companion, vibrato, forty or fifty readily identifiable sounds emerged, a few closely related to one another, but most entirely distinctive. After this examination of Louis Armstrong's voice, four renowned tenor saxophonists, an array of trumpeters, amplified instruments in fusion, and tone colors in Sun Ra's Arkestra, a listener might continue examining the most distinctive voices, instruments, and bands in jazz. Then, having grasped several hundred sounds made by the creators of jazz, he or she might plunge deeper and begin separating out several thousand sounds—not just the most original ones, but the modified and imitative ones as well.

As the title indicates, *Trumpet No End* is a showcase for Ellington's trumpeters. How does each trumpeter sound? How many soloists are there? Who are they? Depending upon a listener's level of expertise, these questions might be addressed in several ways.

One approach would be to focus purely on sound, not on identification. In the following description, the sounds are tagged by formal markers (positions within the succession of four 32-bar *aaba* choruses) to fasten down the location of each one. These signposts are convenient but not absolutely necessary. Even those who find counting bars, bridges, and choruses difficult, or just tedious, should nonetheless be able to delineate various trumpet sounds and their order of appearance. This is the most democratic approach to the fine details of jazz sound, an approach open to anyone willing to make the effort to listen closely (track 7).

> Introduction (track 7, beginning). A clarinet solo break finishes off the introduction.
>
> First chorus (0:08). Trumpet solos begin. The first soloist plays with a bright tone, centering his melody in a fairly high range. He uses a slight trace of vibrato in finishing off occasional held notes, but then, while reiterating a note during the bridge, he introduces a dramatically expressive form of vibrato: a shake.[9]
>
> Second chorus, first 16 bars (0:42). Without notice the sound

changes. A second soloist takes over, playing with a burred tone in a lower range. That burr remains as the melody ascends, with the subtle consequence that this tone is not quite as bright as the first, even when the two men are working in the same moderately high range.

Second chorus, bars 1–6 of the bridge (1:00). The sound changes abruptly to wa-wa trumpeting.

Second chorus, bars 7–8 of the bridge (1:06). After a brief pause, there is a phrase of bright, open trumpeting.

Second chorus, last *a* section (1:08). The bright, open sound overlaps with a return of the burred tone.

Third chorus, first *a* section (1:17). After 4 bars of ensemble work, the soloing resumes. The trumpeter's middle-register sound is hard to distinguish from the burred tone that preceded it. Perhaps it is slightly hollower and smoother.

Third chorus, remaining 24 bars (1:25). The second *a* section begins with another brief passage of ensemble playing; then a high-pitched solo gets under way. At first the trumpeter's articulation and vibrato are corny, the one too stiff, the other too slow and wide; these faults drop away, but as a whole the soloist's delivery lacks confidence. Interrupting this melody at the bridge are three off-beat ensemble punctuations, each one topped by a clean, stratospheric note that casts the idea of high-note trumpeting in a new light.

Fourth chorus, first 16 bars (1:50). Again without a pause one high-note trumpeter gives way to another. This new soloist is more secure in the top range, and his articulation and vibrato seem idiomatic rather than corny.

Fourth chorus, first half of the bridge (2:07). The solos overlap slightly, with a high-pitched upward glissando running over into a phrase of wa-wa trumpeting.

Fourth chorus, second half of the bridge (2:12), to the end of the piece. After a pause, an identical wa-wa sound resumes. This carries on unbroken into a spectacular display of open-toned, high-note trumpeting. The soloist shakes notes in his last phrase, evidently to soften the effect of his whistling tone.

This sort of listening may reveal a great amount of detail in *Trumpet No End*, but at the same time it can be frustrating, because it is so self-contained, so devoid of historical, stylistic, or personal interest. There seem to be at least four soloists, perhaps as many as six or seven. Who are

they? To approach the performance with this question in mind, some expertise, and probably some outside help, are needed.

A modestly experienced listener who is reasonably familiar with Ellington's music might make one or two deductions based on the list of musicians in the recording notes. At the time, Ellington had a five-piece trumpet section comprising Cat Anderson, Francis Williams, Taft Jordan, Shorty Baker, and Ray Nance. Anderson was the foremost high-note specialist in the history of Ellington's band, and in 1946 no one else in jazz could have approached his artistry. Clearly he is hitting the stratospheric accents in the third chorus, singing out the melody of *Blue Skies* (the original title of the recording) in his moderately high range to start the fourth, and then topping off the ending by popping out those unbelievable notes. Ray Nance was the wa-wa specialist in the band, having assumed a role handed down from Bubber Miley, who created the style in the mid-1920s, via Cootie Williams, who reigned from 1929 through 1940. From this famous fact about Ellington's band, one might reason that Nance is a good bet for the wa-wa solos on *Trumpet No End*.

An experienced listener who is well versed in Ellington might make further deductions. Francis Williams was also a high-note specialist, though not as special as Anderson. That must be Williams getting under way at bar 10 of the third chorus. Taft Jordan earlier in his career had followed closely in Armstrong's footsteps. The playing in the first chorus is as bright as Armstrong's on *Hotter than That*, though fuller, because individual notes are sustained rather than clipped off. If this is Jordan, then that similar but burred tone in the second chorus belongs to Shorty Baker. One would need to spend some time becoming familiar with additional recordings by Jordan and Baker to make sure that the initial order of soloing is not reversed.

Even after all this close attention, some uncertainty remains in the identifications, and some moments are unaccounted for. At this point, it becomes useful to look at a published discography. In *Duke Ellington's Story on Records: 1946* Luciano Massagli, Liborio Pusateri, and Giovanni M. Volanté identify the soloists as follows:

Chorus 1. Taft Jordan (32 bars).

Chorus 2. Shorty Baker (16). Ray Nance (8). Baker (8).

Chorus 3. [ensemble (4)]. Francis Williams (28).

Chorus 4. Cat Anderson (16). Nance (4). Anderson (to the end).[10]

Listen again with these individuals in mind. In addition to these details of personal sound, there are, interestingly, moments in the piece when the trumpeters put aside individuality in order to connect material. Hence Williams begins his solo with a sound indistinguishable from Baker's, and Anderson begins his final solo with wa-wa playing indistinguishable from Nance's. Such examples serve as a reminder that it is important not to get so wrapped up in the search for individual identity that similarities— shared personal sounds, if you will—become overlooked. Sometimes in jazz, particularly in big-band jazz, a leader or an arranger wants a sideman to conform to a set role rather than to deliver a personal sound.

By this point the reader should be completely saturated with listening to *Trumpet No End*, perhaps hoping that it *will* end. But for anyone who enjoys mystery stories and good music, this game of identification can become a lifelong passion that never grows tiresome. The potential for independent thought is enhanced, and the potential for stumbling increased, by the fact that jazz discography is riddled with instances of misindentified, tentatively identified, and unidentified musicians; and even when the musicians are known (as on *Trumpet No End*), the presence of two or more similarly minded players can raise questions about the identity of a soloist. Although the game can be great fun, the historiography of jazz suggests, sadly, that the game is likely to lead to intense and sometimes ugly arguments, probably because the stakes—one's ability to hear—seem so high. For better or worse, this is the most popular listening challenge in jazz: to hear a sound and to *know* the musician's name. Any listener who begins to gain a hold on this skill will be well on the way toward understanding jazz. The danger of this approach is that it can overwhelm other modes of listening. Readers of this book should by now need no reminder that there are other worthwhile paths into this multifaceted music.

8 Epilogue: an Introduction to Style

The design of *What to Listen For in Jazz* has been inspired in great part out of frustration with a stylistic approach. In a little over five decades, from around 1913 to the late 1960s, the term *jazz* came to embrace a collection of five broad stylistic categories: New Orleans jazz, swing, bop, free jazz, and fusion. Because these styles emerged in a rapid and unordered fashion, countless examples of stylistically eclectic pieces resulted. These so-called problematic performances—which, though possibly lacking in stylistic uniformity, may have displayed perfect coherence otherwise—arose as the result of many factors: the fluid transitions from one style to the next; the emergence of substyles; collaborations among musicians of varied stylistic leanings; syntheses of jazz with diverse popular (and more recently classical) styles; and retrospective unifications of styles initially thought to be irreconcilable.

This considerable stylistic interchange may leave the uncomfortable impression that there are simply too many exceptions to prove any given rule. Consequently I have found considerable satisfaction in using concepts and procedures rather than styles as a means of understanding unified trends in jazz history. In this sense *What to Listen For in Jazz* has suggested an alternative approach to listening, independent of style. Among the selections used here, nothing exemplifies this idea better than Charles Mingus's *Fables of Faubus*, a piece that reconciles stylistic eclecticism with internal coherence and that was intentionally selected to demonstrate this consolidated diversity (track 13). Within the theme one hears all of the following: a two-beat and a walking bass line, constant swinging cymbal patterns and a more jagged hard-bop drumming style, unison lines for saxophones and trombone, collective improvisation between saxophone and trombone, double-time hard-bop improvisation, moaning blue notes, the controlled use of dynamics, and a unique variation on popular song form. Following the lengthy statement of the theme, Mingus introduces another element, a tenor saxophone solo in the gospel-influenced soul-jazz style.

If style were to be treated in the same depth as the other subjects in this book, it would require an entire volume, not merely a chapter. It would also require a repertory broader than the twenty-one music selections (which seem to serve well enough to demonstrate concepts and procedures and which therefore suggest, by their very brevity, the usefulness of a unified approach to listening organized along conceptual and procedural lines). Such a volume would have to trace the historical development of personal styles; of instrumental families—the saxophone, guitar, voice, and so on; of instrumental groupings—solos (particularly unaccompanied piano), duos, small groups, big bands; and of the five principal jazz styles, their substyles, their transitional cousins, and their syntheses with external styles.

It might be argued that any listener who wishes to approach this subject in a concretely musical way must begin by learning about concepts and procedures—rhythmic, formal, improvisational, and so forth—before trying to tie up elements of these procedures into assorted stylistic packages. In this sense, this final chapter of *What to Listen For in Jazz* could be thought of as a prelude to further study, a whistle-stop tour through general styles, with observations on stylistic traditions for individual instruments but with no explanation of the complex interworkings of general and instrumental styles with personal styles. The outline follows the usual model in jazz history: it amalgamates evolution (new styles emerge from old styles), expansion (old styles remain viable instead of disappearing), and synthesis (jazz styles merge with other genres).

New Orleans Jazz

New Orleans jazz is somewhat of an imagined style, preserved in oral history more so than in musical documents. From the start of the century or early in its second decade—no one seems to know quite when—a local African-American and Creole folk music emerged in the New Orleans area

out of blues, ragtime, brass band music, vaudeville, and American popular song. By most accounts this jazz style failed to survive intact as new ones evolved (thereby contradicting the principle of stylistic expansion noted above), no doubt because of the lack of recordings, which have proven
crucial to the dissemination and preservation of jazz. There is general (though not unanimous) agreement that the first full-blown jazz recordings date only from 1917; they featured, by the way, a white New Orleans group called the Original Dixieland Jazz Band. (Those who do not agree may, for example, find jazz in James Reese Europe's recordings of 1914.) In any event, the best African-American jazz musicians did not begin to record until the 1920s, and by this decade, their music was already moving toward the swing style.

Whatever the historical truth may be, three selections incorporate musical elements that have presumably been a part of New Orleans jazz since it began: the New Orleans Rhythm Kings' *Tin Roof Blues* (1923) (track 16), Jelly Roll Morton's *Black Bottom Stomp* (1926) (track 15), and Louis Armstrong's *Hotter than That* (1927) (track 1). These three pieces involve a front line of trumpet (or cornet), clarinet, and trombone. The collective interweaving of this instrumental combination, with the cornet (or trumpet) presenting the melody, is the single most fundamental sound in the style.[1]

Among these front-line instruments, the trombone, by its very construction, lends itself to the production of glissandos (continuous slides through pitches). Renowned for their bluesy and comical effect, they occur on all three pieces. In fact, the device is commonplace enough in New Orleans jazz to have acquired its own stylistic label, "tailgate" trombone playing.[2]

The faster-paced pieces, by Morton and Armstrong, demonstrate stop-time and a copious use of breaks. Also worth noting on *Black Bottom Stomp* is a percussive technique known as "slap bass," heard in the string bass accompaniment to the banjo solo (track 15, 2:10). These rhythmic devices were exploited most often in New Orleans jazz and early big-band jazz, though they continued to be used on a limited basis in other contexts as well.

Formal patterns include a 12-bar blues progression (*Tin Roof Blues*), a highly original multithematic composition (*Black Bottom Stomp*), and a 32-bar song form extended in a way that recalls multithematic form (*Hotter than That*). The interest in multithematic form would prove to be a significant element in separating the New Orleans tradition from swing and bop.

The makeup of the New Orleans rhythm section was more flexible than it was to become in swing and bop. Both *Tin Roof Blues* and *Hotter than*

That depend upon chordal instruments only: respectively, the piano alone, and the piano, banjo, and guitar; there is no bass (except for the piano bass) or drums. *Black Bottom Stomp* includes string bass and drums, together with piano and banjo.

If these features exemplify some highlights of New Orleans jazz style as it is thought to have been originally, others demonstrate a style in transition. This is most evident on *Hotter than That*, in which the major changes are a move away from collective playing toward soloists, from duple rhythm toward swing rhythm, and from ragtime and march forms toward popular song forms.

On recordings made in 1920, and probably earlier in live performance, jazz instrumentalists accompanied African-American female blues and vaudeville singers. From this perspective New Orleans jazz may be understood not only as a principal style within jazz but also as a component of classic blues and hence a substyle of blues.

New Orleans jazz stands in an imprecise and largely overlapping relationship to traditional jazz and dixieland jazz. The label *dixieland* was originally reserved for white groups, but by the 1940s (and perhaps earlier) the racial distinction seemed to lessen.

Chicago jazz, a transitional substyle that began in the late 1920s, was more fervent than the relaxed New Orleans approach and further along the road toward swing rhythm and solo improvisation. The irreverent spokesman for this style, Eddie Condon, was uncomfortable with the label, because many of his colleagues were not Chicagoans and because the hybrid style is comfortably neither dixieland (which it is sometimes called) nor swing; as a pithy commentary on this, he entitled his autobiography *We Called It Music* (1947).

A later relation was the New Orleans revival, which began in the late 1930s and which is represented in this book by Kid Thomas Valentine's *Panama*. With the revival, the repertory of New Orleans jazz expanded to include a greater proportion of spirituals and hymns. One of these, *When the Saints Go Marching In*, became the anthem of the style. There was also a renewed interest in an instrumentation that included the clarinet, banjo, and tuba, a portion of the zealous revivalist audience having wrongly determined that the saxophone, guitar, and string bass were heretical. Ironically, while critical attention focused on this alleged return to a traditional instrumentation, the musicians of the New Orleans revival were using swing rhythm and swing improvisatory formulas. Like any jazz style, the revival did not function in a vacuum.

In many quarters the New Orleans revival has been as demandingly professional as any other style of jazz, but it has also had worldwide implications for amateur performers, who can do a credible job of capturing this most transparent of jazz styles (witness the proliferation of dixieland jazz festivals). "Trad," a commercialized substyle of the revival, flourished in Britain in the 1950s and 1960s. Most significantly, the revival has existed, and still flourishes, as a folk music in the peculiar and extraordinarily rich environment of semiprofessional performance in New Orleans itself, where Valentine lived. Qualities of *Panama* (track 20)—the jazzing of a ragtime piece, the oom-pah rhythm, the collectively improvising front line, the tenor saxophonist's use of a heavy vibrato, Valentine's outrageous muted trumpet work, the group's rancid conception of intonation—may represent not merely a revival but a continuous tradition dating back to the origins of New Orleans jazz.

Most independent of the New Orleans style are the unaccompanied piano styles known as boogie woogie and stride. Although boogie woogie does not have direct ties to New Orleans, it originated nearby, in the Mississippi Delta region. A blues style, it set a repeated ostinato in the left hand against syncopated, percussive, rifflike melodies in the right.

By contrast the stride style originated in New York City as a technically advanced outgrowth of midwestern ragtime. More flexible than boogie woogie and more focused on the interpretation of multithematic and popular song forms than on blues progressions, it can be as percussive as boogie woogie or delicately sensitive. Its defining characteristic is a motion in the left hand, striding between an interval in the bass range and a chord in the middle range. (The interval is often a tenth, that is, a note struck with the pinky finger and a second note, an octave and a third higher, struck with the thumb; when the thumb strikes first, stride pianists call the effect backward tenths.) Earl Hines utilizes stride piano techniques in portions of *Sweet Sue* (track 11).

Swing

The second grand style is swing. (Swing style and swing rhythm are not the same thing, although they interact to a great extent.) One convenient historical demarcation of the style is the song *It Don't Mean a Thing If It Ain't Got That Swing,* which Duke Ellington's orchestra recorded in 1932. The title testifies that a public notion of swing was in the air; more important, the performance demonstrates that the musicians knew what they were talking about. Another point of demarcation, probably the most frequently cited one, was the phenomenal success of Benny Goodman's big band, beginning with its tour to California in 1935. Although the swing style was already well in place, that year is said to mark the beginning of the swing era, which extends into the 1940s and marks a merger of jazz and popular music.

Several of the qualities associated with this style developed during the 1920s. They include swing rhythm, an emphasis on solo rather than on collective improvisation, a reliance on popular song forms and blues, with multithematic forms falling by the wayside, and an increase in the size of bands. As was pointed out in the chapter on arrangement, when as many as eight or ten instrumentalists engage in collective improvisation, the result can scarcely be as accessible as the charming and gently controlled chaos of an improvising New Orleans front line. Hence there arose the practical decisions to group instruments into sections (brass, reeds, or rhythm) and to provide the brass and reeds with fixed parts, whether simple riffs or elaborately composed lines.

As the 1930s brought further developments, the swing style crystallized. Having been shown the way by individual masters (above all, Louis Armstrong), whole groups learned how to swing; this elusive, intangible rhythmic phenomenon found its simplest and most explicit expression in a pattern repeatedly tapped out on a cymbal or brushed across the head of a snare drum. More broadly, there was a general smoothening of the beat. As mentioned in the catalog of rhythmic devices (chap. 2), it is difficult to make generalizations about a distinct movement from two-beat jazz to four-beat jazz, because polyrhythmic levels of beat are routine in jazz. A two-beat, a four-beat, and perhaps even an eight-beat may all be a part of the same piece (*Black Bottom Stomp* is an example). Nonetheless, by focusing on bass lines, it is possible to hear, from New Orleans jazz into swing, a major trend away from a rocking oom-pah on beats 1 and 3 toward a smooth and continuous sounding of all 4 beats.

This leveling out was heightened by changes in the central instrumentarium: the normal bass sound became the plucked string bass rather than the tuba, bass saxophone, piano bass, and bowed or slapped string bass. In support of this trend, the banjo was replaced by the less percussive guitar, whose insistent but gentle chording was often more felt than heard. Also a duplication of roles within the rhythm section was increasingly avoided. Pianists endeavored not to get in the way of the bass, because clarity in the bass line enhanced the sensation of swing rhythm and harmony was becoming more complex, making spontaneous agreement between piano bass and string (or brass) bass less likely. As these changes occurred, the rhythm section was generally regularized into a quartet of piano, guitar, string bass, and drums. Independent of these developments in the rhythm section, the piano remained the king of unaccompanied instruments, and the tenor saxophone and clarinet rivaled the trumpet as the king of instruments in ensemble playing.

All these qualities come together on Count Basie's *Jumpin' at the Woodside* (track 2). A rhythmically smooth and swinging swing-style performance recorded at the height of the swing era (1938), it features popular song form, big-band riffs, the standard (indeed the definitive) rhythm section, and an improvisation on saxophone from Lester Young that outshines the contribution on trumpet from his colleague, Buck Clayton. Five other selections in this book also represent swing—in various combinations of the stylistic elements detailed above. Ellington's *Ko-Ko* and *Trumpet No End* (tracks 6 and 7) additionally exemplify the use of intricate compositions and arrangements in big-band swing and a keen sensitivity to orchestral and individual tone color. Billie Holiday's *Georgia on My Mind* (track 12), Coleman Hawkins's quartet recording of *The Man I Love* (track 10), and Earl Hines's unaccompanied piano version of *Sweet Sue* (track 11) represent the small-group and solo swing traditions that flourished side by side with big-band swing. Hines's solo, recorded in 1965, serves as a reminder that, like any jazz style, swing remained vital years after its newness had worn away and that a particular performance can be extraordinarily new, original, and creative, even if its general stylistic characteristics are established and familiar.

It might be mentioned here—just to confuse the essential stylistic distinction—that the signature of New Orleans jazz has stayed alive in swing: collective improvisation among brass and reed instruments is a normal device in small-group swing. Following a string of solos, it adds a sense of climax to the end of a piece.[3]

Symphonic jazz, a style of the 1920s, proved to be a precursor of swing in that it contributed greatly to the development of arranged big-band jazz. From it emerged the long-lived principles of varying an instrumental arrangement of a popular song from chorus to chorus (instead of just playing the melody over and over again) and of organizing these variations along sectional lines. The symphonic jazz orchestra included a string section, as well as brass, reed, and rhythm sections. In a grand misassessment of the future of jazz, symphonic jazz was presented as a sophisticated replacement for "primitive" New Orleans jazz. As it turned out, the greatest achievement of the style would fall outside of jazz, in the symphonic compositions of George Gershwin.

Jump is a substyle of small-group swing of the late 1930s and 1940s. Its prominent features are tuneful saxophone solos, simple riffs, clever lyrics about African-American life, and perky swing rhythms. Although Basie's *Jumpin' at the Woodside* involves a big band and lacks lyrics, its title and musical character are related to this substyle. Jump played a part in the development of rhythm and blues and thereby had a strong secondary influence on rock and roll.

Bop

When bop (equally well known as bebop) began to be recorded in 1944–45 and thereby to reach a substantial audience, critics received it as a revolution in jazz style. Insofar as it was an improvised music played by small groups, it contrasted with those areas of big-band swing that had stifled opportunities for improvisation; insofar as it demanded an unprecedented instrumental virtuosity, it contrasted with the comparatively simpler demands of the revived New Orleans style, which flourished concurrently.

This book is not the place to recount stories of battles within the jazz community; nor is there room for an account of the personalities of Charlie Parker, Dizzy Gillespie, and Thelonious Monk, whose behavior and appearance added extra-musical elements to the sense of revolution. What matters here is a stylistic perspective from a later time, which corrected the first impression. It became apparent that bop resulted not from a revolution but from a gradual, almost seamless transformation of small-combo swing, from which it developed in New York City between the end of the 1930s and the mid-1940s.

Indeed, swing and bop share more musical conventions than any other pair of the five principal styles. After listening to Hawkins's *The Man I Love* and Parker's *Koko*, a newcomer to jazz might well decide that the performances are nearly identical stylistically: each concentrates on improvised soloing based on an *aaba* popular song form, and each features a conception of the rhythm section founded on walking bass lines and swing rhythms in the drums. If anything, Hawkins's recording goes furthest in this direction: whereas *Koko* has an introduction and ending that incorporate a composed line played in unison by Parker and Gillespie, *The Man I Love* has nothing but improvised solos.

An experienced listener will recognize immediately that Hawkins's piece is swing and Parker's, bop. The crucial difference is a rhythmic jaggedness that characterized bop, not swing. On *Koko* (track 17) this jaggedness is evident in the melodic lines, in the rhythms of the drum set, and to a lesser extent in the sparse chords; it contrasts with the deliberate and steady line of the string bass, which in bop carries the principal responsibility for timekeeping.

Hand in hand with this jaggedness comes a lessening of tunefulness. With the diminishing influence of Armstrong, the first genius of jazz improvisation, and the overwhelming influence of Parker's new approach, the saxophone finally overshadowed the trumpet; the contrast between these two improvisers was representative of a far-reaching contrast between the two general styles. In bop, melodic themes take on the same abstract and difficult character as melodic improvisations. Trumpeters and trombonists play with the speed and facility of saxophonists. When soloing, pianists and guitarists imitate the saxophone as well. Riffs are generally avoided as a reaction against their overuse in swing.

Bop also brought other adjustments in the central instrumentarium. The clarinet lost its significance and has been used by only a few exponents of the style. Within the rhythm section the trend toward avoidance of duplication continued. Because the piano supplies sparse chording, the rich jazz tradition of thick, two-handed, unaccompanied piano playing has not melded comfortably into bop. And the majority of rhythm sections have just one chordal instrument—usually piano rather than guitar— because spontaneous agreement between two chordal instruments becomes ever more difficult as harmonic complexity increases.

For some musicians in either swing or bop these stylistic differences created an impassable barrier. But the two styles are in so many ways compatible that many musicians commonly combine them into a hybrid style that might be called swing-bop, by analogy with jazz-rock. (Swing-bop is not an accepted term in the field.) One can find examples of every type of stylistically integrated combination: a swing soloist with a bop rhythm section, and vice versa; a succession of soloists alternating between swing and bop; or swing and bop players mingling within the rhythm section. Among the music selections, a modest example of this integrated style would be the first improvised chorus of Thelonious Monk's *Misterioso*, with Milt Jackson improvising a double-time bop blues solo over Monk's jagged but rifflike accompaniment (track 14, 0:44).

Cool jazz, which got under way in New York in the late 1940s, involves a moderation of musical qualities. Apart from a shared interest in quieter dynamics, however, musicians have varied considerably in their opinion of what is to be moderated. Some of the possibilities include: fleet, quietly differentiated chromaticism or, by contrast, a return to tuneful lyricism; gentle rhythmic attacks, with the drummer favoring brushes over sticks; slower tempos; a balance between improvisation and composition; veiled timbres; the avoidance of vibrato; and the detachment of the audience from the performers, by means of an appeal to classical concert traditions.

West Coast jazz was a direct continuation of cool jazz, centered in the Los Angeles area from the early 1950s on. The pool of musicians has included several fine soloists, but in general the quality of improvising has been somewhat poorer than in other areas of bop. Consequently, and ironically for a style founded on solo improvisation, the main interest of West Coast jazz lies in arranged passages.

In the mid-1950s, the emergence of hard bop marked what was essentially a return to bop. Sonny Rollins's *St. Thomas* is representative from the third solo drum chorus on—that is, from the point where the rhythm changes from calypso to swing (track 18, 3:02). Whether this portion of the piece is labeled bop or hard bop really does not matter. New to hard bop was a repertory of themes with catchier tunes than in the parent style. Again *St. Thomas* provides a fine example. In thus reinstating tunefulness, hard bop tightened the relationship to small-combo swing.

In turn, soul jazz (also known as funk or funky jazz) grew out of hard bop from the late 1950s on. Its most distinctive element is the translation of the improvised, formulaic declamatory style of African-American gospel preachers into an improvised musical style. This approach for improvisation works best on—but is by no means restricted to—tenor saxophone, piano, and Hammond electric organ. To a lesser extent soul jazz also borrows chord progressions characteristic of African-American gospel music and the $\frac{6}{8}$ (or $\frac{12}{8}$) rhythmic feeling associated with some of the songs.

This summary of hard bop and its derivative, soul jazz, should be the place for *'Round Midnight*, because it was recorded by one of the quintessential hard-bop groups, Miles Davis's quintet of 1955–57 (track 5). Yet that breathtakingly beautiful performance scarcely fits into the stylistic model. The idea of hard bop embraces pretty ballads, as do many other styles and substyles, but the central qualities of hard bop are not particularly helpful in accounting for the sound and the continuity of the ballad tradition in jazz. *'Round Midnight* thus serves as a reminder that through all of these stylistic bends and curves, jazz musicians have wanted to play tunes that are lovely, romantic, introspective, sentimental, haunting, and passionate.

Latin influences in jazz date back to the origins of the music. However, not until 1947, when Dizzy Gillespie began experimenting with Afro-Cuban jazz (a derivative of bop), did Latin elements gain enough substance to be called a style. Developments in the 1950s and 1960s included Rollins's blend of hard bop and West Indian calypso music, as in the first portion of *St. Thomas* (track 18); and bossa nova, a blend of cool jazz with a greatly subdued version of Brazilian samba rhythm. It may seem ridiculous to group Cuban, West Indian, and Brazilian influences under Latin jazz, especially since St. Thomas is not a part of Latin culture, the Virgin Islands having been founded by Denmark. Yet musically their union is not ridiculous. These styles jointly represent Latin jazz, because they share the essential rhythmic element of that music: even eighth notes (that is to say, duple subdivisions of the beat) grouped asymmetrically into patterns that recur either every measure or every two measures. In any event, Rollins's West Indian influences belong to his personal style rather than to any large-scale jazz style, and nearly all Latin jazz is probably of Afro-Latin origin both musically and culturally.

There are many examples of the merger of Latin jazz with bop and its substyles, but in the definitive example of Afro-Cuban jazz, Gillespie's *Manteca* (track 8), the most prominent non-Latin elements lean toward swing rather than toward bop: the use of a big band; the tunefulness of the melody at the bridge of each chorus; and Big Nick Nicholas's swing-style solo on tenor saxophone.

Third-stream jazz began in 1957 as an effort to unite two divergent streams, contemporary Western art music and bop, but it has had little lasting influence outside the academy.

Modal jazz began in Miles Davis's sextets and orchestras of 1958–59 and involved a slowing of harmonic rhythm. To obtain this quality, Davis moved away from the standard repertories of New Orleans jazz, swing, and bop. Modal jazz thus became an independent transitional style, leading logically to the last two principal jazz styles: free jazz, in which harmony is not merely slowed but sometimes disappears altogether; and fusion, in which harmony may take on the static character of some aspects of rock and soul music. As a consequence of the slowing of harmonic rhythm, motivic improvisation became a more common means for generating musical ideas.[4] Herbie Hancock's composition *Maiden Voyage* (track 9) is representative of modal jazz.

In the mid-1960s another quintet under Davis's leadership took a tentative step toward free jazz by playing a derivative of hard bop that came to be known as "time, no changes." The style involves improvising to a fast, steady, undifferentiated bop beat (the time) that is largely independent of meter. This beat functions in support of highly chromatic lines (no changes, which is to say, no chord progression). The themes associated with this improvisatory style are not as vague as the improvisations in that they incorporate standard metric schemes, ethereal melodies, and highly challenging, weakly functional chord progressions.

Bop, cool jazz, West Coast jazz, hard bop, soul jazz, ballad playing, Afro-Cuban jazz, jazz calypso, bossa nova, modal jazz, and time, no changes—all of these have been collected under the umbrella of the bop revival, which began in the mid-1970s, after the advent of free jazz and fusion. The bop revival reaches a much wider audience than the New Orleans revival, which remains somewhat a specialized area in jazz. Indeed, since the mid-1980s bop has rivaled fusion in popularity.

During this revival veteran bop musicians (notably, the tenor saxophonist Dexter Gordon) returned to prominence, but a more interesting development has been the emergence of a younger generation of jazz musicians who wish to re-create one or more of the various styles that flourished from the mid-1940s to the mid-1960s. Such widespread interest in tradition indicates that jazz, a music that had previously encouraged an ever-restless search for the new, may be moving away from original performance toward historical performance.

Free Jazz

The truly revolutionary style was not bop but free jazz, which got under way in the late 1950s. More than any other style, free jazz is a conglomerate mortared by a common attitude rather than by a sound. Its proponents aim to challenge any element of jazz that has become conventional. Few musicians, however, have challenged everything all at once. Instead, aspects of tradition and explorations of the new combine in every possible way—hence the diversity of free jazz.

One of the areas explored is tone color, altered by means of a vastly expanded instrumentarium, including many non-Western instruments. Hand in hand with this comes an emphasis on extreme registers of both new and standard jazz instruments to produce squeals, honks, vocalized tones, multiphonics, splats, and other unconventional sounds. Strangely, there have been few significant free-jazz singers; the reason is unclear.

Another area is repertory, including its implications for harmony and intonation. Blues progressions and popular song forms, the bedrock of swing and bop, have been abandoned in favor of ad hoc forms or of truly spontaneous improvisation, independent of form. As with instrumentation, but in a less precise way, non-Western influences have entered via this route. Directly tied to the transformation of repertory is a rejection of the assumption that improvisations ought to be based on the chord progression of a theme. In free jazz there may still be a theme, but the improvisations can be independent of it. In many free-jazz performances, harmony simply becomes unimportant. And once freed from conventional harmony, themes and improvisations can be oriented toward a non-Western conception of intonation.

In the early years of free jazz, drums and bass still functioned mainly as timekeepers, but by the mid-1960s, when John Coltrane recorded *Ascension* (track 4) and Sun Ra recorded *Outer Nothingness* (track 19), some areas of the style broke drastically with tradition by abandoning the beat. In place of rhythm came an irregular ebb and flow of energy and intensity. Directly tied to this transformation of jazz was a redefinition of traditional divisions between soloists and accompanists, so that drums and bass might sometimes participate roughly on an equal footing with other instruments in stating themes and improvising collectively. Another consequence has been the expanded possibility for individual playing, which may be a forum for any instrument rather than solely for piano or guitar.

By the 1980s, perhaps even earlier, the label free jazz had fallen into disfavor, but the style remains active under the banners of "avant-garde jazz" and "improvised music," the latter being an astonishingly preemptive label, given the strength of improvisation in other areas of jazz. With the abandonment of conventional harmony and rhythm, avant-garde jazz moved much closer to contemporary Western art music, with which there has been considerable interchange. This time the union has seemed less strained than in the days of symphonic jazz and third-stream jazz.

There have also emerged, though not as independent styles, stylistic labels for the practice of incorporating techniques of free jazz into a more traditional approach, the most clever of them being "freebop" and "avant gutbucket." Freebop brings a more expansive stylistic vocabulary into bop improvisation without abandoning the foundations of the style. Avant gutbucket incorporates aspects of New Orleans jazz and swing into free jazz.[5] These and less cleverly named stylistic syntheses indicate that free jazz is in the process of being assimilated into the mainstream of jazz. Such an assimilation had seemed inconceivable in 1960.

Fusion

The last of the five main styles is fusion, which originated in the late
1960s and marked a new merger of jazz and popular music (after the swing era). In striking contrast to free jazz, the style emphasizes a return to fundamental dance rhythms and a clear tunefulness, while also introducing a broader spectrum of amplified sound into jazz. Fusion was initially known as jazz-rock, but after it became clear that other types of synthesis were also in operation, the less restrictive label was applied. Whereas fusion owes a debt to rock in the area of electric, electronic, and synthesized instruments, its rhythmic qualities are more affiliated with contemporary African-American popular music: soul, funk, disco, and rap. Weather Report's *Birdland* (track 21) illustrates all these central qualities.

The many mergers encompassed by this single term require some clarification. "Soul jazz," also known as "funk" or "funky jazz," is not the same as "jazz-soul" and "jazz-funk" fusion. Soul jazz, a substyle of hard bop, is based on swing rhythm, whereas substyles of fusion involve duple rhythmic patterns. It is also worth noting that the latest substyle, jazz-rap fusion, has been given a somewhat misleading name, "new jazz swing." As jazz expands, so do meanings of the word *swing*.

From the mid-1970s on, improvisation, which had been an indispensable element in the early years of fusion, has come into balance with, and has sometimes been overshadowed by, composition and arrangement. This increased attention to fixed roles is tied to a widespread interest in achieving a polished studio sound on fusion recordings. The interest in composition has also generated a number of sophisticated new ad hoc forms, also exemplified by *Birdland*.

In the instrumentarium of fusion, the electric guitar has become as important as the saxophone. The electric bass guitar or a synthesized bass has replaced the string bass in most bands. The electric piano and assorted electronic and synthesized keyboard instruments rival the piano. Synthesizers have also been adapted to the configurations and hand coordination characteristic of other instruments (guitar synthesizer, drum machine, saxophone synthesizer), with a consequent breakdown of distinctions among instruments: a device that utilizes a keyboard might sound the same as a device that looks like a guitar. Ensembles often incorporate Latin percussion, because the duple rhythmic patterns of the Latin jazz tradition meld smoothly into the rhythms of fusion. As in free jazz, there have been few significant singers in fusion. Here the reason seems clear: the absence of lyrics—that is, the use of instrumental sound instead of words—alone distinguishes jazz-rock from rock, jazz-funk from funk, jazz-disco from disco, jazz-rap from rap.

At first free jazz and fusion seemed impossibly at odds, but as in all of the earlier styles, jazz musicians found ways to break down barriers. Cutting across both free jazz and fusion is "world music," which since the 1970s has produced a gentle and earnest freshness by presenting diverse ethnic sounds within the context of these leading jazz styles. The two styles have also been linked through the combination of free collective improvisation and a steady beat, as in Ornette Coleman's *Honeymooners*, which offers a playfully distorted vision of African-American funky dance music.

Here ends the tour through jazz styles and their manifestation on recordings associated with this book. Published predictions about the future of jazz style have had the unfortunate tendency of seeming very wrong and very silly once the future becomes the past. It might nonetheless be worthwhile to note where the music has been heading in recent years and what this might mean for the future—ideas that the jazz community always debates.

No musician of overwhelming originality and creativity has dominated and redirected jazz since John Coltrane died in 1967. No new principal style has dominated and redirected jazz since fusion first appeared in 1968. As a substitute for the personality and variety that these leaders and principal styles had fostered from the 1900s into the 1970s, jazz musicians have instead sought to find personality and variety in neoclassic, panstylistic performances of the 1980s and 1990s. Eddie Condon's complaint that his style was neither dixieland nor swing but an amalgamation of the two (*We Called It Music*) can now, fifty years later, be applied across the whole genre (I call it jazz). To be sure, numerous musicians have continued to be devoted to a single style, as was common in the past, and individual styles remain viable and identifiable. But the shift toward eclecticism has been dramatic, and it indicates a trend mentioned above: jazz seems to be moving away from original performance toward historical performance.

Some people find this assessment exceedingly depressing. Certainly I would have given anything to be just a few years older so that I might have gotten into a club to hear the (last?) great jazz musician, Coltrane. And I would be pleased if the music ceased to focus on syntheses and instead resumed its evolution and expansion. But in my lifetime I have had no shortage of ecstatic experiences of live jazz. And there are ten lifetimes of listening in the legacy of recorded jazz: over three hundred thousand tracks, a body of documented sound that is the envy of anyone who prefers a musical genre that existed before the age of recording. I cannot imagine being glum about jazz.

What to Listen For in Jazz is a direct consequence of that enthusiasm. The book is based on the premise that the more carefully one listens to jazz and the better one understands how jazz works, the more jazz reveals its depth and beauty. If any reader and listener is now closer to discovering that depth and beauty, I will have achieved my aim.

Appendix 1
Notating Chords

This appendix presents two systems of chordal notation introduced in chapter 3, fake-book notation and roman
numeral notation. Neither is standardized. For each system
the symbols detailed below represent only one of several ways
of notating each type of chord. Those interested in learning
other versions of these systems should consult Steven Strunk's
"Harmony" and Robert Witmer's "Notation," in *The New
Grove Dictionary of Jazz*, edited by Barry Kernfeld (London:
Macmillan, 1988). Strunk and Witmer together provide a
comprehensive study of possibilities for notating chords in
jazz.

Fake-Book Notation

This system of notating chords has been used for
many years in publications of sheet music of popular songs.
Typically, a melody and a piano accompaniment are
presented, with the melody doubled in the right hand.
Beneath the melody are lyrics; above it there may be two sets
of chord symbols: tablature, showing where to place the
fingers to make guitar chords, and fake-book chord symbols.

Fake books have also been around for many years, but
unlike sheet music these have often been published without
copyright permission, although since the 1980s many more
legitimate fake books have appeared. A fake book presents a
collection of "lead sheets," each offering a shorthand version
of a popular or jazz tune. Typically there will be a melody,
chord symbols, and perhaps lyrics. On rare occasion cues for
inner parts and bass lines appear as well.

In either case the chord symbols are notoriously
inaccurate. For example, some of the chord symbols in the
sheet music of Ray Noble's *Cherokee* disagree not only with

general notions of the tune's harmonies but also with the piano harmonies published directly below them (see chap. 3 for further details). This is a common occurrence. Fake books have had such a reputation for inaccuracy that a now-popular bootleg collection began to circulate in the 1970s in the Boston area under the title *The Real Book*, because its chord symbols gave a generally reasonable indication of the harmonies that a jazz musician really would play, though there are inaccuracies in that version, too.

The unreliability of fake-book notation is in part due to the carelessness of those who have selected the chord symbols or a desire to present a simplified version for amateur performance, but it also is a reflection of the flexibility of jazz and pop performance, and in that sense it is necessary and proper. Rather than pinpointing a precise sound, a fake-book symbol indicates an area of harmony. It names the elements of a chord, with the understandings that:

1. Not every element may actually be played. As an example, one seldom plays all seven notes of a 13th chord: root, 3rd, 5th, 7th, 9th, 11th, 13th. Often the 9th and 11th are omitted; perhaps the 5th is also left out.

2. A chord does not usually sound in strict order from root to top, as the notation suggests. Instead it might be spread out or clumped together in some more pleasing order (or "voicing") appropriate to the style. Typically in swing and bop, a 13th chord would be voiced thus, from bottom to top: root - 7th - 10th (i.e., 3rd) - 13th.

3. There is no indication of where a chord should fall within the range of an instrument.

4. The system describes each chord as if it were in root position, even though it might be inverted (that is, with the root somewhere other than at the bottom), at the discretion of the performer. Exceptionally, an additional symbol appears when a particular inversion might be essential to the sound of a composition. In his description of *Maiden Voyage* (see chap. 6), Herbie Hancock explains: "You start with a 7th chord with the 11th on the bottom." The chord in question, an A minor seventh chord with a D in the bass, could be labeled thus: Ami^7/D.

5. Rhythm is indicated only in the sense that a given symbol is in operation until the next chord appears. Whatever the span of that chord may be, the symbol does not indicate exactly where the chord sounds within it.

So much for disclaimers. The beauty of fake-book notation is that it provides a quick and unchanging way of identifying an area of harmony. There is no need to recalculate a symbol when its context changes, as in the roman numeral system.

Example 58, a table of fake-book chord symbols, describes triads, seventh

Example 58. A table of fake-book chord symbols.

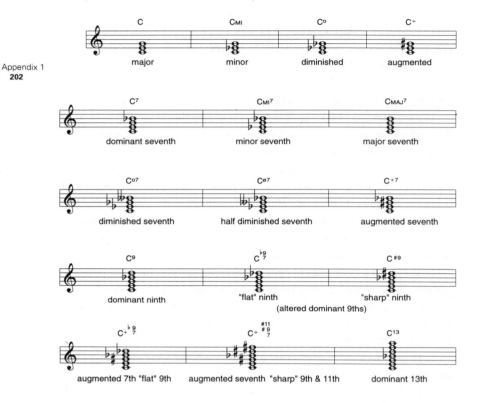

chords, and extended and altered chords. Each symbol is identified by name and also spelled out in music notation.

Roman Numeral Notation

Fake-book notation exists for the sake of performance, not of analysis. Without any cues from the notation, an instrumentalist is expected to learn how to realize individual chords in a way that brings harmonic continuity to the whole.

In a listener's guide that aims at description and analysis, fake-book notation has its uses. But rather than always dealing with chords as if they exist in isolation, such a guide also needs to explain how harmonies relate to one another. To meet this goal, harmonic analyses borrow the roman numeral notational system from classical music. Like fake-book notation, roman numeral notation describes the elements of a given chord, but it also takes an additional step, placing each chord within the context of a harmonic progression in a key.

The type of roman numeral notational system described here has the same limitations as fake-book notation. Among them, this system, as adapted to jazz, ignores inversions. Consequently, the arabic numeral appendages used take on a meaning that sometimes differs from the meaning they have in classical music. In the analysis of a classical composition, arabic numerals may indicate extensions of triads, but they may also specify inversions, which are essential to the success of classical part writing; in analyzing jazz, arabic numerals define extensions but not inversions. Each chord is described as if it were in root position.

The system is designed to allow immediate transposition from one key to another, and in that sense it exists in the abstract, independent of key. For the purpose of introduction and explanation, however, it is best to begin by defining a key. This may be done concisely with a note name (using uppercase for major keys and lowercase for minor) and a colon. "B♭:" means the key of B♭ major; "g:" means the key of g minor.

From there, roman numerals define triads built on each step of the diatonic scale in that key. Flat or sharp signs may modify the roman numerals to define triads built on nondiatonic pitches. In the version of roman numeral notation used in this book, an uppercase roman numeral identifies a major triad; the addition of "♯5" alters that to an augmented triad. A lowercase roman numeral identifies a minor or a diminished triad; context usually determines which of the two is intended, unless the symbol "♭5" or "o" appears, specifying a diminished triad (though the sign "o" may also identify a diminished seventh chord). The following example illustrates diatonic and nondiatonic triads.

Example 59. A table of triads in roman numeral notation.

The arabic numerals 7, 9, 11, and 13 indicate chordal extensions, details of which are identified by continuing to stack up diatonic pitches in the given key. A sharp or flat sign moves a chordal extension one half step away from the scale of the given key, thus creating a frequently encountered distinction between equivalent fake-book and roman numeral symbols. In a simple blues built on dominant seventh chords, the fake-book symbols would all look the same (ex. 60a). By contrast, the equivalent roman numeral symbols do not all look the same, because the system should specify that the sevenths of the tonic and subdominant be lowered a half step away from the scale of the given key (ex. 60b). No such alteration is needed for the dominant (V^7), because that is automatically a dominant seventh chord.

Example 60a. A blues progression in fake-book notation.

C^7 | | | | F^7 | | C^7 | | G^7 | | C^7 | |

Example 60b. The same blues progression in roman numeral notation.

$I^{\flat 7}$ | | | | $IV^{\flat 7}$ | | $I^{\flat 7}$ | | V^7 | | $I^{\flat 7}$ | |

In thirteenth chords, the seventh is usually present. Because inversions are not indicated, the number 6 may be used to define a triad extended to include a sixth, without the seventh present. (In the classical system, it would indicate a chord in first inversion.) Finally, the notation "add 9" indicates an extended chord that does not include a seventh.

Example 61 presents a sampling of extended and altered chords used in this book, particularly in the description of the harmonic progressions of *Manteca* (in the segment based on George Gershwin's *I Got Rhythm*) and Parker's *Koko* (in the body of the piece, based on Ray Noble's *Cherokee*).

Example 61. A table of extended and altered chords in roman numeral notation.

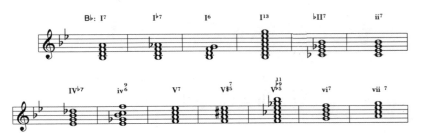

Secondary relationships may be indicated by a slash. For example, the symbols "C: ii^7/V, V^7/V, V^7" indicate a progression from ii^7 (A minor seventh) in the key of V (the dominant, G), to V^7 (D dominant seventh) in the key of V (G), to V^7 (G dominant seventh) in the principal key (C). Writing out these secondary relationships sometimes gets messy, and it is better to redefine the key, as in the bridge to *Cherokee*, which moves downward sequentially in whole tones from ♭II (C♭) to V (F) and then returns to the main key, B♭:

Example 62. Roman numeral notation for secondary chordal relationships in the sequential chord progression in the bridge to Ray Noble's *Cherokee*.

C♭: V^{13}		I^9	A: V^9/V
V^{13}		I I^7	I^6
G: V^{13}		I^9	F: V^9/V
V^{13}		B♭:ii^7	V$^9_{\sharp5}$

Example 24 (chap. 3) spells out these chords, as published in the sheet music to *Cherokee*. Although the passage in C♭ major functions harmonically as ♭II (not ♯I, which would be a strange analytical symbol), for the sake of clarity the notes are written enharmonically, in B major.

Appendix 2
Discography

The following appendix gives details of the twenty-one central music selections and identifies the issue from which they were dubbed in the making of the compact disc that accompanies this book. The selections are listed alphabetically, by leader. There are, in addition, references to other recordings mentioned in the text.

Louis Armstrong and his Hot Five. *Hotter than That.*

Louis Armstrong (trumpet and vocal), Kid Ory (trombone), Johnny Dodds (clarinet), Lil Armstrong (piano), Johnny St. Cyr (banjo), Lonnie Johnson (guitar).

Recorded in Chicago, Dec. 13, 1927.

CD: *The Hot Fives and Hot Sevens*, volume 3, Columbia Jazz Masterpieces CD 44422 (USA).

Count Basie and his orchestra. *Jumpin' at the Woodside.*

Buck Clayton, Harry "Sweets" Edison, Ed Lewis (trumpets), Dicky Wells, Dan Minor, Benny Morton (trombones), Earle Warren, Jack Washington (alto saxes), Lester Young (tenor sax), Herschel Evans (tenor sax, clarinet), Count Basie (piano), Freddie Green (guitar), Walter Page (string bass), Jo Jones (drums).

Recorded in New York, Aug. 22, 1938.

CD: *The Complete Decca Recordings*, GRP Decca Jazz GRD 3–611 (USA). This CD includes Basie's *Doggin' Around*, mentioned in chapter 2. *Doggin' Around* is also on many other anthologies, including both editions of *The Smithsonian Collection of Classic Jazz.*

Ornette Coleman and Prime Time. *Honeymooners.*

Ornette Coleman (alto sax), Charlee Ellerbee and Bern Nix (electric guitar), Al MacDowell and Chris Walker (electric

bass guitar), Denardo Coleman and Calvin Weston (drums and percussion).
Recorded in New York, Sept. 1987.
CD: *Virgin Beauty*, Portrait RK 44301 (USA).

John Coltrane orchestra. *Ascension* (Edition II) (excerpt only).
Freddie Hubbard, Dewey Johnson (trumpets), Marion Brown, John
Tchicai (alto saxes), John Coltrane, Pharoah Sanders, Archie Shepp (tenor
saxes), McCoy Tyner (piano), Art Davis, Jimmy Garrison (string bass), Elvin
Jones (drums).
Recorded in Englewood Cliffs, N.J., June 28, 1965.
CD: *The Major Works of John Coltrane*, GRP Impulse! GRD 2–113 (USA).
The full version of edition II was also issued earlier on the CD *Ascension*, MCA
Impulse! AS 95 (USA) and Impulse! 254618 (Europe).

Miles Davis Quintet. *'Round Midnight*.
Miles Davis (trumpet), John Coltrane (tenor saxophone), Red Garland
(piano), Paul Chambers (string bass), Philly Joe Jones (drums).
Recorded in New York, Sept. 10, 1956.
CD: *'Round about Midnight*, Columbia Jazz Masterpieces CK 40610 (USA).
CD issues of the other versions mentioned in chapter 4 include: Thelonius
Monk's *'Round Midnight* of 1947, on *Genius of Modern Music*, volume 1, Blue
Note CDP 7–81510–2 (USA); Davis's *'Round about Midnight* of 1953, on *Collec-
tor's Items*, Original Jazz Classics OJCCD 071–2 (USA); Davis's *'Round Mid-
night* of 1956 for the Prestige label, on *Miles Davis and the Modern Jazz
Giants*, Original Jazz Classics OJCCD 347–2 (USA).
The first recording of *'Round Midnight*, by Cootie Williams's big band
(1944), circulated for a time on the LP *Big Band Bounce and Boogie: Echoes of
Harlem*, Affinity AFS 1031 (UK).
Dizzy Gillespie's *I Can't Get Started* of 1945 is widely available on editions
of *The Smithsonian Collection of Classic Jazz*, but many readers will have
difficulty finding his versions of *'Round about Midnight* done in the mid-1940s,
unless new issues appear. Sources used for the three versions discussed in
chapter 4 are on the LP *The Development of an American Artist*, Smithsonian
R004-P2–13455 (USA), which includes one of two takes of *'Round about Midnight* recorded by Gillespie's six-piece group on February 6, 1946; the LP
Paris, Prestige PR 7818 (USA), with a version by his big band recorded in Paris
on February 26, 1948; and a version in concert in Pasadena on July 19, 1948,
on the LP *Dizzy Gillespie and His Big Band*, GNP LP 23 (USA).

Duke Ellington and his orchestra. *Ko-Ko* (take 2).

Wallace Jones, Cootie Williams (trumpets), Rex Stewart (cornet), Tricky Sam Nanton, Lawrence Brown (trombones), Juan Tizol (valve trombone), Johnny Hodges, Otto Hardwick (alto saxes), Barney Bigard (tenor sax, clarinet), Ben Webster (tenor sax), Harry Carney (baritone sax), Duke Ellington (piano), Fred Guy (guitar), Jimmy Blanton (string bass), Sonny Greer (drums).

Recorded in New York, Mar. 6, 1940.

CD: *The Smithsonian Collection of Classic Jazz*, RD 033 / A5 19477 (USA).

Take 1 of *Ko-Ko*, discussed in chapter 5, appears on the LP *Jazz Tribune No. 33: The Indispensible Duke Ellington, Volumes 5/6, 1940*, RCA NL 89750 (Europe) and RCA PM 45352 (France).

Duke Ellington and his orchestra. *Trumpet No End*.

Cat Anderson, Harold "Shorty" Baker, Taft Jordan, Ray Nance, Francis Williams (trumpets), Lawrence Brown, Wilbur De Paris, Claude Jones (trombones), Johnny Hodges, Russell Procope (alto saxes), Jimmy Hamilton (tenor sax, clarinet), Al Sears (tenor sax), Harry Carney (baritone sax), Duke Ellington (piano), Fred Guy (guitar), Oscar Pettiford (string bass), Sonny Greer (drums), Mary Lou Williams (arranger).

Recorded in New York, Nov. 25, 1946.

LP: *The Golden Duke*, Prestige 24029 (USA).

Dizzy Gillespie and his orchestra. *Manteca*.

Dizzy Gillespie (trumpet, vocal), Benny Bailey, Dave Burns, Elmon Wright, Lammar Wright, Jr. (trumpets), Ted Kelly, Bill Shepherd (trombones), John Brown, Howard Johnson (alto saxes), Big Nick Nicholas, Joe Gayles (tenor saxes), Cecil Payne (baritone sax), John Lewis (piano), Al McKibbon (string bass), Kenny Clarke (drums), Chano Pozo (conga), Gil Fuller (arranger).

Recorded in New York, Dec. 30, 1947.

CD: (anthology of various artists) *The Bebop Revolution*, Bluebird 2177–2 RB (USA).

Herbie Hancock quintet. *Maiden Voyage* (excerpt only).

Freddie Hubbard (trumpet), George Coleman (tenor saxophone), Herbie Hancock (piano), Ron Carter (string bass), Tony Williams (drums).

Recorded in Englewood Cliffs, N.J., March 17, 1965.

CD: *Maiden Voyage*, Blue Note CDP 7–46339–2 (USA). All CDs, tapes, and LPs of this title include the full version of *Maiden Voyage*.

Coleman Hawkins quartet. *The Man I Love*.

Coleman Hawkins (tenor sax), Eddie Heywood (piano), Oscar Pettiford (string bass), Shelly Manne (drums).

Recorded in New York, Dec. 23, 1943.

CD: *Classic Tenors: Coleman Hawkins and Lester Young*, CBS Special Products AK 38446 (USA).

Earl Hines. *Sweet Sue.*

Earl Hines (piano).

Recorded in Paris, May 27, 1965.

CD: *Special Earl Hines, 1928–1965*, Jazz Time 253.624–2 (France).

Billie Holiday. *Georgia on My Mind* (take 1).

Shad Collins (trumpet), Eddie Barefield, Leslie Johnakins (alto saxes), Lester Young (tenor sax), Eddie Heywood (piano), John Collins (guitar), Ted Sturgis (string bass), Kenny Clarke (drums), Billie Holiday (vocal).

Recorded in New York, Mar. 21, 1941.

CD: *The Quintessential Billie Holiday, Volume 9, 1940–1942*, Columbia Jazz Masterpieces CK 47031 (USA).

Take 2 of *Georgia on My Mind* is on the LP *God Bless the Child*, Columbia KG 30782 (USA) and CBS M 66267 (UK). *Fine and Mellow* comes from the television show *The Sound of Jazz*, available on video (8 December 1957, Kay Jazz KJ-013). It has circulated as a recording on numerous independent and bootleg labels. Listeners should be warned that the so-called sound track, issued on the CBS, Columbia, Coronet, Fontana, and Philips labels, contains entirely different performances from a rehearsal on December 5, 1957, and Lester Young's contribution to this rehearsal version of *Fine and Mellow* bears no relation to the solo mentioned in chapter 5.

Charles Mingus and his Jazz Workshop. *Fables of Faubus* (theme only).

Jimmy Knepper (trombone), Shafi Hadi, John Handy (alto saxes), Booker Ervin (tenor sax), Horace Parlan (piano), Charles Mingus (bass), Dannie Richmond (drums).

Recorded in New York, May 5, 1959.

CD: *Mingus Ah Um*, Columbia Jazz Masterpieces CK 40648 (USA).

All CDs, tapes, and LPs entitled *Mingus Ah Um* include the full version of *Fables of Faubus*.

Thelonious Monk quartet. *Misterioso* (take 1).

Thelonious Monk (piano), John Simmons (string bass), Shadow Wilson (drums), Milt Jackson (vibraphone).

Recorded in New York, July 2, 1948.

CD: *Milt Jackson*, Blue Note CDP 7–81509–2 (USA).

Jelly Roll Morton's Red Hot Peppers. *Black Bottom Stomp.*

George Mitchell (cornet), Kid Ory (trombone), Omer Simeon (clarinet),

Jelly Roll Morton (piano), Johnny St. Cyr (banjo), John Lindsay (string bass), Andrew Hilaire (drums).

Recorded in Chicago, Sept. 15, 1926.

CD: *Original Versions of the Music Inspiring Jelly's Last Jam and Other Morton Classics*, Bluebird 66103–2 (USA).

Black Bottom Stomp appears together with band versions of *Grandpa's Spells*, *The Pearls*, and *Kansas City Stomps*, all mentioned in chapter 4, on many CD collections, including *Jelly Roll Morton*, volume 1, JSP CD 321 (UK); *The Jelly Roll Morton Centennial: His Complete Victor Recordings*, Bluebird 2361–2 RB (USA) and Bluebird ND 82361 (Europe), and *The Pearls*, Bluebird 6588–2 RB (USA) and RCA ND 86588 (Europe). CD issues of Morton's unaccompanied piano versions of these three titles include *Jelly Roll Morton*, Milestone CD 47018–2 (USA) and *The Pianist and Composer*, Smithsonian RD 043 (USA).

New Orleans Rhythm Kings. *Tin Roof Blues* (take B).

Paul Mares (trumpet), George Brunies (trombone), Leon Roppolo (clarinet), Mel Stitzel (piano), [Ben Pollack (drums); no drums audible on this title].

Recorded in Richmond, Ind., March 13, 1923.

CD: *New Orleans Rhythm Kings*, Milestone MCD- 47020-2 (USA). This collection includes only take B. All three takes of *Tin Roof Blues* appear on the CD *New Orleans Rhythm Kings*, Village VILCD 004–2 (Germany) and on several LPs: *New Orleans Rhythm Kings*, BYG 27 (Italy); *New Orleans Rhythm Kings*, volume 1 (1922–23), Kings of Jazz NLJ 18009 (Italy), Classic Jazz Masters CJM 12 (Sweden), and Swaggie S 829 (Australia); *New Orleans Rhythm Kings and Jelly Roll Morton*, Milestone M47020 (USA) and Milestone 2C178–96405/06 (France).

Charlie Parker quintet. *Koko* (take 2).

Dizzy Gillespie (trumpet, piano), Charlie Parker (alto sax), Argonne Thornton (piano), Curly Russell (string bass), Max Roach (drums).

Recorded in New York, Nov. 26, 1945.

CD: *The Smithsonian Collection of Classic Jazz*, Smithsonian RD 033 / A5 19477 (USA).

Sonny Rollins quartet. *St. Thomas* (abridged).

Sonny Rollins (tenor sax), Tommy Flanagan (piano), Doug Watkins (string bass), Max Roach (drums).

Recorded in New York, June 22, 1956.

CD: *The Complete Prestige Recordings*, Prestige 7PCD-4407–2 (USA). The unabridged version of this title appears together with the titles mentioned in the discussion of Roach's drum tuning (chap. 7) on this anthology and on all CD, tape, and LP collections entitled strictly *Saxophone Colossus*, including

Original Jazz Classics OJCCD 291–2 (USA). However, the double-LP *Saxophone Colossus and More*, Prestige PR 24050 (USA), does not include all titles mentioned in the discussion of Roach's drum tuning.

Sun Ra and his Solar Arkestra. *Outer Nothingness* (abridged).

Teddy Nance (trombone), Bernard Pettaway (bass trombone), Danny Davis (flute), Marshall Allen (?piccolo), John Gilmore (tenor sax), Robert Cummings (bass clarinet), Pat Patrick (?percussion), Sun Ra (timpani, bass marimba), Ronnie Boykins (string bass), Jimhmi Johnson (?drums).

Recorded in New York, Apr. 20, 1965.

CD: *Cosmic Equation*, Magic Music 30011-CD (Italy). This CD includes the unabridged version of *Outer Nothingness*, as do all LPs entitled *The Heliocentric Worlds of Sun Ra, Volume 1: "Other Worlds."*

Kid Thomas Valentine and his Creole Jazz Band. *Panama*.

Kid Thomas Valentine (trumpet), Louis Nelson (trombone), Emanuel Paul (tenor sax), Joe James (piano), "Creole" George Guesnon (banjo), Alcide "Slow Drag" Pavageau (string bass), Sammy Penn (drums).

Recorded in New Orleans, May 24, 1959.

LP: *Kid Thomas Valentine and His Creole Jazz Band*, Arhoolie F 1016 (USA).

The session of February 26, 1946, by the Original Zenith Brass Band, mentioned together with Valentine's *Panama* in the discussion of tuning systems (chap. 7), fills half of the collection *George Lewis of New Orleans* on Original Jazz Classics OJCCD 1739-2 (CD) and OJC 1739 (LP) (USA).

Weather Report. *Birdland*.

Wayne Shorter (soprano sax, tenor sax), Joe Zawinul (Oberheim polyphonic synthesizer, Arp 2600 synthesizer, piano, melodica, vocal), Jaco Pastorius (electric bass guitar, mandocello, vocal), Alex Acuña (drums), Manolo Badrena (tambourine).

Recorded in North Hollywood, Calif., 1976.

CD: *Heavy Weather*, Columbia CK 34418 (USA).

The live version of *Birdland* is preserved on the LP *8:30*, Columbia PC2-36030. At the time of this writing it had not yet been issued on compact disc.

Appendix 3
Biographical
Sketches of
Key Musicians

This appendix gives brief biographies of the musicians who figure prominently in the historical anthology of recordings that accompanies this book. The entries list the name by which each musician is known and, where appropriate, a given name (except when it is obvious from a nickname); the place and date of birth and death (and when known, the reason for a seemingly premature death); significant affiliations or activities; the relevant title(s) on the anthology; and his or her contributions to and stature within the world of jazz. The information derives mainly from *The New Grove Dictionary of Jazz*, edited by Barry Kernfeld (London: Macmillan, 1988), with assorted details drawn from an unpublished file of additions and corrections. Sketches of a few of Kid Thomas Valentine's lesser-known sidemen are taken from Al Rose and Edmond Souchon, *New Orleans Jazz: A Family Album* (Baton Rouge: Louisiana State University Press, third edition, revised and enlarged, 1984).

Although it is no coincidence that some of the greatest jazz musicians are included here (the anthology having been selected on this basis), the more far-reaching aim was to illuminate musical concepts and procedures, not to offer a history of jazz. Accordingly this biographical list is incomplete, arbitrary, and disproportionate. No one believes for a moment that Francis Williams, a trumpet soloist on Duke Ellington's *Trumpet No End* and hence a subject in the list below, is one tenth as important as cornetists and trumpeters King Oliver, Tommy Ladnier, Bubber Miley, Jabbo Smith, Henry "Red" Allen, Roy Eldridge, Bobby Hackett, Fats Navarro, Chet Baker, Clifford Brown, Lee Morgan, Maynard Ferguson,

Clark Terry, Booker Little, Don Cherry, Woody Shaw, Lester Bowie, and Wynton Marsalis, none of whom figures in the recordings, or Harry "Sweets" Edison and Rex Stewart, who figure only peripherally, as non-soloing sidemen. Readers seeking a complete and balanced sketch of the giants of jazz are advised to consult Ian Carr, Digby Fairweather, and Brian Priestley, *Jazz: The Essential Companion* (London: Grafton, 1987; new edition forthcoming, ca. 1995).

Acuña, Alex (b. Pativilca, Peru, Dec. 12, 1944), drummer and percussionist. From 1975 to 1977 he was a member of the group Weather Report, in which he played miscellaneous percussion before taking over the drum set in 1976, when the group recorded *Birdland*.

Anderson, Cat (William) (b. Greenville, S.C., Sept. 12, 1916; d. Norwalk, Calif., Apr. 29, 1981), trumpeter. Specializing in high-note passages, he worked in Duke Ellington's big band from 1944 into the 1970s, except for occasional periods when he led his own band (1947–49) or worked as a free-lance musician. *Trumpet No End* was recorded during his first tenure with Ellington.

Armstrong, Lil(lian), née Hardin (b. Memphis, Feb. 3, 1898; d. Chicago, Aug. 27, 1971), pianist, singer, and composer. While working in King Oliver's Creole Jazz Band (1922–24), she married Oliver's second cornetist, Louis Armstrong, whose career she furthered and with whose Hot Five and Hot Seven she made recordings (1925–27), including *Hotter than That*. She led the New Orleans Wanderers and New Orleans Bootblacks in recording sessions that featured her compositions and the playing of Johnny Dodds and Kid Ory (1926).

Armstrong, Louis (b. New Orleans, Aug. 4, 1901; d. New York, July 6, 1971), trumpeter and singer. Known variously as Dippermouth, Pops, and Satchmo (Satchelmouth), Armstrong played the cornet with King Oliver's Creole Jazz Band in Chicago (1922–24) and Fletcher Henderson's big band in New York (1924–25). In the course of a series of recordings with his Hot Five, Hot Seven, and Savoy Ballroom Five in Chicago (1925–29), he switched from cornet to the more brilliant sounding trumpet, and he developed a delightful, entirely original blend of gruff singing and scat singing. These recordings, including *Hotter than That*, established Armstrong as a creative genius who was unprecedented in jazz and who has never been surpassed in his conception of improvised, swinging melody. He starred in the Broadway show *Hot Chocolates*, written by Andy Razaf and Fats Waller (1929), and over the remainder of his career performed in nearly fifty movies. He led a big band from the 1930s to the mid-1940s and in 1947 returned to the traditional instrumentation of a New Orleans ensemble with his All Stars, although the group's style reflected as much swing as New Orleans jazz. The All Stars toured internationally, and Armstrong became an ambassador of goodwill for jazz and for America.

Badrena, Manolo (b. Puerto Rico, ca. 1952), percussionist. He worked with the Rolling Stones, Weather Report (1976–77, during which time it recorded *Birdland*), Spyro Gyra (ca. 1982–83), and Carla Bley (1983–84).

Baker, Shorty (Harold) (b. St. Louis, May 26, 1914; d. New York, Nov. 8, 1966), trumpeter. He played in the big bands of Don Redman (1936–38), Teddy Wilson (1938–39), Andy Kirk (1940–42), Johnny Hodges (1954–55), and especially Duke Ellington (briefly in 1938 and intermittently from 1942 through 1962), with whom he recorded *Trumpet No End*.

Basie, Count (William) (b. Red Bank, N.J., Aug. 21, 1904; d. Hollywood, Apr. 26, 1984), bandleader and pianist. After playing in Walter Page's Blue Devils (1928–29) and Bennie Moten's Kansas City Orchestra (1929–33), he led his own band. In 1935 he rejoined Moten and in 1936 formed a big band that he led for the remainder of his life (except for 1950–52, when financial considerations forced him to reduce its size). The Count Basie orchestra was, after Ellington's, the finest jazz big band, particularly during the late 1930s, when it featured the combination of swinging riffs and improvisation exemplified by *Jumpin' at the Woodside*. The orchestra also boasted the best rhythm section of the swing era, consisting of Basie on piano, Freddie Green on guitar, Walter Page on string bass, and Jo Jones on drums. As an improvising soloist he created a highly personal, understated style.

Bigard, Barney (Albany) (b. New Orleans, Mar. 3, 1906; d. Culver City, Calif., June 27, 1980), clarinetist. While working with King Oliver's Dixie Syncopators (1925–27) he switched from the tenor saxophone to the clarinet. On this instrument he became a featured soloist in Duke Ellington's big band (1927–42). His clarinet soars above the ensemble during the last portion of Ellington's recording of *Ko-Ko*. Bigard also played with Louis Armstrong's All Stars (1947–52, 1953–55, 1960–61).

Blanton, Jimmy (b. Chattanooga, Tenn., Oct. 1918; d. Los Angeles, July 30, 1942), string bass player. As a member of Duke Ellington's orchestra (1939–41) he revolutionized the role of his instrument in ensemble work by uniting well-defined pitch, a roaring tone, and a firm sense of swing to create lines that fulfilled the supporting role of the bass yet also carried interest as melody, as heard on *Ko-Ko*. Tuberculosis ended his brief career.

Boykins, Ronnie (b. Chicago, ca. 1935; d. New York, Apr. 20, 1980), string bass player. From 1958 to 1966 he was a member of Sun Ra's Arkestra, with which he recorded *Outer Nothingness*.

Brown, Marion (b. Atlanta, Sept. 8, 1935), alto saxophonist. He played free jazz with Archie Shepp and John Coltrane (including the recording of *Ascension* in 1965). He has played with his own free-jazz groups since 1967.

Brunis, Georg (b. New Orleans, Feb. 6, 1902; d. Chicago, Nov. 19, 1974), trombonist. His given name was George Brunies. In Chicago he became a member of the New Orleans Rhythm Kings, which recorded *Tin Roof Blues* in 1923. After touring with the entertainer and clarinetist Ted Lewis, he played for decades in hybrid swing and dixieland bands.

Carney, Harry (b. Boston, Apr. 1, 1910; d. New York, Oct. 8, 1974), baritone saxophonist. His entire career parallels that of Duke Ellington's, with whose orchestra he played from 1927 until his death. The first significant baritone saxophonist in jazz, Carney anchored the saxophone section, as on *Trumpet No End*, and sometimes the rhythm section, as on portions of *Ko-Ko*, and he starred as an improvising soloist.

Carter, Ron (b. Ferndale, Mich., May 4, 1937), string bass player. As a member of Miles Davis's groups (1963–68), he formed, together with Herbie Hancock and Tony Williams, an acclaimed rhythm section heard on *Maiden Voyage* (recorded in 1965 without Davis). From 1976 he participated in Hancock's revivals of this mid-1960s style. He toured with Sonny Rollins and McCoy Tyner (1978) and performed in the film *'Round Midnight* (1986). The more than one thousand albums he has recorded with jazz and soul musicians testify to his stature.

Chambers, Paul (b. Pittsburgh, Apr. 22, 1935; d. New York, Jan. 4, 1969), string bass player. After playing bop in Detroit, he became a member of Miles Davis's hard-bop quintet in 1955, recording *'Round Midnight* the following year. He remained with Davis from the years of the trumpeter's famous sextet (1958–59) through 1963. He then worked with Wynton Kelly before illness ended his career.

Clarke, Kenny (b. Pittsburgh, Jan. 9, 1914; d. Montreuil-sous-Bois, near Paris, Jan. 26, 1985), drummer. In the early 1940s he was centrally involved with Dizzy Gillespie and others in the emergence of a new jazz style, bop, and his nicknames Klook and Klook-mop derive from the unpredictably placed drum accents he contributed. Subsequently he recorded *Manteca* with Gillespie's big band. He was an original member of Milt Jackson's quartet (1951–55), which became the Modern Jazz Quartet. As an expatriate he worked with Bud Powell in Paris (1959–62) and formed a big band with Francy Boland (1960–73).

Clayton, Buck (Wilbur) (b. Parsons, Kans., Nov. 12, 1911; d. New York, Dec. 8, 1991), trumpeter. He formed a big band in California that played in Shanghai, China, for one year (1934). From 1936–43 he was a soloist in Count Basie's big band, which recorded *Jumpin' at the Woodside*. After military service he regularly led groups and toured internationally. From 1953–56 he led a series of acclaimed informal recordings for the Columbia label.

Coleman, George (b. Memphis, Mar. 8, 1935), tenor saxophonist. He was a member of Miles Davis's quintet (1963–64) and subsequently recorded *Maiden Voyage* with Davis's sideman Herbie Hancock (1965). Later he mainly led groups, often with pianist Harold Mabern.

Coleman, Ornette (b. Fort Worth, Tex., Mar. 9, 1930), alto saxophonist and composer. In partnership with trumpeter Don Cherry he was at the forefront of, and the center of the controversy concerning, the style of free jazz that emerged in the late 1950s. Without ever losing touch with his early experiences in rhythm and blues, he explored a new conception of pitch, a severing of the relationship between theme and improvisation, new timbral combinations (in pursuit of which he took up the trumpet and the violin), and (most radically) the abandonment of rhythm. In 1975 he founded the group Prime Time, which carried his principles of free jazz into the domain of amplified and rhythmically intense funky dance music. Denardo Coleman, his son (b. ca. 1956), is a member of Prime Time and one of the two drummers heard on *Honeymooners*, recorded in 1987.

Coltrane, John (b. Hamlet, N.C., Sept. 23, 1926; d. New York, July 17, 1967), tenor and soprano saxophonist. His career followed a logical progression from hard bop in Miles Davis's quintet (1955–57), to modal jazz in Davis's sextet (1958–59) and his own quartet (1960–65), and finally to free jazz in his last groups (1965–67). He offered new and widely imitated timbres (a hard-edged sound on tenor saxophone, a plaintive sound on soprano saxophone); an astonishing, at times unbelievable technical command of these instruments; an entirely new conception of improvised melody; and a spirituality of such conviction that he alone managed to make free jazz into a popular music.

Davis, Miles (b. Alton, Ill., May 25, 1926; d. Santa Monica, Calif., Sept. 28, 1991), trumpeter, flugelhorn player, and bandleader. After working in Charlie Parker's bop quintet (1945–48) he led a series of pioneering groups: a recording nonet that helped define cool jazz (1948–50); a hard-bop quintet (1955–57), which recorded '*Round Midnight*; a recording orchestra, under Gil Evans's direction, which expanded the coloristic and harmonic palette of big band jazz and developed modal jazz (1957–60); a sextet that played hard bop and also developed modal jazz (1958–59); a quintet that explored a "time, no changes" style (1963–68); and groups of varied size that established jazz fusion (1968–), on which style Davis finally settled for the remainder of his life. Individually his innovative uses of the trumpet with stemless Harmon mute and of the flugelhorn were widely imitated in jazz, but no one else was able to capture the subtle and sophisticated nuances that were essential to the depth of his improvisations.

Dodds, Johnny (b. New Orleans, Apr. 12, 1892; d. Chicago, Aug. 8, 1940), clarinetist. In Chicago he worked with King Oliver's Creole Jazz Band (1922–24) before recording with Louis Armstrong's Hot Five and Hot Seven (including *Hotter than That*), the New Orleans Wanderers and New Orleans Bootblacks (with Lil Armstrong), Jelly Roll Morton, and his own groups. His playing was strongly colored by blues devices.

Ellington, Duke (Edward) (b. Washington, D.C., Apr. 29, 1899; d. New York, May 24, 1974), composer, bandleader, and pianist. He took over leadership of the Washingtonians during the first year of an engagement at the Hollywood Club (renamed the Kentucky Club) in New York (1923–27). The group expanded to become a big band, which held a famous engagement at the Cotton Club (1927–31) and then toured for over four decades. Under his direction it became by far the most creative of all the big bands. Happily its legacy is preserved on thousands of recordings, of which *Ko-Ko* is often considered among the finest. (The underrated *Trumpet No End* is not, in part because the recording fidelity is so poor.) Ellington's greatest strengths were founded in concise blues and popular songs, though from mid-career on he turned increasingly to suites, ballets and, finally, sacred concerts. Whether arranging and orchestrating borrowed material or composing anew, he had a genius for making entirely original sounds, particularly in the areas of harmony, melody, and timbre.

Ervin, Booker (b. Denison, Tex., Oct. 31, 1930; d. New York, Aug. 31, 1970), tenor saxophonist. He was a member of Charles Mingus's group (1958–62), which recorded *Fables of Faubus*. He then led his own hard-bop groups before succumbing to kidney disease.

Evans, Herschel (b. Denton, Tex., 1909; d. New York, Feb. 9, 1939), tenor saxophonist. He was a member of Bennie Moten's big band (1933–35) before joining Count Basie's big band in 1936. With Basie his soloing followed Coleman Hawkins's approach and thus contrasted with Lester Young's style. He occasionally played clarinet, as on *Jumpin' at the Woodside*. A heart ailment caused his premature death.

Flanagan, Tommy (b. Detroit, Mar. 16, 1930), pianist. He worked with bop and hard-bop groups in Detroit and then began playing in New York in 1956, when he recorded Sonny Rollins's *St. Thomas*. He served as Ella Fitzgerald's pianist and music director (1956, 1963–65, 1968–78), after which time he mainly led small groups.

Fuller, Gil (Walter) (b. Los Angeles, April 14, 1920), arranger and composer.

During the 1940s he wrote for swing, bop, and Afro-Cuban bands, most notably in collaboration with Dizzy Gillespie and various of Gillespie's sidemen on such titles as *Oop-bop-sh'bam* (1946) and *Manteca* (1947).

Garland, Red (William) (b. Dallas, May 13, 1923; d. Dallas, Apr. 23, 1984), pianist. He was a member of Miles Davis's groups (1955–58) and recorded *'Round Midnight* with the quintet. He then led his own trio.

Garrison, Jimmy (b. Miami, Mar. 3, 1934; d. New York, Apr. 7, 1976), string bass player. After working with Ornette Coleman (1961), he was a member of John Coltrane's groups (1961–67), forming an acclaimed rhythm section with Elvin Jones and McCoy Tyner and recording *Ascension* with Coltrane's orchestra in 1965. He continued to explore Coltrane's style in groups with Archie Shepp (1967–68, 1972) and Jones (1968–69, 1973–74).

Gillespie, Dizzy (John) (b. Cheraw, S.C., Oct. 21, 1917; d. Englewood, N.J., Jan. 6, 1993), trumpeter. While working in Cab Calloway's big band (1939–41), he became a leading figure in the development of a new small-combo style, bop. After playing in the big bands of Earl Hines and Billy Eckstine, he recorded the definitive examples of this style, including *Koko*, in partnership with Charlie Parker (1945). His trumpet improvisations showed an audacious sense of harmony (as implied in his melodies) and an unprecedented technical facility. In 1946–47 he established his own big band, developing a blend of swing, bop, and Latin music known as Afro-Cuban jazz, of which *Manteca* is a definitive example. He continued to lead groups, including a big band that toured the Middle East (1956) and his United Nations Superband (1988–92).

Gilmore, John (b. Summit, Miss., Sept. 28, 1931), tenor saxophonist. In 1953 he joined Sun Ra, with whom he remained until 1993, except for two years spent in Art Blakey's Jazz Messengers (1964–65). He pioneered a screaming free-jazz improvisatory style, as heard on *Outer Nothingness*.

Green, Freddie (b. Charleston, S.C., Mar. 31, 1911; d. Las Vegas, Mar. 1, 1987), guitarist. (As an affectation, he spelled his surname Greene.) For almost fifty years, from 1937 on, he was the guitarist in Count Basie's big band. His role was to provide a supple, beat-by-beat rhythm, as on *Jumpin' at the Woodside*.

Greer, Sonny (William) (b. Long Branch, N.J., Dec. 13, ca. 1895; d. New York, Mar. 23, 1982), drummer. From 1920 through 1951 his career paralleled that of Duke Ellington's, with whose big band he recorded *Ko-Ko* and *Trumpet No End*.

Guesnon, "Creole" George (b. New Orleans, May 25, 1907; d. New Orleans, May 5, 1968), banjoist and guitarist. In the 1950s and 1960s he was active in the New Orleans jazz revival. He recorded *Panama* with Kid Thomas Valentine.

Hadi, Shafi (b. Curtis Porter, Philadelphia, Sept. 21, 1929), tenor and alto saxophonist. From 1956–58 and again in 1959 he was a member of Charles Mingus's Jazz Workshop, with which he recorded *Fables of Faubus*.

Hamilton, Jimmy (b. Dillon, S.C., May 25, 1917), clarinetist. As a soloist in Duke Ellington's orchestra (1943–68) he recorded *Trumpet No End*. He settled in the Virgin Islands in 1968 but resumed work in the United States in the 1980s, playing in John Carter's clarinet quartet and Clark Terry's Spacemen.

Hancock, Herbie (b. Chicago, Apr. 12, 1940), pianist, composer, and keyboard player. He played in Miles Davis's groups from 1963 through 1970, beginning in the quintet with Ron Carter and Tony Williams—an offshoot of which recorded his composition *Maiden Voyage*—and continuing into Davis's jazz-rock groups. Toward the end of his tenure with Davis he founded his own jazz-rock group (1969–73). Later he pursued separate careers: one in pop music, leading to the hit video *Rockit*, the other in revivals of his earlier jazz style, leading to the movie *'Round Midnight*, in which he acted and for which he received an Oscar for scoring.

Handy, John (b. Dallas, Feb. 3, 1933), alto saxophonist. He was a member of Charles Mingus's Jazz Workshop when the group recorded *Fables of Faubus* (1958). He rejoined Mingus in 1964.

Hawkins, Coleman (b. St. Joseph, Mo., Nov. 21, 1904; d. New York, May 19, 1969), tenor saxophonist. His nicknames were Bean and Hawk. As a member of Fletcher Henderson's big band (1924–34) he established the tenor saxophone as a solo instrument in jazz. He spent five years in Europe, where he recorded with Benny Carter and Django Reinhardt. After returning to the United States he recorded *Body in Soul* (1939), one of the most famous of all jazz improvisations, exhibiting his characteristic preferences for a pronounced vibrato, florid double-time melody, and a climactic gruff tone, qualities heard also on *The Man I Love* (1943). He led groups and from 1946 toured with Jazz at the Philharmonic. In 1961 he starred in *After Hours*, a brief nightclub performance created for television.

Heywood, Eddie (b. Atlanta, Dec. 4, 1915; d. Miami Beach, Jan. 2, 1989), pianist. He made recordings with Billie Holiday in 1941, including *Georgia on My Mind*, and Coleman Hawkins in 1943, including *The Man I Love*, but his career was devoted mainly to his own groups, which played his hit tune *Canadian Sunset* (1956).

Hilaire, Andrew (b. New Orleans, ca. 1900; d. Chicago, ca. 1936), drummer. He made recordings with Jelly Roll Morton in 1926, including *Black Bottom Stomp*.

Hines, Earl (b. Duquesne, Penn., Dec. 28, 1903; d. Oakland, Calif., Apr. 22, 1983), pianist and bandleader. His nickname was Fatha. In Chicago he joined Jimmie Noone's Apex Club Orchestra (1927) and made famous recordings with Noone, with Louis Armstrong, and as an unaccompanied soloist (1928). He led big bands (1928–47) and then joined Armstrong's All Stars (1948–51). Thereafter he led groups and from 1964 also performed alone, as on *Sweet Sue*, recorded in 1965. He had a spectacular piano technique, an irrepressible sense of swing, and a penchant for interpolating zany flights of fancy into his improvisations on popular songs and blues.

Holiday, Billie (b. Elinore Harris, Philadelphia, Apr. 7, 1915; d. New York, July 17, 1959), singer. Lester Young gave her the nickname Lady Day. From 1935 on she made celebrated recordings, including *Georgia on My Mind* (1941), with a succession of all-star swing groups under Teddy Wilson's name and her own. Her life was troubled by difficult relationships, drugs, and a desire for a deserved level of acclaim that unfortunately came posthumously. The most profound of all jazz singers, she possessed a unique, plaintive voice laden with emotion and an ability to reinvent popular songs.

Hubbard, Freddie (b. Indianapolis, Apr. 7, 1938), trumpeter and flugelhorn player. After touring Europe with Quincy Jones (1960–61) he joined Art Blakey's Jazz Messengers (1961–64). Serving in effect as a substitute for Miles Davis, he recorded *Maiden Voyage* with Herbie Hancock's quintet (1965). He joined Max Roach's group (1965–66) but from 1964 mainly led his own groups, experiencing his greatest success with his albums of 1970–71.

Jackson, Milt (b. Detroit, Jan. 1, 1923), vibraphonist. His nickname is Bags. He worked with Dizzy Gillespie's sextet (1945) and big band (1946–47), recording *Manteca* with the latter. In 1948 he made recordings with Thelonious Monk, including *Misterioso*. He then rejoined Gillespie's big band (1950–52); from that rhythm section came the Milt Jackson Quartet, which in turn became the Modern Jazz Quartet (1952–74, 1981–).

James, Joe (b. Algiers, La., 1901; d. New Orleans, 1964), pianist. He was for many years a member of Kid Thomas Valentine's band, which recorded *Panama*.

Johnson, Lonnie (Alonzo) (b. New Orleans, Feb. 8, 1889; d. Toronto, Canada, June 16, 1970), guitarist and singer. His career was focused on blues, but in the 1920s he worked with jazz bands and toward the end of the decade recorded with Louis Armstrong (*Hotter than That*), Duke Ellington, and Eddie Lang.

Jones, Elvin (b. Pontiac, Mich., Sept. 9, 1927), drummer. As a member of John Coltrane's group from 1960–66, he became part of a renowned rhythm section with Jimmy Garrison and McCoy Tyner and recorded the landmark free-jazz improvisation *Ascension* (1965). He developed a kaleidoscopic style in which rhythm swirled around the drum set without losing its definition. Lacking interest in the radical experiments of Coltrane's final years, he led groups following in the tradition of Coltrane's quartet of the early 1960s.

Jones, Jo(nathan) (b. Chicago, Oct. 7, 1911; d. New York, Sept. 3, 1985), drummer. He was twice a member of Count Basie's big band (1936–44, 1946–48). He softened the role of the bass drum and played the hi-hat cymbals in a sizzling manner; the flowing sound he created, as exemplified on *Jumpin' at the Woodside*, replaced the abruptness of earlier drumming styles. Jones also recorded with Teddy Wilson and Billie Holiday, starred in the film short *Jammin' the Blues* (1944), and toured with Jazz at the Philharmonic. After 1948 he continued to play in Basie's tradition, although mainly in small groups and without finding a setting as satisfying as in his days with Basie.

Jones, Philly Joe (b. Philadelphia, Penn., July 15, 1923; d. Philadelphia, Aug. 30, 1985), drummer. He worked in brief associations with many great jazz musicians before and after his tenure with Miles Davis's quintet and sextet (1955–58). Davis's gentle ballad *'Round Midnight* is not representative of Jones's fiery, aggressive drumming.

Jordan, Taft (b. Florence, S.C., Feb. 15, 1915; d. New York, Dec. 1, 1981), trumpeter and singer. Modeling his performances after Louis Armstrong (as did many trumpeters and singers of his era), he worked in the big band of Chick Webb (1933–39), which continued under Ella Fitzgerald's leadership (1939–42) after Webb's death. He joined Duke Ellington's big band (1943–47), which recorded *Trumpet No End*.

Knepper, Jimmy (b. Los Angeles, Nov. 22, 1927), trombonist. He was a member of Charles Mingus's group (1957–61), which recorded *Fables of Faubus*. He worked with Gil Evans intermittently (1960–77), the Thad Jones–Mel Lewis Orchestra (1968–74), nd Lee Konitz's nonet (1975–81). Following Mingus's death in 1979, he worked with the memorial group Mingus Dynasty.

Lindsay, John (b. New Orleans, Aug. 23, 1894; d. Chicago, July 3, 1950), string bass player. While performing in Chicago he contributed in 1926 to Jelly Roll Morton's finest recordings, including *Black Bottom Stomp*.

McKibbon, Al(fred) (b. Chicago, Jan. 1, 1919), string bass player. He was an intermittent member of Dizzy Gillespie's big band (1947–50), which recorded *Manteca*. He also recorded with Miles Davis's cool jazz nonet (1950). McGibbon played with George Shearing (1951–58) and toured with Gillespie in the Giants of Jazz (1971–72).

Manne, Shelly (b. New York, June 11, 1920; d. Los Angeles, Sept. 26, 1984), drummer. With Coleman Hawkins he recorded *The Man I Love* (1943). From 1946–52 he worked mainly in Stan Kenton's big band, although he also joined Woody Herman and toured with Jazz at the Philharmonic. He then became involved in an offshoot of cool jazz known as West Coast jazz, the center of which was Los Angeles. There he played in André Previn's jazz trio and in a cooperative trio with Barney Kessel and Ray Brown (1957–60), led groups, and was later reunited with Brown in the L.A. Four (1974–77).

Mares, Paul (b. New Orleans, June 15, 1900; d. Chicago, Aug. 18, 1949), cornetist. In Chicago he organized the Friar's Society Orchestra (1921), which under the name of the New Orleans Rhythm Kings recorded *Tin Roof Blues* (1923). After the group disbanded in 1924, Mares attempted unsuccessfully to re-create its success.

Mingus, Charles (b. Nogales, Ariz., Apr. 22, 1922; d. Cuernavaca, Mexico, Jan. 5, 1979), string bass player, composer, and bandleader. He was a member of Red Norvo's trio (1950–51) and participated in a famous bop concert with Charlie Parker and Dizzy Gillespie in Toronto (1953). After 1955 he led his Jazz Workshop, which recorded *Fables of Faubus* (1958). Seamlessly integrating composition and improvisation in several series of unified but ever-changing performances, the Workshop explored hard bop and soul jazz, amalgamations of these and earlier styles, an incipient free-jazz style (in partnership with Eric Dolphy) and, finally, jazz-rock. At one point Mingus served as the pianist in the Workshop (1961–62), but his long-standing instrumental skill was as a virtuoso bassist, which brought him renown both for his solos and for his ability to insert contrapuntal ideas while maintaining a flowing bass line.

Mitchell, George (b. Louisville, Ky., Mar. 8, 1899; d. Chicago, May 27, 1972), cornetist. While working in Chicago he made recordings with Jelly Roll Morton (including *Black Bottom Stomp*) and in groups with Johnny Dodds (1926–27).

Monk, Thelonious (b. Rocky Mount, N.C., Oct. 10, 1917; d. Weehawken, N.J., Feb. 17, 1982), pianist and composer. His ideas at informal sessions contributed to the development of bop, although personally he maintained a direct if eccentric link to the earlier stride piano style. In 1944 Cootie Williams recorded Monk's composition *'Round about Midnight* (also known as *'Round Midnight*). From 1947–56 he had few opportunities outside the studio, where he made seminal recordings, including *Misterioso*. At the Five Spot in New York he led a quartet that included John Coltrane (1957), and thereafter he toured internationally as the leader of small groups. Many of his compositions became standards in the jazz repertory, but his wholly original piano playing, which was known for being harmonically stark, and rhythmically brilliant, remained inimitable.

Morton, Jelly Roll (b. Ferdinand Lemott, New Orleans, Oct. 20, 1890; d. Los Angeles, July 10, 1941), composer and pianist. He claimed to have invented jazz, and in his wide travels he at least contributed to its dissemination before the era of jazz recording. In Chicago he made recordings as an unaccompanied pianist (1923–24) and with his Red Hot Peppers (1926–30), including *Black Bottom Stomp*. These early recordings testify to his stature as the first great jazz composer and one of the first great jazz pianists; Morton displayed a feeling for the blues that was generally lacking among contemporary northeastern stride pianists. Several of his compositions remained in the repertory even after the instrumentation and ragtime-based elements of his style became passé. In 1938 he recorded his extraordinary memoirs for the Library of Congress.

Nance, Ray (Willis) (b. Chicago, Dec. 10, 1913; d. New York, Jan. 28, 1976), trumpeter, cornetist, violinist, singer, and dancer. He worked mainly as a trumpeter in the big bands of Earl Hines (1937–38) and Horace Henderson (1939–40). As a member of Duke Ellington's orchestra (1940–63 and intermittently thereafter) he replaced Cootie Williams in filling the role of a growling, plunger-muted trumpeter (heard on *Trumpet No End*). While with Ellington he also sang, danced, and played the violin; such multifaceted talent earned him the nickname Floorshow. In 1961 he switched from trumpet to cornet.

Nanton, Tricky Sam (Joe) (b. New York, Feb. 1, 1904; d. San Francisco, July 20, 1946), trombonist. His career parallels that of Duke Ellington (1926–46). His soloing featured a talking style, as heard on *Ko-Ko*, in which he adapted Bubber Miley's growling, plunger-muted trumpeting to the trombone.

Nelson, Louis (b. New Orleans, Sept. 17, 1902; d. New Orleans, Apr. 5, 1990), trombonist. He played traditional jazz with Kid Thomas Valentine (1944–80s), with whom he recorded *Panama*. Nelson toured with George Lewis (1950s), Percy Humphrey, and the Legends of Jazz (1973–79), in addition to performing regularly at Preservation Hall in New Orleans.

Nicholas, Big Nick (George) (b. Lansing, Mich., Aug. 2, 1922), tenor saxophonist and singer. In 1947, as a member of Dizzy Gillespie's band, he contributed a solo on *Manteca*. He worked with Hot Lips Page from 1947 until 1954. Nicholas made his first albums as a leader in the mid-1980s.

Nix, Bern (b. Toledo, Sept. 21, 1947), electric guitarist. He was a member of Ornette Coleman's group Prime Time from 1975 to 1987, the year *Homeymooners* was recorded.

Ory, Kid (Edward) (b. La Place, La., Dec. 25, ca. 1889; d. Honolulu, Jan. 23, 1973), trombonist and bandleader. After leading bands in New Orleans, he went to Los Angeles, where he became the first African-American to record in a New Orleans jazz style (1922). In Chicago in the latter part of the 1920s he made recordings with Louis Armstrong's Hot Five (including *Hotter than That*), Lil Armstrong's New Orleans Wanderers and New Orleans Bootblacks, Jelly Roll Morton's Red Hot Peppers (including *Black Bottom*

Stomp), and King Oliver's Dixie Syncopators. He led one of the most successful bands in the revival of New Orleans jazz (1944–66).

Page, Walter (b. Gallatin, Mo., Feb. 9, 1900; d. New York, Dec. 20, 1957), string bass player. He led the pioneering Blue Devils, a southwestern big band (1925–31) and then joined Bennie Moten's Kansas City Orchestra (1931–34). He was a member of Count Basie's big band (1936–42, 1946–49), forming with Basie, Freddie Green, and Jo Jones the renowned rhythm section heard on *Jumpin' at the Woodside*.

Parker, Charlie (b. Kansas City, Kans., Aug. 29, 1920; d. New York, Mar. 12, 1955), alto saxophonist. His nicknames were Bird and Yardbird. He was a soloist in the big bands of Jay McShann (1940–42), Earl Hines (1942–44), and Billy Eckstine (1944). In partnership with Dizzy Gillespie he made definitive recordings in the bop style, including *Koko* (1945). For the remainder of his life he led small bop groups. Possessing a deep feeling for the blues, an intuitively profound sense of melodic structure and its implications for harmony, the musical equivalent of a photographic memory, and the consequent ability to incorporate sensibly into his improvisations whatever he heard, he was the genius of the style. His technical virtuosity and musical wit were widely imitated, as were his drug addiction and depraved life-style (which led to his early death); few have captured his musicality.

Parlan, Horace (b. Pittsburgh, Jan. 19, 1931), pianist. He was a member of Charles Mingus's Jazz Workshop (1957–59), recording *Fables of Faubus*. He played with saxophonists Lou Donaldson (1959–60), Booker Ervin (1960–61), Eddie "Lockjaw" Davis and Johnny Griffin (1961–62), and Roland Kirk (1963–66). Since moving to Copenhagen in 1973, he has been involved with European musicians active in hard bop and swing and with fellow musical expatriates from America.

Pastorius, Jaco (John) (b. Norristown, Penn., Dec. 1, 1951; d. Fort Lauderdale, Fla., Sept. 21, 1987), electric bass guitarist. As a member of Weather Report (1976–81), he was featured on *Birdland* and furthered the possibilities of the electric bass guitar as a fleet melodic instrument, following the lead of Stanley Clarke in Chick Corea's groups.

Paul, Emanuel (b. New Orleans, Feb. 2, 1904; d. New Orleans, May 23, 1988), tenor saxophonist. In New Orleans he played with the Eureka Brass Band (from 1940) and Kid Thomas Valentine's band (ca. 1942–80s), with which he recorded *Panama*. He toured Europe during his tenure with Harold Dejan's Olympia Brass Band (1966–71).

Pavageau, Alcide (b. New Orleans, Mar. 7, 1888; d. New Orleans, Jan. 19, 1969), string bass player. His nickname, "Slow Drag," was taken from a dance. In the New Orleans jazz revival he worked mainly with George Lewis (1943–60s) and Bunk Johnson (1944–46). He is heard on Kid Thomas Valentine's *Panama*.

Payne, Cecil (b. New York, Dec. 14, 1922), baritone saxophonist. He played in Dizzy Gillespie's big band (1946–49), recording *Manteca*. After touring with Illinois Jacquet (1952–54), Payne recorded bop albums. He played with Machito's Afro-Cubans (1963–64), Lionel Hampton (1964), Randy Weston (1966), Woody Herman (1966–67), Gillespie again (1968), and Count Basie (1969–71). He became a member of Jacquet's big band (late 1980s) and led a hard-bop quintet with Junior Cook (1990).

Penn, Sammy (b. Morgan City, La., Sept. 15, 1902; d. Florida, Sept. 18, 1969), drummer. He was a member of Kid Thomas's band (mid-1940s–1960s), which recorded *Panama*.

Pettiford, Oscar (b. Okmulgee, Okla., Sept. 30, 1922; d. Copenhagen, Denmark, Sept. 8, 1960), string bass player. In 1943 he played with Charlie Barnet's big band and Roy Eldridge. While working in a pioneering bop group with Dizzy Gillespie (winter 1943–44) he recorded *The Man I Love* with Coleman Hawkins. He joined the big bands of Duke Ellington (1945–48, recording *Trumpet No End*) and Woody Herman (1949). In the 1950s he led a big band and small bop groups. Pettiford had Jimmy Blanton's skills as a bassist in big bands and was more gifted than Blanton in solo improvisation.

Pozo, Chano (b. Luciano Pozo y Gonzales, Havana, Cuba, Jan. 7, 1915; d. New York, Dec. 2, 1948), conga drummer. As a member of Dizzy Gillespie's big band from 1947 to 1948 (when he was murdered) he was at the center of the development of Afro-Cuban jazz, represented by Gillespie's *Manteca*.

Richmond, Dannie (b. New York, Dec. 15, 1935; d. New York, Mar. 16, 1988), drummer. He was a member of Charles Mingus's groups (1956–70), recording *Fables of Faubus*. He spent a period in rock groups and then rejoined Mingus (1974). After Mingus's death in 1979 Richmond played in the memorial group Mingus Dynasty and in a quartet that included George Adams and Don Pullen, two of Mingus's former sidemen.

Roach, Max (b. New Land, N.C., Jan. 10, 1924), drummer. He participated in informal bop sessions before joining the quintets of Dizzy Gillespie (1944) and Charlie Parker (1945, 1947–49, and, intermittently, 1951–53). As the preeminent bop drummer of the period, he was capable of handling crisply the demands of a quicksilver performance like Parker's *Koko*. He also played in Miles Davis's cool jazz nonet (1948–50). With trumpeter Clifford Brown he led a hard-bop quintet (1954–56). After Brown's accidental death Roach took over leadership of the group, maintaining it on and off into the 1990s. He also made seminal recordings with Sonny Rollins (1955–58), including *St. Thomas*, and moved toward the emerging free-jazz style, particularly as it related to the sociocultural element of civil protest. In 1970 he formed the percussion ensemble M'Boom Re: Percussion.

Rollins, Sonny (Theodore) (b. New York, Sept. 9, 1930), tenor saxophonist. He recorded with leading bop musicians, including Charlie Parker, Thelonious Monk, and Miles Davis (1949–56). He joined the Max Roach–Clifford Brown quintet in 1955. Concurrently, as a leader of his own groups in the studio, he began a series of monumental recordings, a project that extended through 1958. These recordings, including *St. Thomas*, presented him as arguably the finest bop soloist to follow Parker. During this period Brown died (1956), but Rollins remained in Roach's quintet until 1957. Since then he has performed almost exclusively as a leader. He took two leaves of absence to practice alone: following the first (1959–61), elements of free jazz entered into his playing; following the second (1969–71), he presented his bop improvising with accompanists playing in a jazz-soul fusion style. He is renowned for his ability to sustain interest as an unaccompanied saxophonist.

Roppolo, Leon (b. Lutcher, La., Mar. 16, 1902; d. Louisiana, Oct. 5, 1943), clarinetist. In Chicago around 1921 he joined Paul Mares's Friars Society Orchestra, which as the New Orleans Rhythm Kings recorded *Tin Roof Blues* (1923). He was the group's finest soloist. After 1925 Roppolo spent most of his remaining years in a mental institution.

Russell, Curly (Dillon) (b. New York, Mar. 19, 1917; d. New York, July 3, 1986), string bass player. He worked as a free-lance musician in bop groups (mid-1940s–mid-1950s), including the quintets of Dizzy Gillespie and Charlie Parker. With the latter group Russell recorded *Koko*.

St. Cyr, Johnny (b. New Orleans, Apr. 17, 1890; d. Los Angeles, June 17, 1966), guitarist and banjoist. He joined Kid Ory and King Oliver in New Orleans from 1915 to 1917 and played on the Mississippi riverboats with Fate Marable from 1918. In 1923 St. Cyr went to Chicago, where he made recordings with Oliver, Louis Armstrong (1925–27, including *Hotter than That*), and Jelly Roll Morton (1926, including *Black Bottom Stomp*).

Sanders, Pharoah (Farrell) (b. Little Rock, Ark., Oct. 13, 1940), tenor saxophonist. He was an unofficial member of John Coltrane's group (1965–67); his recordings with this group, including *Ascension*, presented the harshest of free-jazz saxophone styles. His work as a leader after Coltrane's death in 1967 combined this abrasive sound with a serene approach. Later his playing became more eclectic, drawing upon swing, rhythm and blues, and bop, as well as free jazz and meditative music.

Shepp, Archie (b. Fort Lauderdale, Fla., May 24, 1937), tenor saxophonist. He played free jazz with Cecil Taylor (1960–62), the New York Contemporary Five (1963–64), and his own groups (after 1964), while also recording *Ascension* with John Coltrane. After the 1970s he turned toward more conventional styles, including rhythm and blues, and bop.

Shorter, Wayne (b. Newark, N.J., Aug. 25, 1933), tenor and soprano saxophonist and composer. He played with Maynard Ferguson (1958), Art Blakey's Jazz Messengers (1959–64), and Miles Davis (1964–70). In partnership with Joe Zawinul he followed Davis's experiments in jazz-rock by founding the group Weather Report (1970-85), which recorded *Birdland*. He also participated intermittently in revivals of Davis's mid-1960s style under the leadership of Herbie Hancock (1976–90s). He performed in the film *'Round Midnight* (1986).

Simeon, Omer (b. New Orleans, July 21, 1902; d. New York, Sept. 17, 1959), clarinetist and saxophonist. He played on the first recordings made by Jelly Roll Morton's Red Hot Peppers (1926), including *Black Bottom Stomp*. He was a member of King Oliver's Dixie Syncopators (1927) and recorded with Jabbo Smith (1929). Simeon joined the big bands of Earl Hines (1931–37), Horace Henderson (1937–38), Hines again (1938–40), and Jimmy Lunceford (1942–50), while also recording with Kid Ory (1944–45).

Simmons, John (b. Haskell, Okla., June 14, 1918; d. Los Angeles, Sept. 19, 1979), string bass player. He had brief associations with many leading jazz musicians, including Teddy Wilson (1937), Roy Eldridge (1940–41), Benny Goodman (1941), Cootie Williams and Louis Armstrong (1942), and Duke Ellington (1943). Among his prolific work as a free-lance musician were his performances in the film *Jammin' the Blues* (1944) and recordings with Sid Catlett (1944) and Thelonious Monk (1948), including *Misterioso*. He was a member of Erroll Garner's trio (1949–52).

Stitzel, Mel(ville) (b. Germany, Jan. 9, 1902; d. Chicago, Dec. 31, 1952), pianist. He made recordings with the New Orleans Rhythm Kings (1923, including *Tin Roof Blues*), Muggsy Spanier (1924–25), and Benny Goodman (1928).

Sun Ra (b. Birmingham, Ala., May 1914; d. Birmingham, May 30, 1993), composer, bandleader, and keyboard player. During 1946–47 he played piano with Fletcher Henderson's big band, at which time he was known as Herman "Sonny" Blount and Le Sony'r Ra. He formed his Arkestra in Chicago in the 1950s, moved it to New York in 1960, and finally settled in Philadelphia in the 1970s. With it he presented theatrical and widely eclectic performances that embraced radical free jazz (as heard on *Outer Nothingness*), funky dance music, cosmic philosophy, and comedy, while also drawing from mainstream swing and hard-bop styles. Utilizing many keyboard instruments, he was a pioneer in the incorporation of electric piano and synthesizers into jazz.

Tchicai, John (b. Copenhagen, Denmark, Apr. 28, 1936), alto saxophonist. After moving from Copenhagen to New York, he played free jazz in the New York Contemporary Five (1963) and the New York Art Quartet (1964). In

1965 Tchicai recorded *Ascension* with John Coltrane. The following year he returned to Denmark, where he has continued his musical career.

Tyner, McCoy (b. Philadelphia, Dec. 11, 1938), pianist. He played in the Benny Golson–Art Farmer Jazztet (1959–60) before joining John Coltrane's famous quartet (1960–65), which formed the nucleus for the recording *Ascension*. The style known as modal jazz was very much characterized by his manner of accompanying Coltrane with chordal patterns that were static and indeterminate harmonically and colored by chromatic wanderings. Concurrently he began to pursue this style in a prolific career as a leader, mainly in small groups, although later he gave acclaimed performances both as an unaccompanied soloist and, in the 1990s, as the leader of a big band.

Valentine, Kid Thomas (b. Reserve, La., Feb. 3, 1896; d. New Orleans, June 16, 1987), trumpeter. Equally well known simply as Kid Thomas, he led bands in New Orleans from the 1930s until his death. Valentine was closely associated with Preservation Hall from its opening in 1961, and he also toured internationally. His trumpet playing was characterized by a distinctively telegraphic manner and an outrageously broad tone.

Warren, Earle (b. Springfield, Ohio, July 1, 1914), alto saxophonist. Warren added the letter *e* to his first name to distinguish himself from Earl Hines. Having joined Count Basie's big band in 1937, he served as its lead alto saxophonist (1938–45). Although he was not one of the stronger soloists in the band, he is heard on *Jumpin' at the Woodside*.

Watkins, Doug (b. Detroit, Mar. 2, 1934; d. near Holbrook, Ariz., Feb. 5, 1962), string bass player. After working with bop groups in Detroit, Watkins moved to New York, where he joined the Jazz Messengers (1954–56) and Horace Silver's quintet (1956). He also began to record frequently as a free-lance musician and is one of the players on Sonny Rollins's *St. Thomas*. He later joined Charles Mingus's Jazz Workshop when Mingus temporarily switched from bass to piano (1961). He died in an automobile accident at the age of twenty-seven.

Webster, Ben (b. Kansas City, Mo., Mar. 27, 1909; d. Amsterdam, Holland, Sept. 20, 1973), tenor saxophonist. He played in many big bands, including those of Bennie Moten (1931–33), Fletcher Henderson (1934, 1937), Cab Calloway (1936–37), and Duke Ellington (1940–43), in which he became a major soloist (though not on *Ko-Ko*). In his work as a free-lance musician, Webster recorded a renowned session with Sid Catlett (1944). In 1948–49 he rejoined the Ellington band, and in the 1950s he toured with Jazz at the Philharmonic. After 1964 he lived and performed in Europe.

Williams, Cootie (Charles) (b. Mobile, Ala., July 10, 1911; d. New York, Sept. 15, 1985), trumpeter. He replaced Bubber Miley in Duke Ellington's big band (1929–40), taking over Miley's role as the growling, plunger-muted trumpeter and developing it into his own distinctive solo voice, which was featured on many recordings (though not on *Ko-Ko*). He joined Benny Goodman's big band (1940–41) before forming his own (1941–48), which made the first recording of *'Round Midnight* (as *'Round about Midnight*). He rejoined Ellington in 1962, remaining with the band for a few years after the leader's death in 1974.

Williams, Francis (b. McConnell's Mills, Penn., Sept. 20, 1910; d. Houston, Penn., Oct. 2, 1983), trumpeter. He played with various big bands, including those of Fats Waller (1940), Ella Fitzgerald (1941–42), Machito (1944), and Duke Ellington (1945–49, 1951). Williams recorded *Trumpet No End* with Ellington.

Williams, Mary Lou, née Scruggs, Mary Elfreida (b. Atlanta, May 8, 1910; d. Durham, N.C., May 28, 1981), pianist, composer, and arranger. She was the foremost writer and, after saxophonist Dick Wilson, the finest soloist in Andy Kirk's big band (1929–42). In the mid-1940s she led small swing groups and wrote arrangements for Duke Ellington, including the version of *Blue Skies* that became *Trumpet No End*. Williams worked as a leader into the 1970s, playing conventional swing and bop while also creating sacred works related to these styles.

Williams, Tony (b. Chicago, Dec. 12, 1945), drummer. As a teenager he joined Miles Davis's quintet to form a marvelously flexible rhythm section with Ron Carter and Herbie Hancock (1963); under Hancock's name they recorded *Maiden Voyage* (without Davis). He played an central role in Davis's move from a swing-based to a jazz-rock rhythmic style. After leaving Davis in 1969 he led his own jazz-rock group, Lifetime (1969–72). From 1976 he occasionally rejoined Hancock in revivals of their style of the mid-1960s.

Wilson, Shadow (Rossiere) (b. Yonkers, N.Y., Sept. 25, 1919; d. New York, July 11, 1959), drummer. He played in many big bands, including those of Lionel Hampton (1940–41), Earl Hines (1941–43), and Count Basie (1944–46). He joined Illinois Jacquet in 1947 and made recordings with Tadd Dameron and Thelonious Monk, including *Misterioso* (1948). Wilson briefly returned to Basie (1948), joined Woody Herman's big band (1949), and rejoined Jacquet (1949–50) before touring in Erroll Garner's trio (1950–52) and in a trio accompanying Ella Fitzgerald (1954–55). He was a member of Monk's quartet at the Five Spot in New York (1957–58).

Young, Lester (b. Woodville, Miss., Aug. 27, 1909; d. New York, Mar. 15, 1959), tenor saxophonist. His nickname was Pres (also spelled Prez), for "president of the saxophone." He was the star soloist of Count Basie's big band (1936-40), in which he offered a new conception of tenor saxophone playing: in stark contrast to Coleman Hawkins's influential style,

Young's—as heard on *Jumpin' at the Woodside*—was gentle and dry yet magnificently tuneful and swinging. He led bands, rejoined Basie (1943–44), and starred in the film *Jammin' the Blues* (1944) before suffering a traumatic experience in the army. After 1946 he toured with Jazz at the Philharmonic and led various jazz groups.

Zawinul, Joe (Josef) (b. Vienna, Austria, July 7, 1932), keyboard player, composer, and bandleader. He joined Maynard Ferguson (1959) and accompanied Dinah Washington (1959–61) before becoming a member of Cannonball Adderley's group (1961–70). He worked intermittently with Miles Davis's jazz-rock groups from the late 1960s to the early 1970s; as an outgrowth of this experience he and Wayne Shorter formed Weather Report (1970–85), which recorded his hit composition *Birdland*. Zawinul continued the group without Shorter, under the new name Weather Update, until about 1989.

Notes

1: Introduction

1. *Money Jungle* was recorded for the United Artists label on Sept. 17, 1962.
2. Brian Priestley, *Mingus: A Critical Biography* (London: Quartet, 1982), 87.

2: Rhythm

Epigraph: Nat Hentoff, "Pres," *Down Beat* 23 (7 Mar. 1956): 10.

1. David N. Baker, Lida M. Belt, and Herman C. Hudson, eds., *The Black Composer Speaks* (Metuchen, N.J.: Scarecrow Press, 1978), 120.
2. Details of composers, pieces, and dates can be found in Edward A. Berlin, *Ragtime: A Musical and Cultural History* (Berkeley: University of California Press, 1980).
3. See the liner notes to Oscar Peterson's album *Soul-O!* (Prestige 7595, issued in 1969).
4. It must be stated emphatically that not all free jazz abandons the beat. The style has gone off in many rhythmic directions, some of which involve a deliberate beat. These variations on free style include Anthony Davis's use of Balinese gamelan music; the World Saxophone Quartet playing to the accompaniment of African drummers; and a host of fusions of free improvisation with American dance rhythms, as on Ornette Coleman's *Honeymooners*.
5. After about one thousand copies were pressed, Coltrane changed his mind about which version he preferred and asked the producer to make a substitution. Thus Edition II was born. The LP was released under the identical catalog number. This caused considerable confusion! Details of LP issues and reissues appear in David Wild, *The Recordings of John Coltrane: A Discography*, 2d ed. (Ann Arbor: Wildmusic, 1979). Both editions are on the CD cited in appendix 2.

3: Forms

Epigraph: Max Jones, *Talking Jazz* (London: Macmillan, 1987), 191.

1. The excerpt from *Maiden Voyage* that is presented on the accompanying CD does not include this portion of the piece; the unabridged version is identified in appendix 2.
2. Additionally, there is a small body of jazz compositions that borrow from the central repertory in an unusual way, that draw from a source outside that repertory, or that find a new way to make a chorus. Among the better-known examples are Thelonious Monk's *Friday the Thirteenth*, based on a cyclic 4-bar chorus; Miles Davis's *Solar*, built on a 12-bar nonblues pattern; and a group of

pieces including Tadd Dameron's *Lady Bird*, Eddie "Cleanhead" Vinson's *Tune-up* (often misattributed to Miles Davis), John Coltrane's *Giant Steps*, Wayne Shorter's *Nefertiti*, and Sonny Rollins's *St. Thomas*, all of which use a 16-bar chorus, with Rollins having borrowed his from West Indian calypso music.

3. The identity of the pianist has been a long-standing controversy. The uncomfortable but prevailing theory is that Argonne Thornton played for the first few seconds, giving Gillespie just enough time to lay down his trumpet and take over the piano.

4. This selection was transcribed by Thomas Owens, "Charlie Parker: Techniques of Improvisation," 2 vols. (Ph.D. diss., University of California, Los Angeles, 1974), 2:207–31.

5. Those who wish to pursue this still further will find the full score of *Koko* among the hundreds of Thomas Owens's transcriptions.

6. Gunther Schuller, *Early Jazz* (New York: Oxford University Press, 1968).

7. Baker, Belt, and Hudson, *The Black Composer Speaks*, 120.

8. The question of how an improviser might approach modal jazz is taken up later, in chapter 6, in a discussion of Freddie Hubbard's solo on *Maiden Voyage*.

9. If such a comment seems strange coming from one who depends heavily on the vocabulary of classical music in endeavoring to explain what to listen for in jazz, the comment is nonetheless heartfelt. Jazz literature can usefully borrow a terminology that has been refined over centuries and that is more precise than jazz jargon, but the literature need not borrow the evaluative standards that come along with that terminology (see, for example, chap. 7, tuning systems, where it is argued that playing out of tune is sometimes a virtue in jazz).

4: Arrangement

Epigraph: Stanley Dance, "The Return of Sy Oliver," *Jazz Journal* 23 (Sept. 1970): 2.

1. Reissues of Morton's early solo piano work and the relevant band titles are listed in appendix 2 under Morton.

2. Many reissues of *Maple Leaf Rag* have appeared on RCA and its subsidiary, Bluebird.

3. In the three years between arrangement and recording, her *Blue Skies* was substantially transformed, owing to the experimentation of the band, which led to a version featuring a succession of trumpet soloists. (A broadcast recording of November 1943 had featured clarinet, trumpet, tenor saxophone, and cornet rather than trumpets only.) Nonetheless the written parts, including the excerpt from chorus 1 reproduced below, remained intact for the 1946 studio recording that has been issued and reissued under both Berlin's title, *Blue Skies*, and Ellington's, *Trumpet No End*.

4. On this recording Charlie Parker masqueraded as a tenor (rather than alto) saxophonist under the name Charlie Chan, owing to Parker's contractual obligations to another company. Chan was the first name of Parker's female companion at the time; of course there also was a joking reference to the popular Chinese-American sleuth Charlie Chan.

5. Dave Dexter, Jr., "Critics in the Doghouse: Basie Examines Basie," *Down Beat* 6 (July 1939): 18.

6. Chris Sheridan, *Count Basie: A Bio-discography* (New York: Greenwood, 1986), 81.

7. The album containing *Jammin' for the Jackpot* is New World Records 217, part of a series given out to many American libraries in celebration of the bicentennial and therefore widely available; Blanche Calloway's *I Gotta Swing* is not easy to find.

8. Examples 40b–40i have been taken from the score transcribed by Dave Berger (published by King Brand Products, Inc., New York), but example 40a is my own transcription, because here (exceptionally) I disagree with his version.

9. Jack Chambers, *Milestones 1: The Music and Times of Miles Davis to 1960* (Toronto: University of Toronto, 1983), 240.

10. George Avakian, letter to the author, Sept. 15, 1991.

5: Composition

Epigraph: Baker, Belt, and Hudson, *The Black Composer Speaks*, 119–20.

1. Owing to limitations of time under the current format for musical compact discs, the collection issued with this book contains only the opening theme of *Fables of Faubus*, not the introduction, not the ensuing solos (spanning 1 1/2 choruses), and not the restatement of the second half of the theme. Listeners will find the complete track on the CD *Mingus Ah Um*; see appendix 2.

2. For brief excerpts of the parts for brass and reeds, see chap. 4, exx. 37 and 38. Those interested in more detail should purchase the score (see Sources and Permissions for Music Examples for information on publication).

3. At the end of chapter 6, I present a sophisticated example of this two-stage process, as manifested in the complex workings of composition and improvisation in Billie Holiday's approach to the song *Georgia on My Mind*.

6: Improvisation

Epigraph: Janet Coleman and Al Young, *Mingus/Mingus: Two Memoirs* (Berkeley: Creative Arts, 1989), 36.

1. Such musical dialogues are not represented on the CD that accompanies this book. For examples available at the time of writing, listen to *The Best of the Gerry Mulligan Quartet with Chet Baker*, Pacific Jazz B21Y-95481; Brubeck's CD *Dave Goes to College*, Columbia Jazz Masterpieces CK-45149; and the Modern Jazz Quartet's CD *Django*, Original Jazz Classics OJCCD 057-2.

2. Ekkehard Jost, *Free Jazz* (Graz, Austria: Universal, 1974), 89.

3. See Jost's *Free Jazz*, which surveys the history, workings, and aesthetics of the style. This extraordinary book enabled me to appreciate music that I had previously completely misunderstood.

4. *Air Lore*, Arista Novus AN 3014.

5. Ira Gitler, "Julian 'Cannonball' Adderley," *Jazz: A Quarterly of American Music* 3 (1959): 203–04.

6. André Hodeir, *Jazz: Its Evolution and Essence*, translated by David Noakes (New York: Grove Press, 1956), 144.

7. Rollins has taken credit for this melody, written in the spirit of West Indian calypso tunes. According to Martin Davison, the borrowing is rather more than spirit alone: Rollins actually appropriated a traditional song, *Fire Down There* ("Call and Response: Letters," *Cadence* 16 (Jan. 1990): 66). Thus there arises yet another item for confusion in the area of who wrote what.

8. Roach, by the way, had taken exactly such a departure on Parker's *Koko*, when near the end he played a snare drum solo so completely removed from the rest of *Koko* that it did not even have the same tempo.

9. See Milman Parry, "Studies in the Epic Technique of Oral Verse-Making, I: Homer and Homeric Style," *Harvard Studies in Classical Philology* 41 (1930): 73–147;

Albert Lord, *The Singer of Tales* (Cambridge: Harvard University Press, 1964); Leo Treitler, "Homer and Gregory: The Transmission of Epic Poetry and Plainchant," *Musical Quarterly* 60 (1974): 333–72; Lawrence Gushee, "Lester Young's 'Shoeshine Boy,'" in *International Musicological Society Congress Report, XII Berkeley 1977*, ed. Daniel Heartz and Bonnie Wade (Basel: Bärenreiter-Kasel, 1981), 151–69.

10. For listeners who wish to pursue this further, the number and letter labels are those of Owens's catalog, in "Charlie Parker: Techniques of Improvisation." There would be even more brackets on the page if the analysis included material that is repeated sequentially (as in bars 5–8, 33–39, 97–102, and 105–07); but that involves something quite different, the working out of a single idea in a bit of motivic development, not the interweaving of diverse formulas into a variegated whole. Owens, however, raises the possibility of the two processes coming together: he points out that Parker uses that last motive (the one heard in bars 105–07) in so many contexts that it takes on the character of a formula—it appears roughly ninety times in the several hundred solos that Owens analyzed.

11. See Robert D. Rusch, *Jazztalk: The Cadence Interviews* (Secaucus, N.J.: Lyle Stuart, 1984), 21–22.

12. John Chilton, *The Billie Holiday Story* (New York: Stein and Day, 1975), 25.

7: Sound

Epigraph: Robert George Reisner, *Bird: The Legend of Charlie Parker* (New York: Citadel, 1962), 17.

1. Stanley Dance, *The World of Earl Hines* (New York: Scribner's, 1977; reprint, Da Capo, 1983), 120.

2. Barry Martyn, ed., *With Louis and the Duke* (London: Macmillan, 1985), 89.

3. Whitney Balliett, *Jelly Roll, Jabbo, and Fats: Nineteen Portraits in Jazz* (New York: Oxford University Press, 1983), 196.

4. Thanks are due to T. Dennis Brown for passing my inquiry along to Max Roach, his colleague at the University of Massachusetts, Amherst.

5. The clarinet remains prominent in continuations of New Orleans and swing styles, but it has been relegated to the status of a secondary instrument in bop and free jazz, and it is virtually nonexistent in jazz-rock and other fusion styles. The reasons are unclear. If Weather Report can make the English horn work convincingly in a jazz-rock context (listen to *Unknown Soldier* on the CD *I Sing the Body Electric*, Columbia Jazz Contemporary Masters CK-46107), why not the clarinet?

6. There is one uncertain element in this particular example. On the back cover of Weather Report's album *Heavy Weather*, Pastorius is identified as playing bass— that is to say, electric bass guitar—and mandocello. I have failed to find the mandocello in standard reference works, and a query to Zawinul (via his publisher) yielded no answer. I therefore cannot say exactly where on *Birdland* Pastorius plays mandocello. In any event, this uncertainty does not undermine the point about the twangy timbre of his instrument, or instruments.

7. The ability to identify individuals by their personal sound is a skill that many jazz listeners develop. This skill, which comes easily for some and not so easily for others, is discussed in detail later in this chapter, but readers might find the present example rather daunting and deserving of explanation. How does one identify the soloist in a group that has two improvising electric bass guitarists (MacDowell and Chris Walker)? The expert answer would be that one becomes so fluent in MacDowell's work that one immediately recognizes his personal sound. The honest answer is that I asked the members of Prime Time and thereby identified MacDowell.

8. Ekkehard Jost, letter to the author, Feb. 5, 1993. The transcription of the solo appears in Jost, *Free Jazz*, 189.

9. Produced on a brass instrument, a shake involves an oscillation between well-separated pitches. Its rhythm is more deliberate and its character sometimes intentionally sloppier than that of a trill. It often spans a interval of a third or a fourth, and occasionally extends as far as an octave, although in this specific instance on *Trumpet No End* it covers roughly the interval of a whole step.

10. Luciano Massagli, Liborio Pusateri, and Giovanni M. Volanté, *Duke Ellington's Story on Records: 1946* (Milan: Musica Jazz, 1971), 223.

8: Epilogue

1. Of course different combinations of wind instruments, and occasionally a violin, were also used in New Orleans jazz. See chapter 6 for a more detailed discussion.

2. This technique was revived in a completely different context, that of free jazz, as a means of reintroducing a non-Western conception of pitch and thereby freeing the trombone from convention.

3. In the 1950s writer Stanley Dance coined the term *mainstream* to describe exactly this sort of small-group swing involving instrumental combinations and improvisational methods characteristic of New Orleans jazz. Vic Dickenson's recordings of 1953–54 for Vanguard exemplify the style. By the 1970s, when free jazz and fusion were well established, bop had acquired a traditional flavor by comparison with these newer styles, and consequently it too came to be described as mainstream. By the 1990s the term had lost all specific meaning, because some free-jazz and fusion performances had acquired a classic status and hence gained membership in the mainstream. A similarly vague term—*straight ahead jazz*—encompasses performances centered on, but by no means confined to, bop and its derivatives.

4. The omission from the present chapter of paraphrase and formulaic improvisation (which were discussed at length in chap. 6) is not an error. Rather, their importance is too pervasive to be classified within a single style.

5. The gutbucket caught alcohol drippings from barrels in American saloons; by extension *gutbucket* became a term for a rough musical style in early blues and early jazz.

Glossary of Percussion Instruments

This selected glossary lists instruments that figure prominently in the book and that may be less familiar to readers than, say, the piano or saxophone. The information is taken from *The New Grove Dictionary of Jazz*, 2 vols., edited by Barry Kernfeld (London: Macmillan, 1988), as well as from a file of unpublished corrections for these volumes.

Conga. An Afro-Cuban drum with a tapered or barrel-shaped shell. Played with the fingers and palm of the hand, it can be tuned to a specific pitch. The percussionist alters pitch by cupping the striking hand, by striking in different locations on the drum head, or by pressing the drumhead with the other hand while striking. When two or three congas are used, each is tuned differently. On the evidence of surviving photos, Chano Pozo plays one conga to produce the pitches B♭, F, and A♭ on Dizzy Gillespie's *Manteca* (see, for example, Orrin Keepnews and Bill Grauer, Jr., *A Pictorial History of Jazz: People and Places from New Orleans to Modern Jazz* [New York: Crown, 1966], 237; Frank Driggs and Harris Lewine: *Black Beauty, White Heat: A Pictorial History of Classic Jazz, 1920–1950* [New York: William Morrow, 1982], 333).

Drum set (or drum kit). A collection of cymbals and drums, and often additional accessories (for example, cowbell and woodblock), designed to be played by an individual. The drummer strikes the instruments with sticks or wire brushes (or, less commonly, with mallets or bare hands), while also using foot pedals as detailed below. The kit is not standardized. Essential components, as heard in Max Roach's solo on Sonny Rollins's *St. Thomas*, include the following:

(1) Hi-hat cymbal. A pair of cymbals mounted one above the other and controlled by a foot pedal. A wide array of timbres can be produced by striking the upper cymbal in different locations (from the edge to the center) as well as by depressing the pedal while striking, which dampens the sound.

(2) Ride cymbal. A single cymbal suspended on a metal stand. Larger in diameter than the hi-hat, it produces a generally louder and more shimmering sound.

(3) Bass drum. A large double-headed (or, less commonly, singleheaded) drum that stands upright on a shell, the heads vertical to the ground. The drummer produces sound by means of a beater attached to a foot pedal.

(4) Tom-tom. A medium-size double-headed (or, less commonly, single-headed) drum mounted horizontally or at a slight angle (to facilitate striking). Drummers routinely use different sizes of tom-tom, tuning each to a general area of pitch.

(5) Snare drum. A double-headed drum, not as tall as the tom-tom, that sits at a slight angle. It takes its name from wire snares attached to the lower head. The crackling, unpitched sound this drum produces can be accentuated by striking the upper rim (known as a "rim shot") rather than the head itself. When the snare mechanism is released from contact with the lower head, the snare can function as a high-pitched tom-tom.

Marimba. A tuned set of wooden bars, arranged like a piano keyboard. Each bar is suspended over a tube resonator. On *Outer Nothingness* Sun Ra plays the bass marimba, which spans a lower area of pitch than the marimba.

Vibraphone (or vibraharp). A tuned set of metal bars, arranged like a piano keyboard. Each bar is suspended over a tube resonator in which an electrically powered vane rotates to produce a mechanical vibrato (hence the name). A tubular loop controlled by the foot makes notes resonate in much the same manner that the sustaining pedal of a piano does. Milt Jackson plays vibraharp on Thelonious Monk's *Misterioso*.

Index

Barry Kernfeld is the editor of *The New Grove Dictionary of Jazz* and *The Blackwell Guide to Recorded Jazz*.